Islamophobia in America

Islamophobia in America

The Anatomy of Intolerance

Edited by

Carl W. Ernst

First published in 2013 by
PALGRAVE MACMILLAN®
in the United States—a division of St. Martin's Press LLC,
175 Fifth Avenue, New York, NY 10010.

Where this book is distributed in the UK, Europe and the rest of the world,
this is by Palgrave Macmillan, a division of Macmillan Publishers Limited,
registered in England, company number 785998, of Houndmills,
Basingstoke, Hampshire RG21 6XS.

Palgrave Macmillan is the global academic imprint of the above companies
and has companies and representatives throughout the world.

Palgrave® and Macmillan® are registered trademarks in the United States,
the United Kingdom, Europe and other countries.

ISBN: 978–1–137–29006–9 (hardcover)
ISBN: 978–1–137–32188–6 (paperback)

Library of Congress Cataloging-in-Publication Data is available from the
Library of Congress.

A catalogue record of the book is available from the British Library.

Design by Newgen Imaging Systems (P) Ltd., Chennai, India.

First edition: March 2013

10 9 8 7 6 5 4 3 2 1

Contents

Introduction
The Problem of Islamophobia
Carl W. Ernst

In the summer of 2010, the attention of Americans was riveted by two controversies that erupted over the presence of Islam in the United States. One was the theatrical announcement of Pastor Terry Jones, leader of a small religious group in Florida, that he had put the Qur'an on trial for "crimes against humanity" and was planning to burn copies of it on the anniversary of the 9/11 terrorist attacks against American targets. This threat attracted worldwide condemnation, as well as pleas from international leaders and American officials to abstain from a highly provocative action, and ultimately Jones abandoned that particular plan. The other controversy was related to an attempt by an American Muslim group to establish an interfaith community center and place of worship known as Park 51 in downtown Manhattan, not far from the site of the World Trade Center. Although the project had been approved by a normal zoning process without objection, anti-Muslim bloggers created an enormous dispute by arguing that this so-called Ground Zero mosque was really intended to be a celebration of the 9/11 attacks as a victory of Islam over America. Eventually, the controversy died down shortly after the 2010 elections, leading some commentators to observe that it was a "manufactured story" that had been opportunistically used by politicians as a wedge issue to generate votes.[1] In any case, the massive publicity given to both incidents illustrated the extent to which popular fear and suspicion of Islam, often linked to the 9/11 attacks, had become a widespread element in the climate of opinion in America. As this volume goes to press, new controversies have erupted worldwide over a trailer of an anti-Islamic film, disingenuously entitled "The Innocence of Muslims," evidently distributed by Islamophobic networks for the express purpose of fomenting both Muslim outrage and the predictable denunciations of Islamic irrationality. The forms and implications of this anti-Islamic prejudice in America, commonly referred to as Islamophobia, are the subject of the essays in this volume.[2]

Islamophobia is a complex phenomenon, and the authors represented here have approached it from a variety of perspectives. Peter Gottschalk and Gabriel Greenberg treat it as a largely unwarranted social anxiety about Islam and Muslims, although they focus on the element of fear of Islam rather than other stereotypes. Kambiz GhaneaBassiri considers it to be a prejudice against Islam that is particularly associated with violence in media representations, although he emphasizes the similarity of Islamophobia to prejudice against other minority "out-groups" like Catholics, Jews, and blacks. Edward Curtis highlights the element of racism in Islamophobia, which he links to state repression of political dissent. Juliane Hammer draws attention to the importance of gender in images of terrorists and the construction of Islamophobia, although she cautions that particular examples of Islamophobia must be analyzed in terms of the particular political and intellectual currents that drive them. Andrew Shryock focuses on Islamophobia as an ideology related to nationalism and the problems of minority identity; he contrasts Islamophobic identification of "the Muslim as enemy" with the equally simplistic concept of "the Muslim as friend," as found in Islamophilia. The basic point is that, for the many Americans who have no personal experience knowing Muslims as human beings, the overwhelmingly negative images of Islam circulated in the popular media amount to prejudice—defined by the *Oxford English Dictionary* as "preconceived opinion not based on reason or actual experience...unreasoned dislike, hostility, or antagonism towards, or discrimination against, a race, sex, or other class of people."[3]

This book does not aim to defend Islam or present an idealized portrait of "good Muslims." Nor does it intend to deconstruct all of the fantastic and exaggerated conspiracy theories, alleging that

Muslims are intrinsically violent because of their religion, and also inevitably hostile to the United States—a proposition that is sociologically inconceivable and unsupported by facts.[4] No attempt is made here to go into the distorted and hysterical campaign to banish the sharia as a source of American law, which is a solution for a nonexistent problem, and one that in its most extreme form would outlaw Muslim religious practices such as marriage contracts and wills.[5] Furthermore, this is not the place to examine the fraudulent and alarmist argument that a higher Muslim birthrate will overwhelm the white populations of Europe and America—a familiar claim from the racist playbook of other anti-immigration bigots.[6] Instead, this book offers important insights into Islamophobia as a conflict over American identity, which draws upon a deep well of bitterness toward racial and religious minorities.

There is a long history of negative stereotypes of Islam in European and American culture, parts of which are sketched here in the essay by Peter Gottschalk and Gabriel Greenberg. This history goes back to medieval diatribes against Islam by Christian clerics, although it took on especially potent forms during the colonial era, when European colonial administrators and Orientalist scholars justified the conquest of Asian and African lands by the "civilizing mission" that was being brought to inferior peoples.[7] The term "Islamophobia" was popularized in a 1997 report by a British think tank, the Runnymede Trust, drawing attention to this form of prejudice as a serious social problem.[8] Before 2001, survey data on American opinions regarding Islam revealed a fairly even split between positive and negative impressions of Islam, although the majority of Americans registered no opinion at all because of lack of any knowledge. But that balance has shifted over the past decade, as negative perceptions of Islam have become more widespread. Focusing more precisely on the association between Islam and violence, ten years ago, only 25% of Americans believed that Islam encourages violence, while 51 percent disagreed with that position; as of 2011, 40 percent say that Islam encourages violence, while 42 percent do not.[9]

The opposition to the Park 51 community center in New York is only one example of a larger phenomenon of opposition to the establishment of mosques and Islamic centers in the United States. This opposition has taken the form of vandalism and arson as well as organized attempts to block mosque construction by legal challenge.[10] The American Civil Liberties Union has documented the extent to which anti-mosque activity has taken place in dozens of different locations around the United States.[11] One unlikely site for such a protest was Murfreesboro, Tennessee, where the local Muslim community had been holding prayer services for years without attracting any notice. When the construction of a new Islamic Center was approved in 2010, organized resistance by mosque opponents took the form of arguing that Islam was not a religion protected by First Amendment guarantees, but a political movement aiming at the imposition of sharia law in America. The US Department of Justice disagreed and filed a brief maintaining that Islam has been recognized as a religion since the time of Thomas Jefferson (this action contrasts with the 1964 case in which the Department of Justice unsuccessfully argued against the religious status of the Nation of Islam, as discussed below by Edward Curtis).

The rise of anti-Muslim propaganda in the United States has connections with right-wing activists, whose attacks on Islam are often well funded. A recent report by People for the American Way has documented the menu of tactics that is often used by anti-Muslim extremists. In addition to claiming that Islam is not a religion and that Muslims have no First Amendment rights, these ideologues use misinformation to argue that all Muslims are dangerous, and that liberty must be defended by taking freedoms away from Muslims. The political angle is evident in attacks on Islam that are also linked with criticism of President Obama, but the enemies list is often expanded to include "leftist radicals" as alleged Muslim allies.[12] Another report, by the Center for American Progress, draws attention to seven right-wing foundations that have provided over US$40 million to support Islamophobia between 2001 and 2009, particularly through five dedicated anti-Islamic think tanks headed by Frank Gaffney, David Yerushalmi, Daniel Pipes, Robert Spencer, and Steven Emerson. These professional Islamophobes are supported in a less-formal manner by a network of websites, bloggers, and news outlets that systematically amplify anti-Islamic messages, frequently in a tone that is crude, aggressive, and intolerant. In turn, there is a notable group of elected officials and former presidential candidates—all Republicans—who regularly employ anti-Islamic rhetoric to make political capital.[13] Similar documentation has been provided by the Southern Poverty Law Center, which has also tracked an increase in anti-Islamic hate groups.[14] What is especially remarkable, with all the money flowing into this propaganda machine, is how profitable it can be to bash Muslims. A reporter for *The Tennesseean*, Bob Smietana, noticed how much attention the Murfreesboro mosque controversy was getting from outside groups, and his investigative reporting unearthed a veritable treasure trove of money being made by key players on the anti-Islam circuit.[15] Millions of dollars, funneled through shadowy front organizations, have also supported the distribution of anti-Islamic propaganda on a massive scale. Only weeks before the presidential election of 2008, 100 newspapers and magazines across the country distributed millions of DVDs of a documentary entitled "Obsession: Radical Islam's War against the West," in Sunday editions, and 28 million more DVDs were mailed directly to voters in swing states. The film has also been repeatedly shown on Fox News TV. In lurid and alarming scenes, the film (distributed by an otherwise unknown organization called the Clarion Fund, Inc.) bluntly intercut images of Muslims and Nazis to make the point that they are basically the same.[16] These are only a few examples of the kind of anti-Muslim activity that seems to be carried out on a wide scale with significant funding in a highly politicized context.

One of the especially troubling aspects of institutionalized Islamophobia has been in the area of police training, especially given the vast amounts of funding diverted to the new security regime immediately following on the 9/11 attacks. Vast new powers of surveillance, spying, jailing, and interrogation (including the "enhanced techniques" often considered to be torture) were being regularly employed by American officials, largely against Muslims. It was perhaps inevitable that this regime should prove vulnerable to manipulation by anti-Muslim ideologues eager to be paid as "experts" on terrorism. Investigative reporting by Wired.com has revealed that the Federal Bureau of Investigation (FBI) has sponsored training for its counterterrorism agents presenting mainstream Islam as violent and radical, and depicting the Prophet Muhammad as a "cult leader."[17] Other reports have shown that the pressure on the FBI to produce results has often relied upon questionable use of informants and agents provocateurs to create flimsy plots that could be then broken up and paraded as investigative successes.[18] On the level of local policing, it is even more remarkable to see how easy it is for self-proclaimed "terrorism experts," with no professional qualifications whatever, to get hired in order to provide deeply flawed anti-Islamic guidance for local police forces.[19] Companies that provide "training" for thousands of law enforcement agents and security personnel commonly portray Islam as a terrorist religion intent on subverting the United States from within, and they dismiss mainstream Muslims and prominent Muslim organizations as nothing but radical extremists attempting to impose the sharia on America.[20] In light of this national pattern of police indoctrination with Islamophobic materials, it is perhaps unsurprising that the New York Police Department showed an anti-Islamic film to over a thousand officers in another training exercise. This film, "The Third Jihad" (a sequel to the "Obsession" film mentioned above), actually included a cameo appearance by Police Commissioner Raymond Kelly, despite the fact that he had earlier denied that the film was being shown to the police; Kelly was forced to make a public apology amid cries for his resignation, though he was defended by Mayor Bloomberg.[21] The essential message of this film, again, was that American Muslims are planning to infiltrate and dominate America, and so any claims by Muslims to be "moderate" are part of a devious pattern of deception. The impact of this mentality seems to be demonstrated by Associated Press reports revealing over six years of New York City police spying on Muslims in mosques, small businesses, and universities over a wide region. The secret "Demographics Unit" responsible for this apparent abuse of civil liberties has not generated a single lead or uncovered any evidence of terrorism.[22]

It is also disturbing to see evidence of the dissemination of anti-Islamic propaganda by US military forces in counterterrorism training similar to what has been found in police forces. There is unfortunately a track record of the use of classic textbooks of racist ideology being employed and recommended by military authorities, for instance in books purporting to explain "the Arab mind."[23] It is particularly alarming to see a military leader like Lt.-Gen. William Boykin, who has played a prominent role in the "war on terror," make public denunciations of Islam as a threat to America, and claim that Islam does not deserve religious freedom protections under the First Amendment.[24] Repeated complaints about training courses with anti-Islamic content led the Chairman of the Joint Chiefs of Staff, General Martin Dempsey, to order a comprehensive review of these courses in April 2012 to expunge bigoted materials.[25] One of the most extreme examples was a course for senior military officials that dismissed Geneva Convention protections for Muslim civilians and contemplated Hiroshima-like destruction of Islam's holy cities.[26] Another instance was a target at a Navy SEAL firing range depicting a Muslim woman wearing a head scarf and firing a gun, with framed verses from the Qur'an over her shoulder; this was removed by Navy officials after protest by an American Muslim group.[27] While top military officials clearly regard Islamophobia as incompatible with American foreign policy and military doctrine, the presence of anti-Islamic prejudice in the military is evidently still a problem, to judge from notorious recent events involving US troops abusing bodies of Afghan fighters and burning Qur'ans.

It is hard to say whether the organized networks of Islamophobia have in fact had the chief responsibility for pushing American opinion against Islam. There are clearly sectors of American culture that are predisposed to be hostile to Islam in any case. While it is true that conservative and evangelical circles typically hold anti-Islamic attitudes, as Juliane Hammer points out in her essay, there are also plenty of liberals who are quick to denounce the alleged sins and shortcomings of Muslims. Furthermore, as Kambiz GhaneaBassiri observes, news media and elected officials benefit from the fear of Muslim terrorism with enhanced revenue or political power. So, in effect, Islamophobia fits into certain structural aspects of the way American society deals with recent minorities during times of crisis. Anti-Islamic rhetoric draws upon the repertoire of religious bigotry as well as traditional American racism, but it is given a particular spice by the element of gender and stereotypes about oppressed Muslim women. Ultimately, as Andrew Shryock concludes, this kind of prejudice is a distortion and a distraction from the real issues that confront America. Understanding the nature of this kind of prejudice is therefore essential for getting beyond it.

*   *   *

The five articles presented in this book display a broad spectrum of analyses of the phenomenon of Islamophobia from a variety of angles. All of them are based on thorough research on the history and sociology of anti-Islamic prejudice. All the authors are specialists who have written extensively on Muslims and Arabs in America and the way they have been perceived. Their findings reveal important moments and incidents in the story of American Islam, and they provide thoughtful reflections on the causes and consequences of the hostility toward Muslims that has become such a common attitude in recent years.

Historical background is provided by Peter Gottschalk and Gabriel Greenberg, who are well known for their trenchant study of anti-Islamic political cartoons.[28] Exploring the connections between British and American views of Islam over three centuries, they address enduring stereotypes and anxieties focused on Muslims, beginning with the standard eighteenth-century portraits of Muhammad by Humphrey Prideaux and Voltaire, which depicted him (with somewhat contradictory logic) as both an impostor and a fanatic. Perhaps, because of their limited contact with Muslims (outside of Tripoli and the Philippines), Americans tended to rely on the advice of the British, who claimed extensive experience with Muslim subjects in their Indian colony.

Gottschalk and Greenberg dwell at length on how Islam became perceived as a threat in America, despite the lack of any recognized Muslim presence in the Western hemisphere (since enslaved African Muslims were not normally counted). It is striking to see how the fictional possibility of American Muslims was used as an extreme hypothetical example, as when the 1789 Constitutional debates on the "religious test" for the presidency entertained the notion that even a "Mahometan" could be considered for that office. It was evidently only after the 1857 Indian revolt (largely blamed on the Muslims and the last Mughal emperor) that British officials began to subscribe to a paranoid suspicion of a Muslim threat to their dominion, and American missionaries went along with fears of a global Muslim conspiracy. This British and American antipathy toward Islam fostered the belief that Islam was spread only by the sword—for who could accept this fanatical religion except under threat of violence? This ideological portrait of Islam (the historical record does not support the notion of conversion to Islam by force) fulfilled the imperatives of the European concept of world religions in conflict seeking world domination.[29] This Manichean vision of struggle between forces of light and darkness has left its legacy in apocalyptic depictions of Islam, alongside the Catholic Church, as vehicles of the Antichrist in opposition to evangelical truth. The recurring theme of the fear and threat of Islam in eighteenth- to twentieth-century America, reinforced in this fashion by the perspective of British colonialism, helped to consolidate the concept of Islam as a single homogeneous whole, an essentialized portrait that was severed from any historical context. The continuing global circulation of these stereotypes from America has encouraged Muslims to draw the conclusion that the US security regime (the global "war on terror") is an assault on Islam, the fulfillment of the clash of civilizations.

Focusing on the contemporary situation, Kambiz GhaneaBassiri draws upon survey data and American religious history to discuss the treatment of Muslims as "out-groups," like other racial and religious minorities that have come under suspicion and persecution in the past. Anti-Muslim prejudice today, driven by fears of threats to national security, sees Islam as a dangerous movement bent on world domination, and therefore views Muslims as potentially disloyal and un-American. While it is true that a small group of individuals and well-funded organizations are responsible for manufacturing anti-Muslim propaganda, often channeling it into protest against the construction of mosques, there are larger factors behind this complex and multifaceted problem. Both the news media and the political elite seem to thrive on the fear of Muslim violence. Journalists routinely refer to religion as the basis of terrorism, and their lack of incentive to explain complex issues often ends up reinforcing existing prejudices. Politicians of all stripes have been quick to meet fears of violence by expanding state power, which is rarely curtailed. Crises of confidence in democratic institutions have a long history in America of raising suspicions about minorities, who can be seen as deviants from the mainstream of the American civil religion. Anti-Catholic prejudice questioned the loyalty of American Catholics, whose true allegiance was believed to be due to a foreign leader (the Pope), and anti-Muslim ideologues make the same charge against Muslims today. In a similar fashion, anti-Semitism was widely fashionable and is still quite common, despite its public condemnation in recent years. The multiple ethnic identities of American Muslims added the element of racial difference to their religious identity. So despite efforts by Muslims to assimilate to American norms since the 1950s, the perceptions of Muslims as "other" inevitably drew upon the exclusion of Africans and Asians from equality with whites. It should not be forgotten that racial minorities have been treated differently by state and local governments over the years, and that only since 1964 did civil rights legislation permit nonwhites to defend their liberties.

Thus, it was that early African American Muslim movements, such as the Moorish Science Temple of Noble Drew Ali, found their attempts to claim religious freedom undermined by racial prejudice and the imposition of state surveillance. A major shift came with the popular success of Alex Haley's "Roots," a TV serial that for the first time conveyed to a broad audience of white Americans a compelling narrative about the history of enslaved Africans (including Muslims). While the Nation of Islam had alarmed white Americans with its racial rhetoric, Elijah Mohammed's son and successor, W. D. Mohammed, proclaimed his acceptance of an American Islamic identity as he steered his community out of their former confrontational stance. Ironically, although President Barack Obama has proclaimed his Christian faith, his racial otherness and his Muslim family connections have once again raised suspicion that any association with Islam may be un-American. GhaneaBassiri concludes that, while bigotry and prejudice have regularly played roles in the building of American cultural unity by suppressing diversity, attacks on out-groups divert attention from real crises and often lead to the expansion of state power and the erosion of civil liberties.

The article by Edward Curtis takes us further into the subject of race and its connection with anti-Islamic prejudice. Curtis assembles extensive documentation of state repression of political dissent related to Islam. He argues that this state surveillance was accompanied by an FBI disinformation campaign carried out through the media and counterintelligence measures. Things were not always so; since the eighteenth century, a handful of educated Muslim slaves from Africa, like Job Ben Solomon, attained celebrity status and elite sponsorship in England and America, although they were often expected to serve Western commercial interests and avoid raising questions about equal rights. But in the atmosphere of 1920s' America, with the rise of nativism and the exclusion of nonwhite immigration, conversion to Islam by African Americans took on a sharp political profile, raising FBI suspicions about the foreign connections of American Muslims. The Nation of Islam was only one of several African Muslim organizations that took form at this time, and the presence of Indian missionaries of the Ahmadi sect plus other organizers with African connections raised further concerns among American officials. FBI surveillance during the Second World War (including the arrest of members of the Nation of Islam for draft evasion) conflated demands for civil rights with communism and a possible alliance with the Japanese. The Black Muslim scare of the 1960s continued this pattern, as the Department of Justice unsuccessfully argued in the Supreme Court that the Nation of Islam was a cult undeserving of First Amendment protections of religious freedom. Overt FBI actions against the Nation of Islam went beyond wiretapping to include briefings of journalists and the leaking of damaging information about Elijah Mohammed in an attempt to undercut him. The problem for African American Muslims was that immigrant Muslims from the Middle East were classified as whites, while the Black Muslims were discredited on racial lines. The situation worsened when an American Muslim, Muhammad Ali, challenged the US war in Vietnam on religious grounds as a conscientious objector, with the result that he was imprisoned and stripped of his Olympic boxing medals.

As Curtis observes, in the post-9/11 era, the focus of American anxiety has shifted from Black American Muslims to brown foreigners, but regular procedures continue to include the suppression of critiques of US policies and the rewarding of Muslim groups that remain apolitical and uncritical. Thus, surveillance is being carried out on an unprecedented scale, with further actions including selective suspension of civil rights, false accusations against critics like Army chaplain James Yee, shutting down Muslim charities, and outlawing even training in peace techniques for groups labeled as terrorists. Despite legal challenges to such policies in some court decisions, the official policy of the Obama administration includes authorization for assassinating US citizens without trial, if they are declared to be supporters of terrorism. The FBI and major police departments still interact with Muslim groups by enrolling informants and employing them as agents provocateurs, creating cases that can then be successfully "solved." Under the current incentives of the security regime, it is likely that the application of state Islamophobia will continue, with race being a continuing factor.

There is another element of Islamophobia that has received surprisingly little attention, and that is gender. Juliane Hammer argues that Muslim women are on the center stage of the construction of Islamophobia and the images of terrorism. Like GhaneaBassiri, she sees Islamophobia as a complex phenomenon that cannot be reduced to the conspiracies of anti-Muslim ideologues. But she widens the field of associations to include domestic politics, imperial wars, feminist negotiations, and "Western" claims of superiority—and it includes the polite Islamophobia of liberals as well as conservatives.[30] The gendering of terrorism is explicit in the stereotypes of male Muslim terrorists, who by definition must be suppressing Muslim women. Oddly, the American news media condemn Muslims for being homophobic (as in the Abu Ghraib scandal), at a time when homosexuality continues to be denounced by leading American political and religious leaders. Yet, Muslim women, whose voices are rarely sought out, are regularly both attacked in anti-Muslim hate crimes and viewed with pity as victims who need to be saved from their own religion. Genuine issues of domestic violence (which exists in every community) have been seized by opportunistic Islamophobes as another weapon for bashing Islam. Real discrimination against Muslim women exists in America, including discrimination in the workplace, different public treatment, and abuse of veiled women. Hammer cites examples of Islamophobia directed against Muslim women that underline the importance of racism and fear of minorities as motives. Hysterical attempts to create anti-sharia legislation implicitly target Muslim women, by creating paranoid fantasies of

Muslim takeovers of the Constitution and the imposition of veils and burqas on American women.

In the political realm, as Hammer points out, neoconservative attacks on Islam generally include a gender-egalitarian and women's rights perspective. This ostensible intervention on behalf of women oppressed by the sharia reinforces Islamophobia among Americans; it claims to be interested in saving Muslim women while simultaneously casting them as foreign and dangerous, in this way turning women's bodies into the tools of political agendas of imperialism and minority discrimination. Nowhere is this more evident than in the condescending feminist concern about the oppression of Afghani women, which conveniently justified the 2002 invasion of Afghanistan, although such concerns did not arise in the 1980s when Ronald Reagan praised the Afghan mujahidin as freedom fighters. The picture of gender and Islamophobia is further complicated by a notable presence of strident anti-Muslim women, such as Pamela Geller, whose organization Stop the Islamization of America has been designated as a hate group by the Southern Poverty Law Center. Another regular feature is the prominence of "native informants," self-proclaimed Muslims or ex-Muslims (often women) who offer insider denunciations of Islam to eager audiences in best-selling books and lucrative appearances on the lecture circuit.[31] It is, nevertheless, difficult to categorize secular feminists, who may not always line up with neoconservative agendas, though there are plenty of examples of what Gayatri Spivak called "white women saving brown women from brown men." Likewise, some Muslim feminists may criticize gender oppression while maintaining a Muslim position. Hammer concludes by pointing out that Muslim women remain at the intersections of feminist leftist agendas with liberal and neoconservative ones. Clearly, further research is needed on related topics such as Muslim masculinities, homophobia, and women's agency and voices responding to Islamophobia.

In the final article of the volume, anthropologist Andrew Shryock offers a case study of what is clearly the most Arab and Muslim city in America: Dearborn, Michigan (or in the words of anti-Muslim blogger Debbie Schlussel, "Dearbornistan"). He situates Islamophobia primarily as an ideology related to nationalism and problems of minority identity. The problem is that

Islamophobia defines Islam as unacceptable in the modern state, and Muslims as incapable of being true citizens—though this turns out to be difficult to define in practice. In this murky situation, national identity ends up being defined by a negotiation between law (legal citizenship) and custom (true Americanness). Shryock then takes the further step of pointing to the shortcomings of Islamophilia, the multicultural opposite of Islamophobia, which claims that Muslims are "good" while still sharing assumptions with Islamophobia about the nature of citizenship and national identity. One problem is that Muslims do not benefit from unity-building exercises like Holocaust commemorations in Europe, or American affirmative action—existing stereotypes condemn Muslims for retrograde positions on religion, gender, and politics. Surprisingly enough, Muslims in the United States are nevertheless very trusting in public institutions, perhaps because they are generally well educated and prosperous in comparison with European Muslims. In effect, according to Shryock, simultaneous processes of mainstreaming and marginalizing Arabs and Muslims regularly take place during Middle East conflicts or US wars against Muslim countries, since Arabs and Muslims inescapably retain an ambiguous role that is not seen as fully American.

Dearborn has become the principal venue for anti-Muslim figures (like the Qur'an-burning pastor, Terry Jones) to come and rail against Islam in public. Officials in the city, which has a 40 percent Arab population, have become accustomed to handling these provocations by legal maneuvers that skirt on abridging the freedom of speech. Interfaith groups and journalists in Dearborn have defended Jones's freedom of speech while condemning his ignorance. However, mixed messages are the rule, as civic officials routinely congratulate Arabs and Muslims in the Detroit area when newly constructed mosques are inaugurated, while at the same time, new levels of police surveillance are enforced. FBI monitoring of mosques leads to enthusiastic efforts by Muslim leaders to demonstrate full Americanization, even while they stay on alert for infiltration by informers. The FBI informs Muslim leaders that they will be fine as long as they only talk about "true Islam"—evidently as understood by the US government.

Shryock points out that the pressure for Americanization is nothing new for Detroit Arabs. This has been a regular feature of political crises for years, because the Arab and Muslim communities have been solidly established in the Detroit area since the late nineteenth century. The assumption that Muslims are either foreign-born or African American means that Muslim Americans must be new, alien, and from somewhere else—not fully American, in other words. This exclusion buys into the Orientalist banishment of Islam from the West, and the assimilationist model of American citizenship that calls for the abandonment of all foreign ways. Continuing ties to Arab homelands may have generated advocacy for Palestine or opposition to US-supported dictators, but such moves have frequently collided with American public culture and US foreign policy; in the post–Cold War era, having a Muslim enemy has become a key part of American national identity.

But Islamophobia cannot be cured by simply saying that Muslims are good people. To use the language of political scientist Carl Schmitt, shifting Muslims from the category of enemies (Islamophobia) to friends (Islamophilia) simply perpetuates the same essentializing logic, but with an equally distorted positive view of Islam. The shortcomings of the "good Muslim, bad Muslim" model are all too evident, since there are real differences among Muslims, and Shryock demonstrates this point with an amusing recital of the characteristics of the "good Muslim" stereotype. Requiring the "good Muslim" to be the unimpeachable US citizen automatically alienates any Muslim who has criticism of particular US policies. Islamophilia therefore is bound to be a failing proposition, for even as Muslims become more American, the bar for acceptance is set higher, since no one really believes that they have even denounced terrorism.[32] A better remedy is to call for a situation in which no religious group is singled out to prove their loyalty (consider Rep. Peter King's investigation of Muslims as un-American); opponents of Islamophobia should criticize racism and bigotry rather than attempt to idealize Islam. Shryock acknowledges that Arab and Muslim Americans have been subjected to "processes of marginalization and mainstreaming that are abusive and extreme," having to demonstrate patriotism and loyalty while simultaneously being exhibited by the State Department as examples of American tolerance and minority success. But the friend–enemy distinction can only be overcome if Muslims and non-Muslims recognize each other as an inescapable part of the same zones of interaction.

Obviously, much more could be said on the subject of Islamophobia, particularly in relation to the hatred of Islam that is so prominent in evangelical circles. It is also worth exploring in detail the way in which right-wing politicians exploit the fear of Islam in a cynical and opportunistic manipulation of credulous public opinion. In any case, it is to be hoped that calm and dispassionate exploration of the roots of prejudice, as presented in this volume, will be helpful in allowing Americans to move beyond the scapegoating and demonizing of religious minorities; American citizenship and the freedoms that go with it are far too valuable to be compromised in the name of irrational and bigoted identity politics.

NOTES

1. Justin Elliott, "Whatever Happened to the 'Ground Zero Mosque'?" Salon.com (December 31, 2010), www.salon.com/2010/12/31/park_51_a_look_back/, accessed September 15, 2012.
2. Earlier versions of these articles were presented in a plenary panel session on "Islamophobia in America" at the annual conference of the Middle East Studies Association of North America in December 2011.
3. "Prejudice," *Oxford English Dictionary* (3rd edition, March 2007), online version June 2012, www.oed.com/view/Entry/150162, accessed September 8, 2012.
4. Charles Kurzman, *The Missing Martyrs: Why There Are so Few Muslim Terrorists* (New York: Oxford University Press, 2011); David Schanzer, Charles Kurzman, and Ebrahim Moosa, *Anti-Terror Lessons of Muslim Americans* (National Institute of Justice Report, 2010), www.sanford.duke.edu/news/Schanzer_Kurzman_Moosa_Anti-Terror_Lessons.pdf, accessed September 15, 2012.
5. "Court Upholds Ruling Blocking Oklahoma Sharia and International Law Ban," American Civil Liberties Union (January 10, 2012), www.aclu.org/religion-belief/court-upholds-ruling-blocking-oklahoma-sharia-and-international-law-ban, accessed September 15, 2012.

6. Doug Saunders, *The Myth of the Muslim Tide: Do Immigrants Threaten the West?* (New York: Vintage, 2012).

7. Carl W. Ernst, *Following Muhammad: Rethinking Islam in the Contemporary World* (Chapel Hill, NC: University of North Carolina Press, 2004), pp. 3–36.

8. *Islamophobia: A Challenge for Us All* (Runnymede Trust, 1997), available online at www.runnymedetrust.org/publications/17/32.html, accessed September 15, 2012.

9. "Continuing Divide in Views of Islam and Violence," *PewResearch Publications* (March 9, 2011), http://pewresearch.org/pubs/1921/poll-islam-violence-more-likely-other-religions-peter-king-congressional-hearings, accessed September 15, 2012.

10. The recent burning of a mosque in Joplin, Missouri, is discussed by Glenn Greenwald, "Combating Islamophobic Violence," Salon.com (August 9, 2012), www.salon.com/2012/08/09/combating_islamophobic_violence/, accessed September 15, 2012.

11. "Map—Nationwide Anti-Mosque Activity," American Civil Liberties Union, www.aclu.org/maps/map-nationwide-anti-mosque-activity, accessed September 15, 2012.

12. "The Right-Wing Playbook on Anti-Muslim Extremism," People for the American Way (2011), www.pfaw.org/rww-in-focus/the-right-wing-playbook-anti-muslim-extremism, accessed September 15, 2012.

13. Wajahat Ali, Eli Clifton, Matthew Duss, Lee Fang, Scott Keyes, and Faiz Shakir, "Fear, Inc.: The Roots of the Islamophobia Network in America" (Center for American Progress, August 26, 2011), www.americanprogress.org/issues/religion/report/2011/08/26/10165/fear-inc/, accessed September 15, 2012.

14. Robert Steinback, "Jihad against Islam," Southern Poverty Law Center Intelligence Report (Summer, 2011, Issue Number 142), www.splcenter.org/get-informed/intelligence-report/browse-all-issues/2011/summer/jihad-against-islam, accessed September 15, 2012; Robert Steinback, "The Anti-Muslim Inner Circle," www.splcenter.org/get-informed/intelligence-report/browse-all-issues/2011/summer/the-anti-muslim-inner-circle, accessed September 15, 2012.

15. Bob Smietana, "Anti-Muslim Crusaders Make Millions Spreading Fear," *The Tennesseean* (October 24, 2010), www.tennessean.com/article/20101024/NEWS01/10240374/The+price+of+fear, accessed September 15, 2012.

16. Pam Martens, "The Far Right's Secret Slush Fund to Keep Fear Alive," *Counterpunch* (October 26, 2010), www.counterpunch.com/martens10262010.html, accessed September 15, 2012; Erik Ose, "Pro-McCain Group Dumping 28 Million Terror Scare DVDs in Swing States," *Huffington Post* (September 12, 2008), www.

huffingtonpost.com/erik-ose/pro-mccain-group-dumping_b_12596
9.html, accessed September 15, 2012. See also Omid Safi, "Who Put
Hate in My Sunday Paper?" (September 29, 2008), http://omidsafi.
com/index.php?option=com_content&task=view&id=42&Itemid=9,
accessed September 15, 2012.

17. Spencer Ackerman, "FBI Teaches Agents: 'Mainstream' Muslims Are
'Violent, Radical,' " *Wired* (September 14, 2011), www.wired.com/
dangerroom/2011/09/fbi-muslims-radical/all/, accessed September
15, 2012.

18. Petra Bartosiewicz, "To Catch a Terrorist: The FBI Hunts for the
Enemy Within," *Harper's Magazine* (August, 2011), http://harpers.
org/archive/2011/08/0083545, accessed September 15, 2012.

19. Meg Stalcup and Joshua Craze, "The Shocking Way US Cops Are
Trained to Hate Muslims," *Washington Monthly* (March 10, 2011),
www.alternet.org/story/150209/the_shocking_way_us_cops_are_
trained_to_hate_muslims?page=entire, accessed September 15, 2012.

20. Thomas Cincotta, *Manufacturing the Muslim Menace: Private Firms,
Public Servants, and the Threat to Rights and Security* (Political Research
Associates, 2011), www.publiceye.org/liberty/training/Muslim_Menace_
Complete.pdf, accessed September 15, 2012.

21. Tom Robbins, "NYPD Cops' Training Included an Anti-Muslim
Horror Flick," *The Village Voice* (January 19, 2011), www.villagevoice.
com/2011–01–19/columns/nypd-cops-training-included-an-anti-
muslim-horror-flick/, accessed September 15, 2012; Jeremy Walton,
"America's Muslim Anxiety: Lessons of *The Third Jihad*," *The Revealer*
(February 2, 2012), http://therevealer.org/archives/10349, accessed
September 15, 2012.

22. Adam Goldman and Matt Apuzzo, "NYPD: Muslim Spying Led to No
Leads, Terror Cases," Associated Press (August 21, 2012), www.ap.org/
Content/AP-In-The-News/2012/NYPD-Muslim-spying-led-to-no-
leads-terror-cases, accessed September 15, 2012.

23. Raphael Patai, *The Arab Mind*, with a new preface by Col. Norvell
B. De Atkine ([1973]; reprint edition, New York: Hatherleigh Press,
2007). De Atkine, who has been an instructor at the JFK Special
Warfare School in Fort Bragg, NC, is also the author of "Why Arabs
Lose Wars,"*Middle East Quarterly* (December 1999), www.meforum.
org/441/why-arabs-lose-wars, accessed September 15, 2012, which
argues in favor of Samuel Huntington's "clash of civilizations."

24. William G. Boykin, "Sharia Law or Constitution? America Must
Choose," *Texas Insider* (February 11, 2011), www.texasinsider.org/?
p=42440, accessed September 15, 2012; see also http://en.wikipedia.
org/wiki/William_G._Boykin, accessed September 15, 2012.

25. Spencer Ackerman, "Senior US General Orders Top-to-Bottom Review of Military's Islam Training," Wired.com (April 24, 2012), www.wired.com/dangerroom/2012/04/military-islam-training/, accessed September 15, 2012.
26. Noah Schachtman and Spencer Ackerman, "US Military Taught Officers: Use 'Hiroshima' Tactics for 'Total War' on Islam," Wired. com (May 10, 2012), www.wired.com/dangerroom/2012/05/total-war-islam/all/, accessed September 15, 2012; id., " 'Institutional Failures' Led Military to Teach War on Islam," Wired.com (June 20, 2012), www.wired.com/dangerroom/2012/06/failure-oversight-war-islam/, accessed September 15, 2012.
27. Kate Wiltrout, "SEAL training range won't show woman as target," *The Virginian-Pilot* (June 30, 2012), http://hamptonroads.com/2012/06/seal-training-range-wont-show-woman-target, accessed September 15, 2012.
28. Peter Gottschalk and Gabriel Greenberg, *Islamophobia: Making Muslims the Enemy* (Lanham, MD: Rowman & Littlefield, 2007).
29. On the concept of contest between religions for world domination, see also Carl W. Ernst, *Following Muhammad*, pp. 37–69.
30. Bruce B. Lawrence, "The Polite Islamophobia of the Intellectual," *Religion Dispatches* (June 1, 2010), www.religiondispatches.org/archive/politics/2635/the_polite_islamophobia_of_the_intellectual_/, accessed September 15, 2012.
31. On this "native informant" phenomenon, see Pankaj Mishra, "A Critic at Large: Islamismism—How should Western intellectuals respond to Muslim scholars?," *The New Yorker* (June 7, 2010), www.newyorker.com/arts/critics/atlarge/2010/06/07/100607crat_atlarge_mishra, accessed September 15, 2012.
32. For those who still are under the impression that Muslims have not ever denounced terrorism, see the extensive list of "Islamic Statements against Terrorism" compiled by Charles Kurzman, at http://kurzman.unc.edu/islamic-statements-against-terrorism/, accessed September 15, 2012.

Chapter 1

Common Heritage, Uncommon Fear
Islamophobia in the United States and British India, 1687–1947

Peter Gottschalk and Gabriel Greenberg

When confronted with the commonality of Islamophobic themes of the fanatic Muslim man, the oppressed Muslim woman, and an intolerant Islamic religion, defenders of these views often respond that their prevalence must reflect their truth. After all, they argue, all stereotypes have some seed of truth. The ironclad quality of this tautology—that past repetition of an allegation is justification for its reiteration—recommends a different tack in refutation. A historical evaluation of these claims that demonstrates their persistence despite historical changes helps demonstrate how the core of American and British Islamophobia derives from received truisms that have established—and continue to establish—basic expectations about how Muslims behave. These expectations shape how information about Muslims is interpreted so that what fails to fit within this frame of reference (e.g., Muslim tolerance, nonviolent Muslim pro-test) often is overlooked.

> If a Mohammedan, Turk, Egyptian, Syrian or African commits a crime the newspaper reports do not tell us that it was committed by a Turk, an Egyptian, a Syrian or an African, but by a Mohammedan.

If an Irishman, an Italian, a Spaniard or a German commits a crime
in the United States we do not say that it was committed by a
Catholic, a Methodist or a Baptist, nor even a Christian; we desig-
nate the man by his nationality.[1]

Perhaps, the only thing that exceeds the accuracy of Mohammed
Alexander Russell Webb's observation is the surprise that this New
Yorker made it more than a century ago. Such a comment would
not seem out of place in the United States or Great Britain following the attacks of 9/11 and 7/7. Americans and Britons have
struggled not only with domestic Islamist violence but also with
the question of how to respond, in terms of both national defense
and community engagement. Since the 2001 attacks, non-Muslim
Americans have crowded classrooms to learn about Islam, churches
and synagogues have invited Muslim speakers to conversations, and
mosques and Muslim organizations have heightened interfaith outreach. Nevertheless, Muslims have continued to suffer heightened
suspicion in both countries, drawing worried looks, enduring inva-
sive scrutiny, and even being removed from airliners. But the fact
that Webb's criticism—too often, even if decreasingly, appropriate in the United States and the United Kingdom of today—dates
from so long ago demonstrates that Anglo-American Islamophobia
is not new.

A historical exploration of British and American literature between
1690 and 1947 demonstrates the roots and qualities of Islamophobia
that Britons and Americans have shared. Meanwhile, significant
differences between the perspectives found in the two countries
demonstrate how these were fashioned by differing concerns about
their own societies. In order to emphasize this difference, we choose
to compare American views of Muslims with those found among
Britons who had lived in India. In the latter context, predominantly
white Christian Britons found themselves a minority in a land once
ruled by successive Muslim rulers who left impressive vestiges of
their once-mighty empires. As a ruling elite, Britons had to adapt
their Islamophobic inheritance to the exigencies of governing tens
of millions of Muslims. In the United States, engagements with
Muslims appeared to be a matter of international affairs alone,

"Mohammedans" representing an "other" far more distant than the Jews, Catholics, and other religious minorities who lived among the Protestant majority.

Before beginning, we need to outline the parameters of this study. First, by "Islamophobia," we refer to a largely unwarranted social anxiety about Islam and Muslims. Much more could be said about British and American stereotypes about Muslims. Other groups have also suffered negative stereotypes in these societies, but few communities have been perceived as so threatening. Hence, our argument here focuses only on the features of Muslims that have evoked such fear among the majority without exploring many of the other accusations about Muslims—such as their misogyny, their opposition to modernity, their commitment to a sensual religion, and their association with specific races. Other essays in this collection deal with these important issues, as does our previous work.[2]

Second, some might argue that American concerns about certain threats (e.g., the Barbary pirates) did not focus on Islam at all. We agree that in certain confrontations, American representations may have fixed primarily on the supposed race, ethnicity, and/or nation of an antagonistic group that happened to be Muslim. However, even such depictions almost invariably included Islamophobic inflections that proved Islam to be a damning quality of that group. For instance, the Barbary pirates might be "Arabs" but that included—if it was not exacerbated by—the unfortunate quality of being Muslim as well. Meanwhile, missionary literature continually reinforced the supposedly inherent conflict between Islam and Christianity. Third, we note that a focus on British perspectives in India should not suggest that South Asians did not have their own views, that they did not differ from Britons', or that they simply subsumed their understandings to British ones. Earlier scholarship has demonstrated the significant and changing dynamics of interaction and representation between many of the myriad groups of the subcontinent both preceeding and during British rule. However, our particular endeavor to track the shared heritage and divergent expressions of Anglo-American Islamophobia mandates the exclusion of these voices.

The Anglo-American Heritage

In the seventeenth and eighteenth centuries, no one influenced British and American attitudes toward Islam more than Humphrey Prideaux. In 1697, this Anglican theologian published his seminal book on the topic, *The True Nature of Imposture Fully Display'd in the Life of Mahomet*. The book's popularity led to eight editions in 25 years with copies finding their way to the American colonies as early as 1746.[3] Although the volume's central thesis—that a self-serving Muhammad intentionally deceived his followers by masquerading as a prophet—had long existed in Europe, his work made the allegation commonplace.[4] Originally, Prideaux sought to write a history of Constantinople's fall but, overwhelmed by a concern for what he perceived as British indifference to religion led him to narrate Muhammad's biography instead. The author highlighted the so-called prophet's fraud, tyranny, and fanaticism[5] in order to demonstrate the qualities of a *real* impostor and counter deist claims of Christianity's imposture.[6] Indeed, a section addressing deist claims took up half the original book's length. By the end of the eighteenth century, two American publishers released new editions to an audience shaped by revolution and religious schisms both at home and in France. The publisher of the second American edition sought to address the twin hazards of centralized government and oppressing dissent and omitted altogether the section devoted to the deist "apostacy" that so motivated Prideaux. To the editor, John Adams was the real threat, a modern Muhammad.[7] Thus, the same denigrations of Muhammad were adapted to critique different Anglo-American situations over the course of a century.

Continental views also influenced British and American perspectives. The French *philosophe* Voltaire intended his 1742 play, *Le fanatisme ou Mahomet le Prophete*, as both a warning against religious intolerance and praise of secular humanism. Clergyman James Miller translated Voltaire's work into English in a manner that supported the secular humanism theme while using the image of the lust-filled Mahomet to criticize fanaticism and the abuse of power. In England, it was reprinted annually between 1745 and 1777, while the play premiered in New York and Philadelphia in 1780 and 1796, respectively.[8]

These two early examples demonstrate three significant dimensions of Anglo-American Islamophobia that would be rehearsed repeatedly over succeeding centuries. First, depictions of Muslims—and of the final Islamic prophet in particular—often served as a foil serving social critiques of British and American domestic issues entirely unconnected to Islam. Just in the various editions of the two influential examples noted above, depictions of Muhammad's life aided endeavors to warn Britons and Americans against deism, federalism, political tyranny, religious apathy, and religious zealotry.

Second, the perception of Muslims and Islam as a threat pervaded so broadly that even the most ardent secularists and Christians (these groups were not mutually exclusive) could utilize them as foils serving quite divergent agendas. Prideaux saw Islam as the anti-Christian product of a power-hungry imposter. Voltaire viewed Muhammad's excesses as a warning to governments that espoused religion. As we shall see, secularists like Thomas Jefferson often included Muslims as an extreme example marking the lengths to which toleration should be practiced. Simultaneously, Christians often viewed Islam as—if not the greatest threat to Christianity—the largest obstacle to its universal expansion.

The third and final dimension of Anglo-American Islamophobia demonstrated by the example of Prideaux and Voltaire's works is how certain lines of communication facilitated the transcontinental transmission of Islamophobic ideas. Given the popular authority of those with personal experience of Muslims and the British empire's involvement with Muslim communities across the world, information and opinions often flowed westward across the Atlantic. Clearly, Britain and the other European powers with a stake in North America contributed the seeds for the first sad blossoms of Islamophobia there. This current continued through the next century as evidenced in a variety of ways by the American Charles Godfrey Leland. In 1874, he concluded his satirical travelogue by quoting an article from London's *Daily Telegraph*.

We are very glad to announce that the annual pilgrimage to Mecca has gone off this year with remarkable success. "Glad to announce!" we hear good Mrs. Grundy ejaculate; "why should a Christian newspaper rejoice over the happy conduct and termination of the rites and ceremonies of Mahound?" But the estimable lady in question ought to understand that this great custom of the Moslem world is no longer a matter of indifference to ourselves. The East and the West are nowadays so closely knit together by commerce and intercourse that, upon sanitary grounds alone, we have every reason to watch with the utmost interest the accounts form the holy cities of Arabia. Twice has Europe received the plague of cholera from the crowds that throng from all parts of the eastern world to Mecca and Medina.[9]

Clearly, the journalist anticipated antagonistic Christian responses to his news item. He used a fictional reader's objections to argue his case regarding the increasing relevance of information about Muslims. At a minimum, they represented a pathogenic threat.[10]

Leland's inclusion of the article was more than incidental. Imperialism both quickened the spread of information about Muslims and produced authoritative Western commentators on Islam. British imperial officials often served as sources of information both in their own country and in the United States. Although the experience of such officials with Muslims might be restricted to one region, others might extrapolate it to reflect on other or all Muslims. For instance, as the twentieth century opened, American James L. Barton prefaced his *Daybreak in Turkey* with a quote from Lord Cromer, the acerbic British agent and consul-general who served in Egypt for 24 years following duty in India.[11] Although many imperial officials and even many missionaries had a more nuanced view of Islam tempered by their direct experience of Muslim cultures, few attempted to dispel the popular perception regarding Islam's threat.

British and American experience of Muslims could diverge significantly. Throughout the two centuries of British rule in South Asia, Britons consistently differentiated Indians according to what they presumed to be mutually exclusionary, if not antagonistic, communities. Hence, Britons had constant contact with people they primarily described as Hindus and Muslims (ignoring the other identities individuals often held that defied this division) and their descriptions of India persistently included generalizations about these two groups.[12] On the other hand, few Americans other than sailors and missionaries knowingly encountered Muslims. Only in episodic moments of crisis—notably the Tripolitan War

(1801–1805), the Philippine–American War (1899–1902), and the Turkish question preceding and following the First World War— did many Americans have a sense of engagement with people who happened to be Muslims. Even then (and in contrast with the British in India), they often characterized their opponents chiefly by "nation" or "race," such as "Arab" or "Turk." Nevertheless, an incipient Muslim quality pervaded these identifications, as evidenced in period representations. Given the lack of contact with Muslims except in moments of crisis and through missionaries, Americans often relied on British views to inform their apprehensions about Islam. Thus, Thomas S. Kidd has observed, "Although one should hesitate to describe early Americans as conversant with Islam, they certainly conversed about Islam regularly."[13]

The Threat of Islam

For British and American audiences, the menace of Islam existed at a variety of different levels. Politically, socially, religiously, and theologically, Muslims and their religion were seen to threaten in varying degrees and in different ways Britain and America, secularism and Christianity.

The perception of threat to the state obviously differed between the United States and British India because of the disparity in the proximity of Muslims to the state. Very few Muslims lived in North America and those who did—enslaved African Muslims—seldom were recognized by European Americans as such. Recent scholarship estimates that, among the millions of Africans forced into American servitude, perhaps one out of five was a Muslim. Yet, severely repressive conditions meant that Islamic practices and identities seldom passed to successive generations. Expressing the view shared by most of his contemporaries, Puritan leader Cotton Mather declared, "We are afar off, in a Land, which never had (that I ever heard of) one Mahometan breathing in it."[14] Nevertheless, the currency of the inherited medieval view of Muslims as a twin peril—political and theological[15]—made Muslims an ideal hypothetical threat to be used in various political disputes within the early republic. Both Robert

J. Allison and Denise Spellberg have demonstrated how Muslims figured into the political rhetoric of constitutional debates in various states. Muslims represented an outlier group whose objectionable character—particularly the tyranny associated with the Ottoman court—made them the ultimate test case in many debates.[16] For instance, during the North Carolina debates regarding the requirement of a religious test for political candidates, delegates mentioned Muslims six times. Many references dealt with the issue of a Muslim becoming president.[17] Of course, such a possibility served only as a hypothetical, given that no delegate likely believed that Muslims existed in the new nation.

While controversies around new schemes of representation demonstrated how Muslims served as a worst-case scenario, disputes regarding governance provided opportunities to question whether fictive resident Muslims would be tolerated as Americans. For instance, a petition by citizens of Chesterfield County, Virginia, to their state assembly argued in 1785, "It is mens [sic] labour in our Manufactories, their services by sea and land that aggrandize our Country and not their creeds... Let Jews, Mehometans, and Christians of every denomination find their advantage in living under your laws."[18] More famously, Thomas Jefferson disapproved of an effort to insert "Jesus Christ" into a Virginia bill for religious freedom. He noted, "the insertion was rejected by a great majority, in proof that they meant to comprehend, within the mantle of its protection, the Jew and the Gentile, the Christian and Mahometan, the Hindoo, and Infidel of every denomination."[19] Of course, before Americans adopted Jefferson as a model of toleration, he had taken John Locke as his ideal. Demonstrating again the cross-Atlantic flow of ideas, Locke's *Letter of Toleration* (1689) influenced many Americans besides Jefferson. In it, he promoted the inclusion in public life of all Protestants—whatever their sect—before going a step further: "Nay, if we may openly speak the truth, and as becomes one man to another, neither pagan, nor Mahometan, nor Jew, ought to be excluded from the civil rights of the commonwealth, because of his religion. The Gospel commands no such thing."[20]

Locke and others used *fictive* Muslims to indicate the extremity of their inclusivity, knowing how acutely their audiences would view any *actual* Muslim presence as a threat. Each time statesmen took Muslims as an extreme example, they helped reinscribe the liminality of Muslims in the popular imagination. For instance, Locke declared in his *Letter* that toleration could not extend to those whose religion compels them to be faithful to a foreign prince. His one example was the Muslim who lives under a Christian magistrate "whilst at the same time he acknowledges himself bound to yield blind obedience to the mufti of Constantinople; who himself is entirely obedient to the Ottoman emperor, and frames the famed oracles of that religion according to his pleasure."[21] Islam, according to Locke, may incline a Muslim to unthinkingly obey a religion that ultimately sways at a tyrant's whim. If such a Muslim lives in a non-Muslim country, she introduces this tyrannical, foreign jurisdiction there. Locke's comments voiced three aspects of contemporary Anglo-American Islamophobia. First, that the Ottomans represented an exemplar of bad government and, second, that Muslims offered a nascent threat (of varying degrees according to the author) to every non-Muslim political order under whose jurisdiction they lived. Third, Locke, like Jefferson and the citizens of Chesterfield County, expressed the possibility that (at least some) Muslims *could* coexist under a non-Muslim government. Although such a threat remained in the abstract for Americans until the large-scale Muslim emigrations of the twentieth century, it haunted British administrators and others in British India following the uprising of 1857–1858. This wide-scale, virulent rebellion not only ushered in an end to the East India Company (EIC) as the British government assumed direct control over its Indian territories, it also instilled an overall British distrust toward Muslims.

For perhaps three reasons, British publications—at least when not written by missionaries—demonstrated few Islamophobic tendencies before 1857. First, the Mughals' precipitous decline meant that no Muslim group credibly challenged British domination. Despite the increasingly disruptive changes that the EIC made to the social and economic order, Muslims seldom questioned British ascendancy and few Islamic revivalists of the period openly contested British rule.

Second, inspiring Mughal architecture impressed many British observers even as it attested to Muslim decline. The Mughals may have been despotic—as seemed an inevitable conclusion in the Anglo-American view of any "oriental" and "Muslim" state—but the benefits of their governance could be appreciated too, now that they posed no threat. James Mill, whose *History of British India* (1817) represents one of the most influential and tartest British appraisals of South Asians, praised Muslims for their sophistication relative to Hindus. India's "Mahomedan conquerors" manifested "an activity, a manliness, an independence, which rendered it less easy for despotism to sink, among them, to that disgusting state of weak and profligate barbarism, which is the natural condition of government among such a passive people as the Hindus."[22]

Mill demonstrates here a dynamic common among Britons in India: the identification of a specific characteristic supposedly unique to one religious group might be the reason that one Briton *praised* Muslims relative to Hindus and the reason another *condemned* Muslims in favor of Hindus. The manliness that Mill saw curtailing despotism would be viewed as the very engine of Muslim tyranny by others. However, as with Mill, few Britons considered either community superior to their own. In this manner, Britons often positioned themselves as the normative middle ground between two extremes of human behavior and belief. If most Hindu men seemed passively effeminate and Muslim men fanatically violent, then the British man represented the proper poise of action and restraint. If Hinduism promoted a retrograde idolatry similar to Catholicism and Islam represented an apostate's arrogance similar to heresy, then the Church of England provided the truth of the only god.

The third aspect of pre-1857 conditions that mitigated British Islamophobia was the model of tolerance some Britons saw as instrumental to Mughal success. For instance, long after Mughal political power had evaporated, Anglican bishop Reginald Heber reported in his Indian travelogue (1828) that "the fierce Mohammadans" only had begun to question British control because Britons had disrespected the Mughal court.[23] The same year, Walter Hamilton in his gazetteer of India stumped for a respectful British policy toward the downfallen Mughal lineage, "The most rational course appeared to be, to leave the king's authority exactly in the state in which it was found, and to afford the royal family the means of subsistence…not unsuitable to a fallen but illustrious race."[24] A quarter century later, Edward Thornton noted in his gazetteer "The feelings of deference for the throne of Delhi extended to provinces very remote from the seat of its former grandeur, and to Hindoos not less than to Mahomedans. It was in fact universal."[25] Undoubtedly, this transcommunal respect must have struck some Britons in India as evidence of toleration's advantages, just as Locke and others promoted at home. Depictions of Aurangzeb's reign—characterized by temple destruction, Sikh oppression, and the *jizya* tax—conformed much more closely with the prevalent picture of the Ottomans, the exemplar of Muslim prejudice and tyranny. For most, though, this last great Mughal provided the exception that proved the rule, his stereotypical Muslim intolerance for non-Muslims standing in unwelcome contrast with the remarkable inclusiveness of his predecessors Akbar, Jahangir, and Shah Jahan. This pre-1857 generosity toward the erstwhile Mughal empire would be significantly undermined by the mutiny of many of the Company's Indian soldiers, the uprising among parts of the population, and the slaughter of British civilians.

    W. W. Hunter most infamously voiced this change in *The Indian Musalmans: Are They Bound by Conscience to Rebel against the Queen?* (1871). His initial chapter titles amply portray the volume's tenor: "The Standing Rebel Camp on Our Frontier" and "The Chronic Conspiracy within Our Territory." Although British authors often qualified their concerns about Muslims by reassuring their audiences of the loyalty of most Indian Muslims,[26] Hunter began his book with the assertion, "While the more fanatical of the Musalmáns have thus engaged in overt sedition, the whole Muhammadan community has been openly deliberating on their obligation to rebel."[27] As a long-time officer in the Bengal Civil Service and member of numerous learned societies, Hunter was highly influential with his opinions. He reversed the formula found in other works in which Aurangzeb served as the intolerant outlier among Mughal emperors, demonstrating how even Akbar's tolerance was overshadowed by the pervasive religious chauvinism of his courtiers. Overall, however, Hunter said little about the dynasty, reflecting primarily on the positive sea change accomplished by the British administration of India, especially in Bengal. For instance, Hunter characterized government under Muslims as "an engine for enriching the few, not for protecting the many"[28] (a characterization not ill-fitted to describe contemporary Indian conditions under British governance). Although the author dedicated a chapter to describing the wrongs Muslims alleged to have suffered under British domination, he mostly placed the onus for change on them, not the government.

The repetition of his claims by later authors reflects the persistent popularity of Hunter's perspectives. As W. A. Wilson, a Canadian missionary in Indore, made his own case for the distrustfulness of Muslims in 1911, he quoted Hunter, "The Mussulmans of India are and have been a source of chronic danger to the British power in India." Wilson went further, claiming obliquely that, "There are many who doubt the loyalty of the Mohammedan people as a whole." For evidence, Wilson followed Hunter by pointing to the so-called Wahhabi conspiracies, Qur'anic injunctions to overthrow infidel rule, and Muslim resistance on the northwest frontier. But as with most Islamophobic authors in British India, Wilson viewed one event to hang particularly heavily over Muslim heads: "They remind us of the part they played in the terrible mutiny, when they pressed to the front and through rivers of blood made a furious dash to seize the standard of empire."[29] As the terrible series of vengeful reprisals reaped immediately following the end of the rebellion demonstrated, Muslims took the brunt of British blame although they were no more seditious than Hindus and many Muslim soldiers and officials had remained loyal. However, at the revolt's height, the Mughal emperor had reluctantly sided with the mutineers who pressed for his support. In the later effort to explain the seemingly sudden reversal of reverence for British rule, many Britons described a resentful monarch leading disenfranchised nobles and sullen soldiers in a vain struggle to reestablish the decrepit former order of Muslim position and prestige. As Wilson's comment demonstrates, a half century later, this view and the passion behind it had not dissipated much among Britons and many members of the colonies.

Meanwhile, at least one commentator in the United States drew a larger lesson from the rebellion. D. H. Wheeler, president of the Chautauqua Institution, despaired in 1885 that Britons had ignored "the religious source" of the uprising and continued their twin practices of arming some Muslims and slaughtering others. "[England] is uniting Islam, and teaching Islam how to make war...A Moslem victory is proclaimed in every Arab tent, and in every Indian village." While decrying the European atrocities, Wheeler preferred that Islam "should be locked fast in the iron arms of the British empire" for the sake of Christendom.[30]

Wheeler reflected yet another Islamophobic concern among many Britons and Americans: a global surge of Islamism meant to bring the world under singular Muslim domination. Much of this centered on Istanbul (or Constantinople, the name many commentators preferred), "the capital of Mohammedanism" as an American missionary there put it in 1835. In his overview of religions that went through at least five reprintings in the first half of the nineteenth century, John Haywood explained that Muslims' "spiritual head" lived in Turkey, a man equivalent to the "Roman Pontiff, or the Grecian Patriarch."[31] He was referring to the *khalifa* (caliph), an office of leadership of the entire Muslim community dating back to the successors of Muhammad. The Ottoman sultans had claimed it for themselves since 1517. In 1892, the American Catholic priest Charles C. Starbuck cautioned that this Muslim "Pope" might yet unite all Muslims whom he characterized as "simply a vast agglomeration of disconnected atoms, like its own sand-wastes," conflating Muslims with the people of the desert.[32] Wheeler did not seem to fear the caliph per se, but believed that pan-Islamism awaited only for another Muhammad to galvanize the expectant Muslim masses. "When the Prophet is once crowned with the diadem of military success, there is an army of Mohammedans in India wearing the queen's uniform, there are vast resources at Constantinople ready to fall from the helpless hands of the Sultan...There are two hundred millions of Mohammedans waiting for a leader to restore the glories of Islam."[33]

In contrast with these American anxieties, Britons in India only became alarmed at the prospect of an Ottoman-oriented pan-Islamism as the nineteenth century concluded. Officials began to fear that Turkish agents were stirring discontent in India. Important intellectuals like Sir Muhammad Iqbal and Abul Kalam Azad promoted an Islamic identity that transcended national borders, a widespread sentiment among the *ulama*.[34] Pro-British Muslims such as Sir Saiyid Ahmad Khan and Mirza Ghulam Ahmad felt compelled to write tracts defending loyalty to the British government as popular support grew for the Turkish sultan.[35] However, no uprising ever pursued any Ottoman-oriented ends.

At the start of the First World War, when the Ottomans allied with Briton's enemies, British anxiety deepened. Immediately, the Government of India telegraphed all districts describing pan-Islamism to officials, directing them to warn certain Muslim preachers of the consequences of criticizing the government, and requiring all householders to report foreigners.[36] Despite such concerns, after the war, some authorities aimed to use pan-Islamic thought to British advantage. In 1919, the Government of India sent to at least one provincial government a copy of a fatwa that called "upon all Muhammadans to oppose Bolshevism" and the central government sought to publicize it by feeding it to Muslim newspapers.[37] Independence leader Mohandas Gandhi saw advantage too in pan-Islamist sentiment and allied his Congress Party with the Khilafat movement that sought to prevent the victorious Allies from removing the caliph and dismembering the Ottoman empire. In 1924, the entire issue vanished when the Turkish National Assembly eliminated the caliphate in the course of establishing a fully secular republic.

Although Americans and Britons shared a trepidation regarding a global Islamic movement that never emerged, the British continually fretted about local uprisings. The event that most inculcated this fear and until 1857 served as the primary justification for it was the "Wahhabi movement." As Hardy put it, "In thinking about Muslims after 1857, the so-called Wahhabis were for the British the great unthinkable that was always thought." British belief in Indian-based Wahhabis originated in the 1820s, as Saiyid Ahmad Shahid and his followers moved to the northwest territories to launch a jihad against the Sikhs who ruled there. Their Tariqah-i Muhammadi may have shared a notion of jihad with Arabia's Wahhabis, but its efforts at reform drew much more from Sufi traditions. Saiyad Ahmad's jihad failed but some of his followers remained on the frontier into at least the 1870s. British concerns loomed more menacingly than the actual threat, the *mujahidin* numbering perhaps 600 in 1852.[38]

Although this so-called conspiracy began twice as long ago as the 1857 rebellion—which had far more immediate effect on Britons— Hunter's *The Indian Musalmans* includes far more references to the former. Hunter, like many other Britons, collapsed diverse Muslim movements seeking divergent goals in disparate parts of India into the category "Wahhabi." This phantasmal conspiracy thus ranged across a great swath of territory over a long period of time. Britons erroneously conflated a wide range of Muslim political endeavors with "Wahhabism" such as Bengal's Faraizi movement, a coup attempt by the Nizam of Hyderabad's brother, and the assassinations of a viceroy and chief justice.[39] In fact, no such unity existed among Islamist groups and a puny proportion of Muslims evinced interest in any of them. In fact, the popular Muslim movements of the nineteenth century primarily focused on Islamic reform and revival, many of them on an entirely personal level.[40] Yet, as late as 1937, the Government of India could not be certain that the Wahhabi threat had entirely dissipated.[41] Sir Saiyid blamed three factors for the recent public scrutiny of Muslim loyalty: trials of supposed Wahhabis, the murder of the chief justice, and Hunter's book, to which he wrote a rejoinder.[42]

Of course, the final act of Muslim anti-imperialism would be the Pakistan movement. Initiated in 1930 with Iqbal's call for a separate Muslim homeland, it culminated with the partition of the subcontinent's British-held territories and semi-independent states into an independent India and Pakistan at the very moment when Britain relinquished its control in 1947. For many Pakistan proponents—certainly for its ultimate leader, Muhammad Ali Jinnah—separatism represented less an anti-imperial and anti-Hindu agenda than a political threat to obtain minority concessions from the British-led government and Hindu-dominated Congress Party. Indeed, once the endgame had played out and the sought concessions failed to materialize, Jinnah steered the movement into close alliance with the British during the Second World War in order to best obtain his objectives even as Gandhi and the rest of the Congress leadership sat imprisoned for their wartime efforts to undermine British rule.

Although Britons in India differed from Americans because of the active (if exaggerated) threat to their political order, both shared a conviction regarding two alleged qualities of Islam that made it a perennial menace: the proclivity of Muslims to spread their religion and to do so violently. In their reflections on the proselytizing power of Muslims—an issue among Europeans since at least the eighth century when predominantly Christian north Africa and Spain converted almost entirely to Islam—Americans and Britons almost universally explained mass conversion as the result of coercion. In the preface to his book on Muhammad's "imposture," Prideaux emphasized how the Eastern churches abdicated Christianity with "the Sword at their Throats."[43] Such sentiments persisted throughout ensuing centuries, not being limited to publications by Christian apologists. In 1872, the British government in Calcutta (Kolkata) published Edward Tuite Dalton's ethnology of Bengal, which argued that Muslim rulers had forced or induced "aborigines" and Hindus to accept Islam.[44] Some warned that coercive conversions did not belong just to the past but may again menace Christians. For instance, in 1835 Eli Smith, an American missionary in Turkey, imagined for his audience in a Boston magazine that the dead ancient Christians of Western Asia warned American Christians today, "Hereafter, upon the fair face of your beloved America, as now upon that glory of all lands which was once our country, a night of apostasy may settle down, and hordes of yet unnamed barbarian invaders fasten deep the blight of some new Mohammedanism" [sic]. Smith shamed his coreligionists by contrasting their lack of ardor with Muslim zealotry: "Is a mere *handful* of missionaries all that enlightened Christian benevolence can send forth, where the superstition of the dark ages sent forth *armies*?"[45]

Smith's reference to the armies of Islam reflected a troubling question: Why had the armies of Christendom been unable to halt the rapid Muslim expansion? Why were current missionaries unable to convert Muslims today? After all, many Christians considered the steady global advance of their religion as a testament to its truth. How to explain yesterday's setbacks and today's stalemate? One answer that most Americans and Britons seemingly accepted was that the inherent fanaticism of (male) Muslims produced their violent success. According to the well-respected and widely read Briton Claudius Buchanan (1807), Muslims were a "dagger-drawing people" who maintained a "vindictive spirit."[46] Smith, in 1835, opined that religious fanaticism was "the strongest principle of obedience in the Turkish citizen, and of bravery in the Turkish soldier."[47] Meanwhile, their concerns for the chaos of revolutionary France and the march of Napoleon's armies gave Americans opportunities to demonstrate how "fanatic" and "Muslim" seemed almost synonymous. In 1814, Thomas Jefferson likened the "military Fanatic" Napoleon to Achilles, Alexander, Caesar, and "Mahomet."[48] Five decades later, a Boston literary journal published an article that reflected on the extreme fanaticism once seen in France: "The only historical phenomenon to which this transformation of France can be compared is that of the rise of such a religion as Mahometanism... The fanatical Frenchman believes in the ideas of '89 very much as the Mahometan believes in the Koran. He hates a noble or a priest as a Mahometan hates a Giaour [non-Muslim]."[49] Early in the next century, President Theodore Roosevelt compared Muslims with a more domestic model of fanaticism when answering critics of his policies toward a rebellious minority in the Philippines: "To abandon the Moro country as our opponents propose in their platform, would be precisely as if twenty-five years ago we had withdrawn the Army and the civil agents from within and around the Indian reservations in the West, at a time when the Sioux and the Apache were still the terror of our settlers."[50] Popular portrayals of Muslim Arabs, Turks, and Moros demonstrated the near universal association of fanaticism with Muslim men and helped to explain the initial expansion and contemporary entrenchedness of Islam.

When commentators did not attribute coercion as the cause of conversion, they blamed Muslim success on some negative quality of the proselytized. In his review of world religions (1842), Haywood blamed Islam's early gains not only on "the terror of Mahomet's arms" but also Islamic law, which suited "the manners and opinions of the Eastern nations." Islam's few doctrines were simple, its duties easy, and nothing was "incompatible with the empire of appetites and passions" that characterized Arabs and most Easterners.[51] In 1892, a publication of the Church of England's Church Missionary Society (CMS) credited the prophet's success to a combined strategy of carrot and stick, arguing that Muhammad took a decrepit form of Judaism and Christianity and "added to it elements of worldliness and sensuality which rendered it acceptable to the natural mind, and by establishing the principle of enforcing his tenets by the sword, he ensured their zealous propagation."[52] While these Americans and Britons avoided any suggestion that someone, drawn by a positive characteristic of the religion, might willingly accept Islam, others argued that if there had been a good reason for South Asians to convert, it reflected less the value of Islam than the deficits of Hinduism, specifically caste prejudice and the proscription of widow remarriage. Reverend John Takle—a New Zealander working as a missionary in Bengal—used the most recent "scientific" evidence of phrenology that tracked intermarriage between Muslim and native races to supposedly prove a long-standing conclusion. In 1911, he stated, "The anthropometric survey made by government proves conclusively that the vast majority of the Mohammedans in India are converts from among the depressed Hindu communities."[53]

The "scientific" dimension of European imperialism not only seemed to affirm existing views about Muslims and Islam, it also helped deepen fears by proving how many Muslims existed. Anglo-American literature about Muslims repeatedly stressed their considerable population. Recall that in Smith's essay on Turkey, he warned Americans of "hordes of yet unnamed barbarian invaders" that might sweep the United States if enough missionaries did not meet the Islamic threat. In 1842, Hayward indicated a world population of 140 million Muslims.[54] An 1850 letter in the *Missionary Herald* by a "Mr. Hume" began with a reckoning of the relative numbers of Muslims and Hindus in Bombay, drawing on data derived from the recently instituted census there.[55] Although some European states had begun to develop demographic tools to better understand their populations by this time, the British were creating a more thorough and expansive census for their Indian territories than they exercised at home. The first all-India census (1872) and the several city and provincial counts that preceded it each required those polled to give their religion. The resulting numbers alarmed Britons because the population of Muslims exceeded their expectations. But more than statistics on the *overall* Muslim population, those tracking its *growth* only worsened Anglo-American fears. Muslims appeared to out-proliferate Hindus and Christians. For instance, two authors detailing the missionary work of the United Free Church of Scotland opened their 1910 book with a quote from the census commissioner followed by their own prognostication.

"In East Bengal two-thirds of the inhabitants and in North Bengal nearly three-fifths are followers of the Prophet." As the Mohammedans in those regions increase faster than Hindus, it is quite possible that within a few decades Hinduism may be banished from those parts of Bengal...The influence of Islam is the most powerful engine destroying Hinduism in North and East Bengal at the present day.[56]

The next year, Takle cited U. N. Mukherjee of the Indian Medical Services whose pamphlet "A Dying Race?" made much the same argument. Official demography added to the stream of knowledge about Muslims that imperialism made available to Britons and Americans.[57]

Reflecting on the overall expansion of Islam, the American missionary Samuel M. Zwemer, a recognized authority who published repeatedly on Islam, declared of "the Moslem Peril," "It is now or never; it is Islam or Christ!"[58] Zwelmer's sentiment signals the last quality of Islamophobia that featured prominently in Anglo-American discourse: Islam as Christianity's inherent and inexorable nemesis. In his deliberations on the demographic eclipse of Hinduism in India, Takle approvingly quoted another author who claimed, "India, unless all is changed by the intervention of some new force, must become a Mohammedan country... The intervening spiritual force which ought to prevent this is, of course, Christianity."[59] The most prominent qualities of Muslims that threatened Christians included their universal resistance to conversion, consistent success in proselytization, and their flawed belief in Jesus Christ that denied his divinity. The latter claim often meant that Western Christians considered Muslims as heretics or apostates, a threat to the doctrinal orthodoxy central to many churches.

Christians feared Muslims both as a radically other religious competitor *and* a despoiled fraction of Christians. Deprecating Muslims often served efforts to police the doctrinal boundary circumscribing "true Christianity," as seen in Roger Williams's answer to Quaker founder George Fox in *G. Fox Digg'd out of His Burrows* (1676). Although he tolerated Quakers in his colony of Rhode Island, Williams distrusted their theology. So, when Fox claimed that the growth of the Quaker community demonstrated its credibility, Williams retorted that Islam and Roman Catholicism had grown equally as quickly. Elsewhere, Williams wrote of his anticipation that the destruction of Islam and Catholicism would coincide, along with the mass conversion of the Jews, with the apocalypse. Contemporaneously, Cotton Mather reflected on the eschatological promise both of Protestant royal power ascending in England over Catholicism and of the perhaps imminent fall of Rome and the Turkish sultan.[60] In 1912, Bruce Kinney wrote *Mormonism: The Islam of America*, the book's title stemming from the perceived similarities between the two religions in terms of topics such as polygamy and ideas on heaven. The resemblance was not intended to be a salutary one, as the book, written by a former superintendent of Baptist missions in Utah, dealt with "the Mormon problem."[61] Jews, too, featured in this Christian boundary policing, and it is not incidental that some of the authors whose books on Muslims we have considered also published on Jews: Prideaux wrote on the Bible and Jewish history (1725), Buchanan described the Jews of south India (early 1800s), and Starbuck penned "The Jew in Europe: Christianity's Antagonist" (1900).

Many authors portrayed Muslims as more dangerous than just misled Christians: Islam and Christianity had locked into (im)mortal combat. When John Dickinson, delegate to both the Continental Congress and Constitutional Convention, described the advancement of nations, he (mistakenly) noted that the Portuguese arrival in India disrupted the advent of Muslim power. This proved providential since "there [is] the least reason to question, that they would have strenuously employed the increase of wealth and power in their favourite design of reducing all *Christendom* to the same miserable slavery, with which by their oppressive superstition, so many celebrated parts of it, including the Birthplace of its religion, have already been overwhelmed."[62] Muslims had "contempt towards the gospel," as Smith said in 1835, drawing on his experience in Turkey. Starbuck concluded in 1892, "Christendom and Mohammedanism have been misled by no false instinct in their unconquerable and deadly antipathy to each other."[63] "The Gospel in the Mission Field has no more powerful or bitter foe than Islam, or the religion of the false prophet Mohammed" as a CMS article reported the same year. In its competition with Islam in West Asia, Christianity "was driven to the wall and lost nearly everything."[64]

The successful resistance of Muslims to conversion and flourishing Islamic proselytizing seemed twin roadblocks to the cherished goal of Christianizing humanity. Without any apparent sense of irony, Hume wrote "We are well aware that Mohammedans, wherever found, constitute a difficult, and hitherto a comparatively unfruitful field...They regard themselves as God's peculiar people, and look with feelings of hatred and contempt upon all opposing religions."[65] Although Anglican missionary James Long referred in 1875 to both "the Brahmanical pride and Moslem arrogance" that consigned Bengali children "to the dungeons of ignorance and degradation,"[66] most missionaries equated only Muslims with stubbornness and resistance. Notably, Long did not refer to "Hindu pride" as an obstacle to conversion, indicating that his frustration extended only to Brahmans, not all Hindus. Christian missionaries in India tended to have the most success among the very groups they alleged Muslims to have converted: the lowest ranking castes and most impoverished classes. The view of this inherent, ultimate conflict persisted into the twentieth century (and longer), especially in British India where missionaries from throughout the Anglo-American world labored. The Canadian Presbyterian missionary Wilson believed "There is ground for the opinion that the final struggle for the religious conquest of Eastern nations will be between Christianity and Islam."[67]

Many Americans and Britons drew the ultimate conclusion to this Christian Islamophobia: Islam had to be destroyed. Muslims needed to be converted for the sake of their souls. As Hume had asked, "Shall we be content to leave the followers of the false prophet to perish in their pride and unbelief? No, surely. Mohammedans, as well as the heathen, have been given to Christ for his inheritance; and for their conversion the church of Christ must labor and pray."[68] Many agreed with Wilson that without redemptive power, Islam could only ever thwart salvation.[69] Some imagined the struggle more cosmologically. As we have seen, Williams and Mather expected an eschatological conclusion to the battle. John Prentiss Kewley Henshaw, an American evangelical who later became Episcopal bishop of Rhode Island, used the book of Revelation to anticipate the destruction of anti-Christian powers, including Muslims and the "Papal Apostacy." He expected that before long Islam will "be overthrown, and sunk in the pit whence it emanated."[70] Such convictions connected Muslims with Satan and/or the Antichrist. Comparing the Qur'an with the Gospels, missionary C. B. Leupolt found "The former is calculated to lead me daily farther away from God, and unite them closer with the prince of darkness."[71] Even the sober Benjamin Franklin made this association among the maxims penned for *Poor Richard's Almanack* in 1741:

Turn Turk *Tim*, and renounce thy Faith
in Words as well as Actions:
Is it worse to follow *Mahomet* than the Devil?[72]

In colonial America, many Protestants associated Islam and Catholicism with the Antichrist.[73] Indeed, Prideaux considered related the rise of Muhammad and the bishop of Rome's claim to reign over all churches. Hence, the *"Antichrist* seems at this time to have set both his Feet upon *Christendom* together, the one in the *East*, and the other in the *West*."[74] As already seen, many authors viewed Christian division and degradation as the cause of the successful rise of Islam. How better to reconcile the triumphant truth of Christianity with its historical setbacks beginning in the seventh century than to portray the conquered churches as corrupted? Prideaux viewed Muslims as a tool used by God to punish the sinful Eastern churches. God raised "the *Saracens* to be the Instruments of his Wrath, to punish them for it."[75] Simultaneously such an explanation chastised contemporary dissenting Christians with the threat of God's possible punishment and explained the loss of Christendom's heartland while denigrating Islam.

Despite the shared conviction among many Britons and Americans that Islam stood in inherent antagonism to Christianity and the sentiment among some that it should be destroyed, Britons in India—especially those serving the government—remained conflicted about how to proceed. Although some of its servants viewed Muslims as antithetical to Company aims, the EIC initially preferred to minimalize Christian missionary activity, concerned that resulting antagonisms might disrupt commerce. Detecting this, Buchanan wrote in 1807 to the governor-general of India and alleged that the Company was "hostile to the progress of Christianity." The Bengal government justified itself to the Court of Directors through allusion to the principles of toleration practiced in England toward minorities, notably Jews and Catholics. The directors initially both supported the government's strictures on missionaries and warned against restrictions on "the British faith, on which [Indians] rely for the free exercise of their religion." Buchanan responded that because Muslims were violent and vindictive, he expected that peace could be achieved only by educating Muslim children in Christian schools, Christianizing them even as their parents resisted.[76] Meanwhile, James Owen of the British and Foreign Bible Society contended that government should promote the Bible because "the sooner it supersedes the Shaster [Hindu scripture] and the Koran, the sooner will the happiness of India be consummated."[77] Others objected. Thomas Twining, a senior merchant for the Company in Bengal, argued that either the conversion of India's people should be left to God, or else British efforts would be met with unrelenting hostility.[78] In the end, Buchanan's publications proved particularly consequential (as did the efforts of the evangelical Christian, William Wilberforce) and when Parliament renewed the Company's charter, they included greater latitude for missionary work.

The rising tide of British evangelicalism ensured the persistence of the issue. William Buyers, a 20-year veteran of the London Missionary Society in north India, sought greater government attention on "the destruction of Hinduism and Muhammadanism, and on the speedy extension of Christianity."[79] Nearly a century later, a government publication reflecting on this period celebrated the support government had provided to missionaries in India as part of the effort by which "Christian Europe is spreading the Light of the World from the north to the south pole."[80] If the successful conversion of Muslims had not shown god's favor on Christianity, then the success of Christian Europe's empires did. Samuel M. Zwemer, one of the most famous—and perhaps the most well-published— missionaries to Muslims summed up this view: "In India and Malaysia God's favor has given us an open door to 100,000,000 Mohammedans. Under Queen Wilhelmina, the Christian Queen of Holland and under George V, the Christian Emperor of India, 100,000,000 Mohammedans are enjoying the blessings of Protestant Christian rule." [81] Robert Stewart, United Presbyterian missionary from the United States, put the overall matter succinctly in 1896 when he declared of the British empire that "its motto, like that of the old Romans, can be nothing else than this, *Carthago delenda est*, 'Carthage must be destroyed.'"[82]

Conclusion

It must be reemphasized that not all Americans or Britons shared extreme Islamophobic sentiments. Some positively valued the religion and the cultures associated with it. Some converted, as perhaps had the New Yorker Mohammed Alexander Russell Webb. However, the preponderance of publications from the late eighteenth to the middle of the twentieth century demonstrates recurring themes of fear and threat beyond the sentiments of disapproval and loathing also present. Leupolt found some beautiful Quranic passages and Muslim traditions, even if—as he believed and stressed—these were ones that Muslims never mentioned.[83]

Americans and those Britons serving in India often differed in their perception of Muslims. Few Americans benefited from actual contact with Muslims that many Britons experienced occasionally, if not daily. However, after 1857, Britons in India eyed Muslims more warily as a source of potential rebellion. In both the American and British cases, European imperialism made more known about Islam than ever before, although such information was often inflected by administrative anxieties and Christian concerns. Zwemer explained, "We know to-day something of the true horror of Islam. Our women are no longer ignorant of the unspeakable degradation to womanhood in Mohammedanism. We know that this religion is inadequate intellectually, socially, morally." Islam was Christianity's "competitor."[84]

Such convictions presumed a singular Islam that required all adherents to act in prescribed ways. This helped make a pan-Indian conspiracy plausible in many British imaginations. The stereotype of the inherently intolerant, aggressive jihadi that informed British concerns for a potentially India-wide Wahhabi conspiracy rested on a reified understanding of Islam that pictured the religion as a self-motivating agent. For instance, a government ethnography of Indians (1937) stated "Islam is a unity in which there is no distinction and this unity is secured by making men believe two simple propositions, *viz.,* the unity of God and the mission of the Prophet," even as it went on to describe Muslim "sects."[85] Missionaries, too, often referred to an essentialized Islam, as Zwemer demonstrated 30 years earlier, "In India Islam has abandoned, as untenable, controversial positions which were once thought impregnable."[86] Again, others dissented. For instance, in response to the anti-Muslim sentiment he observed filling a newspaper's columns following the Muslim assassination of a British chief justice, the Orientalist W. Nassau Lees portrayed the multi-vocality of Islamic law, emphasizing how most Islamic jurists had ruled that Muslims could live under a Christian government, although some groups—such as Wahhabis—would not.[87]

Our essay began with a century-old contention about the accuracy of media portrayals of Muslims that appears pertinent today. Many of the Islamophobic allegations described still reverberate, especially in conversations, websites, blogs, and viral emails in the United States, United Kingdom, and India. On the governmental level, the Bush administration endeavored to foster pan-Islamic anxiety by imagining al-Qaeda's ambition to establish, in the words of US President George W. Bush (2005), "a totalitarian Islamic empire that reaches from Indonesia to Spain."[88] Meanwhile, currently popular book titles reflect past themes: *Religion of Peace? Why Christianity Is and Islam Isn't*; *Islam Unveiled: Disturbing Questions about the World's Fastest-Growing Faith*; *Antichrist: Islam's Awaited Messiah*; *While Europe Slept: How Radical Islam is Destroying the West from Within.*

Some volumes more than echo past perspectives: *Answering Islam: The Crescent in Light of the Cross* (1993, 2006), for instance, begins by citing Zwemer. This book's goal of providing Christians with counterarguments to Islamic beliefs—"preparing you with strong apologetic answers"[89]—reflects how the perpetuation of Islamophobia often represents more of an effort to positively define those making the allegations than accurately describe Muslims or Islam. The American Catholic priest Starbuck recognized this when he observed in the nineteenth century, "We know Mohammedanism better and worse than Hinduism or Confucianism or Buddhism. It has been implicated inextricably with Christianity as a tremendously aggressive and intensely hostile force during all the twelve centuries of its existence. This, until our own day, has made objective study of it almost impossible."[90]

The globalization and democratization of the flow of information allow Muslims nearly everywhere to take note of the currency of Islamophobic sentiments. Most recently, in the Pakistani film *Khuda Kay Liye* (2007) a sadistic American official begins his abusive interrogation of a Muslim by declaring, "Not all Muslims are terrorists but all terrorists are Muslims." The film thus connects this truism—regularly repeated in the United States and United Kingdom—with state-sanctioned violence against Muslims. It is precisely through such a dynamic that Samuel Huntington's thesis regarding a clash of civilizations—perhaps more extreme in its reception than its author intended—becomes perceived, if not actuated, reality.

Notes

1. John Wesley Hanson, *The World's Congress of Religions: The Addresses and Papers Delivered before the Parliament, and an Abstract of the Congresses Held in the Art Institute, Chicago, Aug. 25 to Oct. 15, 1893, Under the Auspices of the World's Columbian Exposition* (Chicago, IL: Monarch Book, 1894), pp. 523–524.
2. Peter Gottschalk and Gabriel Greenberg, *Islamophobia: Making Muslims the Enemy* (Lanham, MD: Rowman & Littlefield, 2007).
3. Thomas S. Kidd, *American Christians and Islam: Evangelical Culture and Muslims from the Colonial Period to the Age of Terrorism* (Princeton, NJ: Princeton University Press, 2009), pp. 6, 9.
4. Thomas S. Kidd, " 'Is It Worse to Follow Mahomet than the Devil?' Early American Uses of Islam." *Church History* 72:4 (December 2003), p. 773.
5. Robert J. Allison, *The Crescent Obscured: The United States and the Muslim World, 1776–1815* (New York: Oxford University Press, 1995), p. 37.
6. Humphrey Prideaux, *The True Nature of Imposture Fully Display'd in the Life of Mahomet: With a Discourse Annex'd for the Vindication of Christianity from this Charge: Offered to the Consideration of the Deists of the Present Age* (8th edition, London: E. Curll, 1723), pp. iii–viii.
7. Kidd, 2003, p. 787.
8. Allison, pp. 43–45.

9. Charles Godfrey Leland, *The Egyptian Sketch Book* (New York: Hurd and Houghton, 1874), p. 326.
10. In *The Satanic Verses* (1988), Salman Rushdie would recycle "Mahound" for English literature, noting its objectionable origins as a slur.
11. James Levi Barton, *Daybreak in Turkey* (Boston, MA: Pilgrim, 1908), p. 10.
12. For a history of British constructions of a religiously defined and bifurcated India, see Peter Gottschalk, *Religion, Science, and Empire: Classifying Hinduism and Islam in British India.* (New York: Oxford University Press, 2012).
13. Kidd, 2003, p. 766.
14. Kidd, 2003, p. 767.
15. John L. Esposito, *The Islamic Threat: Myth or Reality?* (New York: Oxford University Press, 1992), p. 45.
16. However, Muslims did not serve as the ultimate outlier for all early Americans. In New Hampshire's ratification convention, one delegate commented that "a Turk, a Jew, a Rom[an] Catholic and, what is worse than all, a Universal[ist], may be President of the United States." Denise Spellberg, "Could a Muslim Be President? An Eighteenth-Century Constitutional Debate." *Eighteenth-Century Studies* 39 (2006), p. 492.
17. Spellberg, p. 493.
18. James H. Hutson, "Founding Fathers and Islam: Library Papers Show Early Tolerance for Muslim Faith." *Library of Congress Information Bulletin* 61:5 (May 2002), http://www.loc.gov/loc/lcib/0205/tolerance.html, accessed February 14, 2009.
19. Thomas Jefferson, *Memoirs, Correspondence, and Private Papers of Thomas Jefferson: Late President of the United States*, volume I, ed. Thomas Jefferson Randolph (London: Henry Colburn and Richard Bentley, 1829), pp. 38–39.
20. John Locke, *John Locke: A Letter Concerning Toleration, in Focus*, ed. John P. Horton and Susan Mendus (London: Routledge, 1991), p. 35.
21. Locke, p. 32.
22. James Mill, *The History of British India*, ed. William Thomas (Chicago, IL: The University of Chicago Press, 1975 [1817]), p. 309.
23. Hardy, pp. 33–34.
24. Walter Hamilton, *East-India Gazetteer; Containing Particular Descriptions of the Empires, Kingdoms, Principalities, Provinces, Cities, Towns, Districts, Fortresses, Harbours, Rivers, Lakes, &c of Hindostan, and the Adjacent Countries, India Beyond the Ganges, and the Eastern Archipelago*, volume I (Delhi: Low Price, 1993 [1828]), p. 497.
25. Edward Thornton, *A Gazetteer of the Territories under the Government of the East-India Company, and of the Native States on the Continent of India* (Delhi: Low Price Publications, 1993 [1858]), pp. 264–265.

26. For instance, see W. Nassau Lees, *Indian Musalmáns: Being Three Letters Reprinted from the "Times" with an Article on the Late Prince Consort, and Four Articles on Education, Reprinted from the "Calcutta Englishman"* (London: Williams and Norgate, 1871).

27. W. W. Hunter, *The Indian Musalmans: Are They Bound in Conscience to Rebel against the Queen?* (2nd edition, London: Trübner and Company, 1872), p. 10.

28. Hunter, p. 164.

29. W. A. Wilson, "The Situation in India." *Islam and Missions: Being Papers Read at the Second Missionary Conference on Behalf of the Mohammedan World at Lucknow, January 23–28,* 1911, ed. Elwood Morris Wherry, Samuel Marinus Zwemer, and C. G. Mylrea (New York, London: Fleming H. Revell, 1911), pp. 144, 146.

30. D. H. Wheeler, "England and Islam." *The Chautauquan* 5 (October 1884–July 1885), pp. 402–404.

31. John Hayward, *The Book of Religions: Comprising the Views, Creeds, Sentiments, Or Opinions, of All the Principal Religious Sects in the World, Particularly of All Christian Denominations in Europe and America, to which are Added Church and Missionary Statistics, Together with Biographical Sketches* (2nd edition, Boston, MA: I. S. Boyd and E. W. Buswell, 1842), p. 229.

32. Rev. Charles C. Starbuck, "Missions and Civilization. II." *The Andover Review: A Religious and Theological Monthly* 18 (July–December 1892), pp. 69–70.

33. Wheeler, p. 404.

34. Francis Robinson, *Islam and Muslim History in South Asia* (New Delhi: Oxford University Press, 2000), pp. 192–194.

35. Hardy, pp. 177–180.

36. Telegram from H. LeMesurier, Government of India, Home Department, Simla, August 21, 1914, Public Special, No. 225 of 1914, State Archives of Bihar.

37. Letter from Government of India, Home Department (Political), to G. Rainy, Chief Secretary, Bihar and Orissa, D.O. No. 1965, Simla, September 17, 1919, Political Department, Special Section, No. 345 of 1919, State Archives of Bihar.

38. Hardy, pp. 53–55, 60.

39. Hunter, pp. 42, 100. Hardy, p. 79. Rafiuddin Ahmed, *The Bengal Muslims 1871–1906: A Quest for Identity* (New Delhi: Oxford University Press, 1996 [1981]), pp. 40–41.

40. Harlan O. Pearson, *Islamic Reform and Revival in Nineteenth-century India: The* Tariqah-i Muhammadiyah (New Delhi: Yoda, 2008), p. 173.

41. T. C. Hodson, *India. Census Ethnography, 1901–1931* (New Delhi: Government of India Press, 1937), p. 111.

42. Syed Ahmad Khan Bahadur, *Review of Dr. Hunter's Indian Musalmans: Are They Bound in Conscience to Rebel Against the Queen?* (Benares: Medical Hall Press, 1872), p. 5.

43. Prideaux, pp. viii–ix.

44. Edward Tuite Dalton, *Descriptive Ethnology of Bengal* (Calcutta: Office of the Superintendent of Government Printing, 1872), p. 2.

45. Eli Smith, "Present Attitude of Mohammedanism, in Reference to the Spread of the Gospel." *The American Quarterly Observer* 1 (July–October 1833), p. 114.

46. Claudius Buchanan, *An Apology for Promoting Christianity in India* (Boston, MA: Nathaniel Willis, 1814), p. 86.

47. Smith, 106.

48. James H. Hutson, ed., *The Founders on Religion: A Book of Quotations* (Princeton, NJ: Princeton University Press, 2007), p. 116.

49. "The Hatred of Priests." *Littell's Living Age* 79 (October–December 1863), p. 165.

50. Theodore Roosevelt, *Presidential Addresses and State Papers, Volume III: April 7, 1904, to May 9, 1905* (New York: Review of Reviews, 1910), pp. 88–89.

51. Hayward, p. 229.

52. Anonymous, "Islam and Christian Missions." *The Church Missionary Gleaner* 19 (May 1892), p. 68.

53. John Takle, "Moslem Advance in India." *In Islam and Missions: Being Papers Read at the Second Missionary Conference on Behalf of the Mohammedan World at Lucknow, January 23–28, 1911*, ed. Elwood Morris Wherry, Samuel Marinus Zwemer, and C. G. Mylrea (New York, London: Fleming H. Revell, 1911), p. 211.

54. Hayward, p. 221.

55. Hume, "Letter from Mr. Hume, June 22, 1850." *The Missionary Herald* 46 (1850), p. 349.

56. Alexander Tomory and K. S. Macdonald, "Bengal." *Our Church's Work in India*, ed. Alexander Tomory et al. (Edinburgh: Oliphant, Anderson & Co., 1910), p. 13.

57. Takle, pp. 212–214.

58. Samuel Marinus Zwemer, *Islam, a Challenge to Faith: Studies on the Mohammedan Religion and the Needs and Opportunities of the Mohammedan World from the Standpoint of Christian Missions* (2nd edition, New York: Student Volunteer Movement for Foreign Missions, 1907), pp. 233, 244.

59. Takle, p. 214.

60. Kidd, 2003, pp. 777–778.
61. Bruce Kinney, *Mormonism: The Islam of America* (revised edition, New York: Fleming H. Revell, 1912), pp. 5, 7.
62. John Dickinson, *The Political Writings of John Dickinson, Esquire: The Address of Congress to the Inhabitants of Quebec, Dated October 26th, 1774*, Volume 2 (Wilmington, DE: Bonsal and Niles, 1801), p. 303.
63. Starbuck, p. 66.
64. Barton, p. 105.
65. Hume, p. 350.
66. J. Long, *How I Taught the Bible to Bengal Peasant-Boys* (London: Gilbert & Rivington, 1875), p. 1.
67. Wilson, p. 141.
68. Hume, p. 350.
69. Wilson, pp. 141–142.
70. John Prentiss Kewley Henshaw, *An Inquiry into the Meaning of the Prophecies Relating to the Second Advent of Our Lord Jesus Christ: In a Course of Lectures, Delivered in St. Peter's Church, Baltimore* (Baltimore: Daniel Brunner, 1842), pp. 51, 57.
71. C. B. Leupolt, *Recollections of an Indian Missionary* (London: Church Missionary House, 1846), p. 16.
72. Benjamin Franklin, *Poor Richard's Almanack* (New York: Barnes & Noble Publishing, 2004), p. 88.
73. Kidd, 2003, p. 774.
74. Prideaux, p. 13.
75. Prideaux, pp. iii–viii.
76. Buchanan, pp. 49, 86–88, 103, 127–128.
77. John Owen, "An Address to the Chairman of the East India Company Occasioned by Mr. Twining's Letter to that Gentleman, on the Danger of Interfering in the Religious Opinions of the Natives of India, and on the Views of the British and Foreign Bible Society, as Directed to India" (London: Black and Parry, 1807), pp. 24–27.
78. Thomas Twining, *A Letter to the Chairman of the East India Company, on the Danger of Interfering in the Religious Opinions of the Natives of India; and on the Views of the British and Foreign Bible Society as Directed to India* (2nd edition, London: Hazard and Carthew, 1807), p. 30.
79. W[illiam] B[uyers], *Travels in India: Comprising Sketches of Madras, Calcutta, Benares, and the Principal Places on the Ganges;—Also of the Church of England, Baptist, London Society, and Other Missionary Stations* (London: James Blackwood, 1852), p. 539.
80. R. Hand, *Early English Administration of Bihar, 1781–85* (Calcutta: Bengal Secretariat Press, 1894), p. 83.
81. Samuel M. Zwemer, "The Fulness of Time in the Moslem World." *Students and the World-wide Expansion of Christianity: Addresses*

Delivered before the Seventh International Convention of the Student Volunteer Movement for Foreign Missions, Kansas City, Missouri, December 31, 1913 to January 4, 1914, ed. Fennell Parrish Turner (New York: Student Volunteer Movement for Foreign Missions, 1914), p. 74.

82. Robert Stewart, *Life and Work in India: An Account of the Conditions, Methods, Difficulties, Results, Future Prospects and Reflex Influence of Missionary Labor in India, Especially in the Punjab Mission of the United Presbyterian Church of North America* (Philadelphia, PA: Pearl Publishing, 1896), p. 356.

83. Leupolt, pp. 16–17.

84. Zwemer, p. 73.

85. Hodson, p. 110. The passage is quoted in this source from the Census of India report for Punjab, 1911, p. 162.

86. Zwemer, 1907, p. 248.

87. Lees, pp. 9–11.

88. Elisabeth Bumiller, "Watchword of the Day: Beware the Caliphate; White House Letter." *The International Herald Tribune* (December 12, 2005), p. 2.

89. Norman Geisler and Abdul Saleeb, *Answering Islam: The Crescent in Light of the Cross* (Grand Rapids, MI: Baker, 2006 [1993]), p. 1, back cover.

90. Starbuck, p. 58.

Chapter 2

Islamophobia and American History
Religious Stereotyping and Out-grouping of Muslims in the United States[1]

Kambiz GhaneaBassiri

American Anti-Muslim attitudes are as old as the United States. Throughout its history, large segments of American society have identified Islam with tyranny, intolerance, misogyny, violence, sexual promiscuity, and heathenism.[2] These sentiments, however, remained latent in national politics and discourse until recently.[3] One is hard-pressed to find public opinion surveys that inquire into attitudes toward Muslims prior to 9/11. In one of these rare surveys conducted a few days before the 1993 World Trade Center bombing, one can see that the general public for the most part had little knowledge and interest in Islam at this time. When asked to give their impression of Islam, the majority (62 percent) said that they "haven't heard enough to say" or they are "not sure." Fourteen percent had favorable impressions and 22 percent had unfavorable impressions. When asked, "When you think of the religion of Islam, what comes to your mind?," the respondents gave widely disparate answers, with the largest group (36 percent) indicating either "nothing" or "not sure." The second largest group (21 percent) indicated "Mideast" or "Arabs." When asked, if a second thing comes to mind about Islam, the overwhelming majority (80 percent) failed to mention anything.[4]

Less than a decade later, there is a dramatic shift in American public opinion. An ABC News Poll conducted soon after the attacks of 9/11 found that 47 percent of Americans had a favorable opinion of Islam; 39 percent had an unfavorable opinion; and 13 percent expressed no opinion. While the majority of respondents (65 percent) thought they knew little about "the teachings and beliefs of Islam," there was a general consensus (87 percent) that the views of the terrorists who attacked the United States did not represent "the mainstream teachings of Islam" but that of "a radical fringe."[5]

The favorable opinion of Islam measured by this survey immediately after 9/11 resulted most likely from a desire to attain national unity in the face of a tragedy by disassociating Islam from terrorism. Ensuing surveys have found public opinion toward Muslim declining, particularly in light of the controversy around the so-called Ground Zero Mosque in 2010. Another poll sponsored by ABC News and *Washington Post* in August of that year found that only 37 percent of Americans had a favorable opinion of Islam, and 49 percent had an unfavorable opinion. Thirteen percent expressed no opinion.[6]

While favorable opinions toward Muslims have declined since the time immediately after 9/11, an overview of public opinion surveys conducted since 9/11 reveals a polarized nation divided down the middle within a 5–10 percent margin in terms of its opinion toward Muslims.[7] Given that this division persists, even though the majority of Americans admit that they do not "have a good basic understanding of the teachings and beliefs of Islam,"[8] it seems clear that attitudes toward Islam have less to do with the religion and its practitioners than it does with current events and media reports, which have indelibly associated Islam with violence in the American public square. The polarization we see in attitudes toward Muslims reflects political divisions in American society about how America ought define its national identity at home as a multicultural society and abroad as the world's sole superpower.

Searching for the Origins of
Anti-Muslim Attitudes

It should be noted that although there are significant negative attitudes toward Muslim, it is not at all clear what is the nature of these
attitudes. How does the general American population conceive
Muslims? Are they conceived as a racial or ethnic group, a religious
group, an ideological group (like Communists or Anarchists), or
a combination thereof? Attempts to answer these questions thus
far have been of two sorts. The first are empirical approaches that
rely on public opinion surveys to assess the nature of anti-Muslim
attitudes. One prominent empirical study found that anti-Muslim
sentiments are shaped by feelings toward both racial/religious
minority out-groups and cultural out-groups (such as feminists
or people on welfare), but feelings toward cultural out-groups are
more closely related to sentiments toward Muslims.[9] According to
this study, there is nothing distinctive about white American attitudes toward Muslim Americans; they are (unfortunately) subject
to the same kind of negative out-group stereotyping as African
Americans, Latinos, Jews, gays and lesbians, welfare recipients,
and other "non-traditional" groups.

A similar finding was made by another empirical study that
inquired into whether or not attitudes toward religious beliefs and
practices affect public opinion toward Muslims. This study concluded that they did not have a definitive effect. Rather, "Muslim
stereotypes are underpinned by a similar set of factors to those that
underpin stereotypes of blacks, Hispanics, and Asians—notably,
authoritarianism and a preference for cultural homogeneity."[10]

A cross-national study, conducted in the United States, Germany,
France, Spain, and Britain, found that perceptions of an impending
threat to national security drive negative attitudes toward Muslims,
in addition to negative out-group attitudes. This study argued that
"threat perception is a major, and perhaps the single most important
predictor, of ingroup attitudes toward outgroups."[11]

The last empirical study I will mention found a significant cor-
relation between negative attitudes toward mosques as places that

encourage hostility toward the United States and negative attitudes toward Muslims. This finding suggests that there may be some Islam-specific reasons for anti-Muslim attitudes, which correlate with the visibility of Muslims and Muslim institutions in the United States.[12]

The other set of responses to the question of what is the basis of anti-Muslim attitudes in American society have been less empirical and more based on conceptions of Islam and American society. In some of these, explanations of anti-Muslim attitudes are sought in the nature of Islam. Islam in such literature is conceived as a triumphalist, exclusivist religion, and as such it is reasonable for the general public to see Muslims' national loyalties as suspect.[13] Moreover, these arguments conceive Islam as a "way of life" that makes certain demands on Muslims in terms of dress, diet, gender relations, consumptions, and political participation that stand in contrast to an "American way of life."[14] This anxiety, palpable also among the general public, has helped propel a number of recent legislative attempts to ban sharia in state courts, even though the use of sharia has not been an issue in the American judicial system.[15]

Others have sought to explain anti-Muslim attitudes by tracking down the sources of Islamophobic propaganda. A study by the Center for American Progress, for example, attributed the rise of Islamophobia in the United States to the activities of five individuals and their organizations.[16] A report by the Southern Poverty Law Center identified a "closely knit cadre of [ten] activists" behind the "recent surge in popular anti-Muslim sentiments in the United States."[17] According to such approaches, anti-Muslim sentiments are manufactured byproducts of the propaganda campaigns of a limited but influential number of Islamophobes.

From even a cursory look at attempts to ascertain the sources of anti-Muslim bigotry in the United States, it becomes clear that there does not appear to be a single basis for anti-Muslim attitudes; rather anti-Muslim attitudes are complex and multifaceted. While public-opinion scholars and researchers of Islamophobia agree that anti-Muslim attitudes are on the rise and politically significant, there is no clear explanation of its basis. This lack of clarity speaks loudly to the complex nature of antagonistic relations between the general American population and the Muslim minority within it. This is why "Islamophobia," insofar as it reduces anti-Muslim attitudes to a fear of Islam, appears to be too narrow a concept to capture the racial and political factors that underpin current negative attitudes toward Muslims.

Religious Explanations of Terrorism

The realization that anti-Muslim attitudes are embedded in larger social and political processes than the fear of Islam begs the question of why has American society resorted to religion as an explanation for acts of terror committed by a very small portion of the world's vast Muslim population, thereby stigmatizing American Muslims to the point that large number of Americans are willing to tolerate discriminatory profiling of Muslims and to deny American Muslims their constitutional rights to protection against unreasonable searches and seizures and to build places of worship.[18]

Part of the answer to this question lies in the media's and the political elite's reinforcement of the association of Islam with violence. However, do these institutions simply reflect the larger society's understanding of violence in terms of religion, or do they have a stake in promoting the stereotype of Islam as a violent belief system?

In the case of the media, it is very likely that many of its members themselves understand the violence of events such as the attacks of 9/11 in terms of religious ideology, but there are also many economic and structural factors in the way in which news is reported that hinder more complicated explanations. There is no doubt that in the American media market, violence is considered newsworthy and attracts an audience that turns to the media for explanations of it. Islam, or the history of militant Muslim organizations, such as al-Qaeda, or the role of the United States in militarizing Afghanistan during its struggle against Soviet occupation in the 1980s are all complex topics requiring resources, expertise, and money to explore properly, and they are not topics that are likely to attract large audiences. Under these circumstances, the media has little incentive to ask whether or not Islam really explains "Muslim terrorism." Moreover, there have been too few in-depth reports on such topics, and those reports that have appeared have been so spread out over time that they have almost no significant effect on the larger public discourse regarding Islam and violence. We are, thus, left with a media that, rather than providing explanations of the political realities of our time, reflects society's understanding of Islam and violence and has created a looping effect that fuels Islamophobia.

Many among the political elite also understand the violence of events like 9/11 in terms of Islam. The series of hearings conducted by Republican Congressman Peter King of New Jersey on the "radicalization of American Muslims" are a case in point. Religious explanations of the violence of 9/11, however, have helped significantly expand the state's control over its citizens. A few days after 9/11, President George W. Bush, in an address to Congress, reassured Americans that al-Qaeda represents "a fringe movement that perverts the peaceful teachings of Islam." He, nonetheless, associated 9/11 with some aspect of Islam—which, as yet, has never been convincingly defined—that, then, demanded constant surveillance and expanded state powers that would allow the state to monitor more readily and secretly its own citizens, detaining them and persecuting them on suspicion of terrorism. By attributing exclusively religious motivations to al-Qaeda's acts of terrorism, even while disassociating these motivations from the "mainstream Islam," the state, which in a democratic society is charged with the protection and representation of its citizens, found a way in which it could increase its control over its citizens and erode their right to due process in the name of their own protection. Once the state, and more specifically the executive branch, are given such powers, they do not relinquish them easily. The Obama administration, for example, has, for the most part, avoided religious explanations of 9/11 by eschewing the language of "war on terror" and by identifying America's war as one that is against al-Qaeda rather than "Muslim terrorists," or "Islamic extremism."[19] Nonetheless, President Obama did not veto the 2012 National Defense Authorization Act, which permitted the indefinite detention of American citizens. He indicated that he signed it with "serious reservations," reserving for his administration the right to interpret and implement it according to its own understanding of the proper balance between national security and civil rights.[20]

While the media has very little incentive to challenge religious explanations of events like 9/11, the state has a definite interest in perpetuating them because this association provides a rationale for the expansion of the state's authority and control with the majority of its citizens' consent who seek protection against another violent attack. Consequently, both the media and the state reinforce through their actions, if not always by words, the association of Islam with violence that has ostracized a segment of the American population on the basis of religion.

Beyond Religious Explanations of Violence

If religion alone does not explain the violence of events of 9/11 and if Islamophobia only engenders social paranoia with regard to Muslims—itself the result of the religious explanations given for the tragic events of 9/11—why do many Americans choose to explain 9/11 and the era of insecurity and warfare it has bequeathed to the nation primarily in terms of the Islamic religion? To answer this question, it is useful to turn to the historical role of religion in the development of American national identity. In his landmark study of American nativism, *Strangers in the Land*, John Higham showed that nativism, "defined as intense opposition to an internal minority on the ground of its foreign (i.e., 'un-American') connections," flourished in the United States at times of crisis and great social change. During such times, Americans lose confidence in their national institutions and see them as susceptible to subversion from within.[21] Later in his career, Higham revised his thesis to include competitions over social status among varying ethnic groups as another impetus for nativist impulses.[22] While such competition is important in shaping relations between ethnic groups at the local level—let's say the Irish and Chinese in California at the turn of the twentieth century—it does not explain as well as his earlier work does how anti-foreign sentiments garner national attention at certain times to affect not only public opinion but also federal laws. Keeping with Higham's example of the Irish opposition to East Asian immigrants, Irish Catholics' antagonism toward Chinese immigration on the West Coast may have manifested itself through nativist rhetoric and politics but it does not explain the popularity of exclusionary immigration laws, such as the Immigration Act of 1924, which targeted not only Asians and Africans but also non-Protestant Europeans.

It is the loss of confidence in national institutions to mediate ethnic and religious conflicts at the local level that pushes nativism on the national agenda. The events of 9/11—having happened after a contentious presidential race between Al Gore and George W. Bush and, at a time, when America was still grappling with its own role abroad as the world's sole superpower and its identity as a multicultural society—occurred in just such an era, one of deteriorating faith in America's democratic institutions of governance. Adherence to democratic institutions, such as constitutions, elections, and courts, helps establish individual rights and settle disputes within society peacefully, but it does not necessarily follow that such adherence builds national unity or confidence. Put differently, democratic processes do not forge a cohesive national identity.

Throughout the history of the American republic, Americans have relied heavily on political narratives founded upon religious principles to establish their national identity. Despite the separation of church and state in this county, religion, specifically Protestant Christianity, is deeply rooted in the way America politically self-identifies and defines its enemies. This is a nation founded on the notion that "all men are created equal" and that "they are endowed by their Creator with certain inalienable rights." These conceptions, along with the Establishment Clause and the guarantee of the free exercise of religion in the First Amendment, were in many ways not only the products of the Enlightenment, but also of Protestant theological understandings formed in opposition to the established churches of European states. In the 1960s, sociologist Robert Bellah identified this cherished place of religion in American society as America's "civil religion,"[23] which, much to the horror of many contemporary secular Western Europeans, demands that American politicians, irrespective of their faith commitments, end their speeches with a divine blessing on America and for sessions of Congress to open with prayers conducted in the name of a supreme being irrespective of who delivers it, a Baptist or Methodist minister, a Catholic or Hindu priest, a Jewish rabbi or Muslim imam.

Politicization of Religious Differences

An outcome of this close association of religion with national interest and identity in American history has been to leave religious differences open to politicization. Religious minorities find themselves not only theologically but also politically suspect as doubts are raised about their national loyalties and adherence to democratic principles. In the mid-nineteenth century, as the United States was moving closer to civil war, the nativist American Party elected six governors in 1855 on a platform of national homogeneity and "American feeling" fueled largely by anti-Catholic sentiments and opposition to new Catholic immigrants. Catholicism, by virtue of its institutional hierarchies, was seen as foreign and "un-American." It was also regarded as intolerant and opposed to individual liberty, and Catholics were depicted as the pope's foot soldiers who were coming to the United States with the expressed purpose of reinstituting the religious and political tyranny that "the Roman church" had imposed upon much of Europe. "Americans should be 'Wide Awake,' " warned a popular nineteenth-century song sung to the tune of Yankee Doodle, "For we are free and won't submit/To intolerance and aggression/From papists, who from foreign lands/Come here to rule this nation/Yankee Doodle, Wide Awake/Be silent you should never/Until you drive the popish snake/From off the soil, FOREVER."[24]

As the twentieth century approached, an epoch when industrialism and urbanism were leading to social chaos in America, Catholicism was juxtaposed to "American values." The nativist Josiah Strong admonished Americans in his popular book, *Our Country* (1888), that Rome could not "make 'America Catholic'...without bringing into conflict the diametrically opposed principles of Romanism and the Republic, thus forcing all Romanists in the United States to choose between two masters, both of whom they now confess to serve." In 1928, when Al Smith won the Democratic presidential nomination, newspapers and magazines cast him as "Rome's Tattooed Man."[25]

During the social and economic upheavals in Europe between 1880 and the 1920s, many Central and Eastern European Jews immigrated to the United States, and anti-Semitism became a more prominent aspect of American public life, so much so that it became fashionable. The stereotypical image of Shylock, the miserly Jewish banker, gave way to that of the wealthy Jewish plutocrat, who was ready to take over the world to establish an aristocracy of "Israel's sacred race." This image spread mostly through the *Protocols of the Elders of Zion*. The *Protocols*, which falsely claimed to document a Jewish conspiracy to take over the world, originated in Russia in 1905; Henry Ford, a committed anti-Semite, popularized it in the United States in the 1920s.[26] Nevertheless, long before then, the book had native antecedents. In his 1891 utopian novel, *Caesar's Column*, for example, Congressman Ignatius Donnelly of Minnesota (1863–1869) envisioned a late twentieth century in which

> the Christian world is paying, in tears and blood, for the suffer-ings inflicted by their bigoted and ignorant ancestors upon a noble race...The great money-getters of the world...rose from dealers in old clothes and peddlers of hats to merchants to bankers, to princes. They were as merciless to the Christians as the Christians had been to them...The "wheel of fortune has come full circle;" and the descendants of the old peddlers now own and inhabit the palaces where their ancestors once begged at the back doors for secondhand clothes...This is a sad world, and to contemplate it is enough to make a man a philosopher.[27]

The pattern that stands out from these examples is that while reli-gious bigotry has existed throughout American history, it comes to the forefront in national public life at times when confidence in America's democratic institutions is waning, and it does so by ques-tioning the belonging and loyalty of the minority religion to the American body politic. This questioning of political loyalty based on religious belief politicizes religious differences, and, thus, paints religious minorities as foreigners and pariahs who pose an internal threat to American values and society. Moreover, creating a pariah out of a religious minority serves a purpose since it builds national unity by defining a common enemy, albeit a false one, and, thereby, masks the real sources of political and social instability and discon-tent in society. American Muslims are but the latest recipients of this long-standing tradition; yet, their situation is not identical to those of Jews and Catholics in the nineteenth and early twentieth centuries because Muslims in the United States today are more eth-nically and racially diverse, which further complicates the way non-Muslim Americans perceive their presence in the body politic.

Religion and Assimilation

Because of its prominence in America's national narrative, the politicization of religion has not been solely a means of exclu-sion; it has also served as a means of assimilation, at least for white non-Protestants. The First Amendment allows religious minorities to organize and to establish themselves locally in this country, long before they appear on the national radar. By the time their pres-ence could be politicized as a subversive threat, they usually have developed enough roots and means in the United States to be able to defend themselves against such attacks, and they often do so by reading themselves into America's political narrative in terms of con-stitutional freedoms. We saw this occur with American Muslims during the controversy surrounding the building of a Muslim com-munity center in Lower Manhattan, two blocks away from where the World Trade Center stood. American Muslims stepped onto the national media and political circles asserting their right under the First Amendment and in the process defining religious liberty for the nation as a whole.

Religious minorities have also been able to gain national rec-ognition and acceptance by interpreting their religion in line with national interest. This occurred during the Eisenhower era. As Will Herberg observed in his seminal 1955 study, *Protestant-Catholic-Jew*, religion was a central means of assimilation in the aftermath of the Second World War. Herberg, relying on the work of Marcus Hansen, a historian of immigration, argued that while children of immigrants generally eschew their distinct cultural and linguistic heritage to assimilate, their grandchildren, who feel more comfort-able with their identity as Americans, are keen to "remember" what their parents "forgot," and, having never learned the language of their grandparents, turn to their religion as that aspect of their heri-tage that they are able to revive most readily. This revival of reli-gion, Herberg noted, was further fueled by "the collapse of secular securities in the historical crisis of our time." By the onset of the Cold War, the United States had become a "triple melting pot" of Protestantism, Catholicism, and Judaism.[28]

United against Communism, Americans rallied around "a common 'American religion' of which each of the three great religious communions is regarded as an equi-legitimate expression." "In its crudest form," Herberg explained, "this identification of religion with national purpose generates a kind of national messianism which sees it as the vocation of America to bring the American Way of Life, compounded almost equally of democracy and free enterprise, to every corner of the globe; in more mitigated versions, it sees God as the champion of America, endorsing American purposes, and sustaining American might."[29] Herberg criticized this "fusion of religion with national purpose" because it silenced religious critiques with regard to the purpose of the state. Indeed, as seen by contemporary portrayals of Martin Luther King, Jr., in the South and Malcolm X in the North, it deemed any religious expression that appealed to social purposes and conceptions of justice outside of the state's political and legal apparatus as radical and militant or dangerous.

American Muslims were not immune to these historical processes. As Herberg aptly stated at the time, to "profess oneself a Buddhist, a Muslim, or anything but Protestant, Catholic, or Jew, even when one's Americanness is otherwise beyond question" would "imply being foreign."[30] American Muslims' history demonstrates Herberg's point, as well as the dynamic nature of American antagonism toward Islam, very clearly. Apart from the Nation of Islam, major American Muslim organizations during this period also sought to assimilate their religious community into the national consensus. The Federation of Islamic Associations of the United States and Canada, which began forming in 1952, stated in its constitution that it sought to "point out the common grounds, beliefs, and common ends which other religions share with Islam," and urged its member associations "in this age of international strife and unrest... [to] draw on the spiritual, moral, and intellectual wealth of the Moslem civilization and contribute their proper share in the establishment of world peace."[31] During the Reagan era, when Islam, in the wake of the Iranian Revolution, was vilified as a backward and militant religion, American Muslim organizations rallied their communities to help the US-supported "jihad" against the Soviet occupation of Afghanistan, in the name of shared values. And, the Islamic doctrine of jihad, interpreted in line with national purposes, was not the anathema it became after the fall of the Soviet Union and the 1993 World Trade Center bombing. The Muslim Students Association, for example, established a Jihad Fund in 1981,[32] and, at the White House in 1985, President Ronald Reagan celebrated the Afghani "freedom fighters" or *mujahidin* (literally, those who undertake jihad) as the "moral equivalents of America's founding fathers."[33]

Ironically, while social discrimination against religious minorities is politically activated when confidence in America's institutions is at a low ebb, religious minorities' assertion of their rights through a defense of constitutional liberties speaks to the vitality of America's democratic institutions and their transformative role in assimilating minorities. Whether today's American Muslims' responses to anti-Muslim bigotry will have the same positive results is uncertain because American Muslims are much more ethnically and racially diverse than Catholics and Jews. There is, however, a silver lining in this irony, and it is not one that, as cultural theorist Ali Behdad has suggested, requires Americans to forget the injustices of the past.[34] Rather, the silver lining lies in the fact that forces of homogeneity and diversity have both shaped this nation.

Assimilation of Racial Minorities

The assimilation of racial minorities in America has had a different history from that of religious minorities. While religion has had a unifying role in the development of American national identity, race has not. The religious and ethical notion that "all men are created equal" did not apply to blacks during the formation of the American republic, and institutionalized racial discrimination was legal in large portions of the country until the mid-1960s. The Naturalization Act of 1790 granted citizenship only to "aliens being free white persons." When Congress passed the 15th Amendment to the Constitution in 1870, it extended citizenship "to aliens of African nativity and to persons of African descent," excluding Asians from citizenship, which, thus, permitted discrimination against them in immigration and naturalization laws well into the middle of the twentieth century. When California's attorney general, Earl Warren, who later became the chief justice of the US Supreme Court, testified in Congress in 1942 in relation to the Executive Order 9066, which allowed the US military to incarcerate more than 100,000 Japanese Americans between 1942 and 1945, he lauded the fact that the Asian Exclusion Act had occluded Japanese immigration since 1924, but warned Congress that many Japanese American children were still sent to Japan after the Exclusion Act went into effect, and thus their loyalty was questionable:

> They are indoctrinated with the idea of Japanese imperialism. They receive their religious instruction which ties up their religion with their Emperor, and they come back here imbued with the ideas and the policies of imperial Japan. While I do not cast a reflection on every Japanese who is born in this country—of course we will have loyal ones—I do say that the consensus of opinion is that taking the group by and large there is more potential danger to this State from the group that is born here than from the group born in Japan.[35]

Despite many years of institution building on the part of racial minorities in this country, these communities have had a much greater uphill battle finding a place in America's national narrative and body politic than their white, religious counterparts. While the First Amendment established a relationship between religious minorities and the state that was beyond the reach of governmental authorities, the Constitution did not guarantee any citizenship rights to nonwhite races. It left decisions related to race to state and local governments. Consequently, racial minorities developed varying relations with the governing institutions of this country, depending on where and when they lived. They also could not define their place in America by fighting for their constitutional rights since it offered them no specific shield to guard against discrimination such as the protection that the First Amendment gave to religion; unlike religious freedom, racial equality was not part of America's national narrative prior to the passage of civil rights legislation. Without constitutional protection, they were much more dependent on the government than society at large to establish their place in America. In contrast to the assimilation of white religious minorities, which occurred for the most part through acculturation, civil rights legislation effected the integration of racial minorities. Today it is hard to believe, but it was not until the passage of civil right legislation in 1964 that nonwhites were able to defend their liberties by appealing to the laws of the nation as American citizens.

Islam, Race, and Assimilation

The history of Islam in America is a harrowing reminder of the disjuncture between religious and racial modes of integration in American history prior to the mid-1960s. When in the late 1920s, Noble Drew Ali founded the Moorish Science Temple, he deliberately chose to organize African Americans around a distinct Islamic national identity because he recognized the roles race and religion played in America's national identity and in the economic and social assimilation of minority communities. "Whatever the reasons may be for their opposition" to the Moorish Science Temple, he wrote, "the legal right to oppose citizens, individuals and organizations alike for their religious beliefs does not exist in the United States. The door of religious freedom made by the American Constitution swings open to all, and people may enter through it and worship as they desire."[36] In hindsight, Noble Drew Ali was naive. Religion did not wash away prejudice based on phenotype. His efforts to counter the stigma of black skin by defining a distinct, black, Moorish national identity was up against America's white, Protestant national narrative, and brought him and his followers under state surveillance. His organization and its kindred heir, the Nation of Islam, were monitored by the Federal Bureau of Investigation (FBI), which labeled them as "radical" and "militant."[37]

The passage of civil rights laws in the 1950s and 1960s gradually afforded an opportunity for non-white Americans to read racial diversity into the narrative of America. It was at this point that seeds sown earlier by the Moorish Science Temple and the Nation of Islam were harvested. Alex Haley, who had become intimately familiar with the Nation of Islam's ideology through the process of writing *The Autobiography of Malcolm X*, led the way in reading black Americans' experiences into America's national narrative through his immensely popular book and television miniseries, *Roots*. Haley's book was released in 1976; he dedicated it "as a birthday offering to my country."[38] The 12-hour miniseries aired on ABC for eight consecutive nights, captivating the nation. It had an estimated 130 million viewers.[39] *Roots* built a narrative around one of Haley's ancestors, Kunta Kinte, an enslaved West African Muslim whose descendents—after much hardship in a racist society—gained their freedom and through hard work and ingenuity managed to enter the professional, middle class. Haley's story gave black Americans a collective memory through which they, like white immigrants, could lay claim to the American dream.[40]

When Warith Deen Mohammed (born Wallace Delaney Muhammad) succeeded his father, Elijah Muhammad, as the head of the Nation of Islam, he reformed it along a similar trajectory. He disbanded the Nation of Islam, demythologized its antiwhite teachings, and began instructing its members in beliefs and practices that were accepted by the majority of the world's Muslim population. The changes Warith Deen Mohammed ushered among black Muslims were in large part the consequence of the passage of civil rights legislation in the 1950s and 1960s, which he considered to be a national "invitation" for blacks to join "mainstream America." Unlike the Nation of Islam, which religiously condemned America for slavery, Jim Crow, and other state-sanctioned forms of racism, Warith Deen Mohammed taught his followers that Islam was compatible with American democracy and went so far as to establish a "World Patriotism Day" to be celebrated on the fourth of July. "Let us have a Patriotism Day Parade every year," he told an Atlanta audience of his followers in 1978. "Let us show all American people we were brought here as slaves and treated like work animals or worse. We were invited to come into the mainstream of American life and the law of the land rose up and said, 'We will protect the black, the African-American just as we protect any other citizen.' We accepted it and we're proud of it and we'll hold the American flag high, we'll fight for it, we'll die for it. We're not going to put our burden on another citizen; I accept the burden. I accept the responsibility."[41]

Barack Obama, who is the product of the generation that had seen *Roots* and had read Haley's telling of the *Autobiography of Malcolm X*, eloquently expressed a sentiment similar to Warith Deen Mohammed's in his famous 2008 speech on race to effect a new multiracial narrative of America:

> I have brothers, sisters, nieces, nephews, uncles and cousins, of every race and every hue, scattered across three continents, and for as long as I live, I will never forget that in no other country on Earth is my story even possible. It's a story that hasn't made me the most conventional candidate. But it is a story that has seared into my genetic makeup the idea that this nation is more than the sum of its parts—that out of many, we are truly one.[42]

Furthermore, Obama stated that he saw in his successes in the primary elections "how hungry the American people were for this message of unity." Indeed, in the aftermath of 9/11, when national insecurity eroded governmental commitments to civil rights, Barack Hussein Obama personified a new narrative of America that could restore faith in its democratic institutions. For many American Muslims, Obama's election reinforced their faith in the essential fairness of American society. Furthermore, as some have noted, while American Muslims' civil liberties were neglected after 9/11 in the name of national security, the "mantra" of American Muslim activists was that this is how America has treated its racial minorities. "If all those groups could overcome bigotry in America, then so can we."[43]

History will tell the outcome of the formation of this multiracial, national narrative of America post-9/11. Today, however, there remain numerous economic and social impediments to racial equality despite the rise of this narrative. The conservative right, particularly the Christian right, has vehemently opposed Obama's centrist presidency as "extremist" or "socialist," and the fact that a quarter of Americans question where he was born and falsely believe that he is secretly Muslim, shows quite clearly that the road to full racial integration, though paved, is still steep.

Conclusion: Lessons Learned?

When contemporary anti-Muslim bigotry is viewed in the larger context of the history of religious and racial prejudice in American politics, instructive patterns emerge that have gone unnoticed in the public square because most Americans have sought to understand the violent events like 9/11 and the bigotry against Muslims in terms of religion. The lesson in this history is that bigotry and prejudice have played a central role in US history as a means of controlling racial and religious diversity and building national unity. Today, Muslims may be targets of this pattern of democratic governance, but with tomorrow's crisis, it may be another group. Some American Muslim organizations are even keen to discover this other group, to push it on the national stage, and to shift the target away from American Muslims; they routinely make a point of publicizing and condemning acts of violence committed by fundamentalist Christians as acts of terrorism.

Building national unity at times of crisis by ascribing undesirable values to religious out-groups has been a pattern of governance in America's democracy that has often obfuscated the political and economic sources of the crisis to the benefit of the state. Today's explanations of 9/11 in terms of religion and our contemporary conceptualizations of anti-Muslim bigotry in terms of a social phobia of Islam continue this pattern at a significant cost to every American's civil liberties.

Notes

1. A shorter version of this chapter appeared in *The Islamic Monthly* (winter/spring 2012) as "America's Latest 'Outsiders': The Struggle of Religious Minorities Throughout American History." I am grateful for their permission to reprint that material here. I wish also to thank Rowena Vrabel for her helpful review of earlier drafts of this chapter. Portions of this research were funded by a collaborative grant from the Alta S. Corbett Fund of Reed College for the study of Anti-Muslim attitudes in the American public opinion and policies.

Thanks to Paul Gronke, Adrien Schless-Meier, and Becca Traber for their collaboration on that project.

2. For a historical overview of Evangelical Christian attitudes toward Islam, see Thomas S. Kidd, *American Christians and Islam: Evangelical Culture and Muslim from the Colonial Period to the Age of Terrorism* (Princeton, NJ: Princeton University Press, 2009).

3. Anti-Muslim attitudes surfaced nationally during a controversy regarding a proposal to build a mosque and an Islamic Community Center two blocks from where the World Trade Center stood. This controversy arguably marks the time in US history when Islamophobia became an issue of national and social concern. See, for example, the August 30, 2010, cover of *Time*, which depicted a star and crescent (symbols of Islam) striped by the American flag under the title, "Is America Islamophobic? What the Anti-Mosque Uproar Tells Us about How the U.S. Regards Muslims."

4. *Los Angeles Times*. February 18–19, 1993. "Los Angeles Times Poll: Clinton's Economic Plan." Retrieved from the iPOLL Databank, the Roper Center for Public Opinion Research, University of Connecticut, available at http://webapps.ropercenter.uconn.edu/CFIDE/cf/action/catalog/abstract.cfm?label=&keyword=USLAT1993–308&fromDate=&toDate=&organization=Any&type=&keywordOptions=1&start=1&id=&exclude=&excludeOptions=1&topic=Any&sortBy=DESC&archno=USLAT1993–308&abstract=abstract&x=32&y=9, accessed September 14, 2012.

5. ABC News. October 8–9, 2001. "Military Action in Afghanistan." Retrieved from the iPOLL Databank, the Roper Center for Public Opinion Research, University of Connecticut. Available at http://webapps.ropercenter.uconn.edu/CFIDE/cf/action/ipoll/abstract.cfm?keyword=islam&keywordoptions=1&exclude=&excludeoptions=1&topic=Any&organization=ABC+News&fromdate=1%2F1%2F1935&todate=&sortby=ASC&label=&archno=USABC2001–18499&start=summary&abstract.x=15&abstract.y=11, accessed July 14, 2012.

6. ABC News/Washington Post. August 30–September 2, 2010. Retrieved from the iPOLL Databank, the Roper Center for Public Opinion Research, University of Connecticut. Available at http://webapps.ropercenter.uconn.edu/CFIDE/cf/action/ipoll/abstract.cfm?keyword=islam&keywordoptions=1&exclude=&excludeoptions=1&topic=Any&organization=ABC+News&fromdate=1%2F1%2F1935&todate=&sortby=ASC&label=&archno=USABCWASH2010–1112&start=summary&abstract.x=14&abstract.y=15, accessed July 14, 2012.

7. For an overview of public opinion research on favorability of Islam, see Erik C. Nisbet, Ronald Ostman, and James Shanahan, "Public Opinion toward Muslim Americans: Civil Liberties and the Role of Religiosity, Ideology, and Media Use." In *Muslims in Western Politics*, ed. Abdulkader H. Sinno (Bloomington, IN: Indiana University Press, 2009), p. 165.

8. Fifty-five percent of the respondents in the above-mentioned survey indicated that they do not have a "good basic understanding of the teachings and beliefs of Islam." For an overview of public opinion research on knowledge of Islam, see Nisbet et al., "Public Opinion toward Muslim Americans," p. 163.

9. Kerem Ozan Kalkan, Geoffrey C. Layman, and Eric M. Uslander, " 'Bands of Others'? Attitudes toward Muslims in Contemporary American Society." *The Journal of Politics* 71:3 (July 2009), pp. 847–862.

10. John Sides and Kimberly Gross, "The Origins of Anti-Muslim Stereotyping," paper presented at the annual conference of the Midwest Political Science Association, Chicago, IL, April 2010.

11. Richard Wike and Brian F. Grim, "Western Views toward Muslims: Evidence from a 2006 Cross-National Survey." *International Journal of Public Opinion Research* 22:1 (2010), pp. 4–25.

12. Matt A. Barreto, Karam Dana, and Kassra Oskooii, "The Park 51 (*sic*) Mosque and Anti-Muslim Attitudes in America," paper presented at the annual conference of the Midwest Political Science Association, Chicago, IL, September 1–4, 2011.

13. Peter Skerry, "The Muslim-American Muddle." *National Affairs*, no. 9 (Fall 2011), http://www.nationalaffairs.com/publications/detail/the-muslim-american-muddle, accessed September 14, 2012.

14. Samuel P. Huntington, *Who Are We? The Challenges to America's National Identity* (New York: Simon & Schuster, 2004); Susan Moller Okin, "Is Multiculturalism Bad for Women?" In *Is Multiculturalism Bad for Women?*, ed. Joshua Cohen, Matthew Howard, and Martha C. Nussbaum (Princeton, NJ: Princeton University Press, 1999), pp. 7–26.

15. Anver Emon, "Banning Shari'a," *The Immanent Frame: Secularism, Religion, and the Public Sphere*, http://blogs.ssrc.org/tif/2011/09/06/banning-shari'a, accessed July 15, 2012.

16. Wajahat Ali, Eli Clifton, Matthew Duss, Lee Fang, Scott Keyes, and Faiz Shakir, *Fear, Inc.: The Roots of the Islamophobia Network in America* (Washington, DC: Center for American Progress, 2011). The five individuals' names in this report were: Frank Gaffney at the Center for Security Policy, David Yerushalmi at the Society of Americans for National Existence, Daniel Pipes at the Middle East Forum, Robert

Spencer of Jihad Watch and Stop Islamization of America, and Steven
Emerson of the Investigative Project on Terrorism.

17. Robert Steinback, "The Anti-Muslim Inner Circle." *Intelligence Report*,
no. 142 (Summer 2011), www.splcenter.org/get-informed/intelligence-
report/browse-all-issues/2011/summer/the-anti-muslim-inner-circle,
accessed September 18, 2011. Individuals named in this report are Bill
French of the Center for the Study of Political Islam, Brigitte Gabriel
of ACT! For America, P. David Baubatz of Society of Americans for
National Existence, Pamela Geller of Stop Islamization of America and
the American Freedom Defense Initiative, David Horowitz of Front
Page Magazine, John Joseph Jay of Stop Islamization of America, Terry
Jones of Dove World Outreach Center, columnist Debbie Schlussel,
Robert Spencer of Jihad Watch, and David Yerushalmi of the Society
of Americans for National Existence.
18. For results of some public-opinion surveys on attitudes toward
Muslim civil rights, see Nisbet et al., "Public Opinion toward Muslim
Americans," pp. 172–173.
19. See, for example, an address by John Brennan, Assistant to the
President for Homeland Security and Counterterrorism, at a conference on "A Dialogue on Our Nation's Security" at New York University
on February 13, 2010, www.whitehouse.gov/photos-and-video/video/
john-brennan-speaks-national-security-nyu, accessed July 15, 2012.
20. The White House, Office of the Press Secretary, "Statement by the
President on H.R. 1540," www.whitehouse.gov/the-press-office/2011/
12/31/statement-president-hr-1540, accessed on July 15, 2012.
21. John Higham, *Strangers in the Land: Patterns of American Nativism,
1860–1925*, with a new forward (New Brunswick, NJ: Rutgers
University Press, 1988 [1955]), p. 4.
22. John Higham, "Another Look at Nativism." *Send These to Me: Jews
and Other Immigrants in Urban America* (New York: Atheneum,
1975), pp. 102–115.
23. Robert Bellah, "Civil Religion in America." *Daedalus* 96:1 (Winter
1967), pp. 1–21.
24. William G. Marion, "Wide Awake Yankee Doodle" [n.p., n.d.], in
American Song Sheet Collection, Rare Book and Special Collections
Division, Library of Congress, Washington, DC, Digital ID: as114980,
cited in *Religious Intolerance in America: A Documentary History*, ed.
John Corrigan and Lynn S. Neal (Chapel Hill, NC: University of
North Carolina Press, 2010), p. 64.
25. Corrigan and Neal, *Religious Intolerance*, p. 53. See Josiah Strong,
Our Country (Cambridge, Belknap Press of Harvard University Press,
1963 [1891]).

26. On this fraudulent production, see most recently *The Paranoid Apocalypse: A Hundred-Year Retrospective on the Protocols of the Elders of Zion*, ed. Richard Landes and Steven T. Katz (New York: New York University Press, 2012).
27. Ignatius Donnelly [Edmund Boisgilbert, M.D.], *Caesar's Column: A Story of the Twentieth Century* (Chicago, IL: F. J. Shulte & Company, 1890), p. 37.
28. Will Herberg, *Protestant-Catholic-Jew: An Essay in American Religious Sociology* (Chicago, IL: University of Chicago Press, 1955), pp. 61, 257.
29. Herberg, *Protestant-Catholic-Jew*, pp. 258, 264.
30. Ibid., pp. 257–258.
31. See a reprint of the constitution in Abdo A. Elkholy, *Arab Moslems in the United States* (New Haven, CT: College & University Press, 1966), pp. 153–154.
32. *Islamic Horizons* 10: 4 (March 1981), p. 11.
33. Cited in Mahmood Mamdani, *Good Muslim, Bad Muslim: America, the Cold War, and the Roots of Terror* (New York: Pantheon Books, 2004), 119.
34. Ali Behdad, *A Forgetful Nation: On Immigration and Cultural Identity in the United States* (Durham, NC: Duke University Press, 2005).
35. "Testimony of the Honorable Earl Warren." In *Documents of American Prejudice: An Anthology of Writings on Race from Thomas Jefferson to David Duke*, ed. S. T. Joshi (New York: Basic Books, 1999), p. 449.
36. Noble Drew Ali, "Moorish Leader's Historical Message to America," *Moorish Literature* (n.p.: 1928), p. 13.
37. See the essay by Edward Curtis in this volume.
38. Alex Haley, *Roots* (Garden City, NJ: Doubleday, 1976).
39. Terry Alford, *Prince among Slaves*, 30th anniversary edition (New York: Oxford University Press, 2007), p. 194.
40. Edward E. Curtis, IV, *Islam in Black America: Identity, Liberation, and Difference in African-American Islamic Thought* (Albany, NY: State University of New York Press, 2002), pp. 118–119.
41. W. D. Mohammed, "Historic Atlanta Address." In *The Columbia Sourcebook of Muslims in the United States*, ed. Edward E. Curtis, IV (New York: Columbia University Press, 2008), p. 120.
42. "Barack Obama's Speech on Race," *The New York Times* (March 18, 2008).
43. Peter Skerry and Devin Fernandes, "Interpreting the Muslim Vote," *Boston Globe* (November 26, 2004).

Chapter 3

The Black Muslim Scare of the Twentieth Century

The History of State Islamophobia and Its Post-9/11 Variations

Edward E. Curtis IV

Though Islamophobia has deep roots in both American culture and US society, its vitality in those domains is a result, at least in part, of the state repression of political dissent organized around Islamic symbols and themes. Long before 9/11, the US government was concerned about the possibility that Muslims on American soil would challenge the political status quo. Beginning in the 1930s, this fear resulted in formal government surveillance and prosecution of African American Muslim civil and religious organizations and their members. Organized and state-supported Islamophobia was not confined to the use of state surveillance, local police departments, and the US courts. After World War II, the Federal Bureau of Investigation (FBI) used mainstream media to prosecute a war of disinformation about Muslim groups, and by the 1960s, engaged in aggressive counterintelligence to repress what it deemed to be the threat of political radicalism among Muslim Americans.

Previous scholarship on images of Muslims and Islam has exposed the entanglement of anti-Islamic views with US politics.

From the election of 1800, when John Adams and Thomas Jefferson referred to each other as oriental despots and Mahometans to the evocation of Muslims in the repression of Mormons, Islam was already a potent symbol in US electoral politics in the nineteenth century.[1] Islam's symbolic power was resurrected in the twentieth century when the Nation of Islam (NOI), Malcolm X, and Muhammad Ali came to represent, respectively, the greatest threat to the liberal promise of civil rights, a strong domestic voice for the rising tide of color and pan-Africanism, and perhaps the most prominent symbol of domestic resistance to the Vietnam War.[2] With the Iranian Revolution in 1979 and the end of the Cold War in the 1990s, the labeling of Islam as a form of anti-Americanism only rose.[3] By the time of the 9/11 attacks, the association of all Muslims and Islamic religion with violence, misogyny, and general backwardness had already become an entrenched form of conventional wisdom in some policy circles, especially among neoconservatives.[4]

Scholars have documented the consequences of such fears, images, and appropriations in US politics and society before, but they have not yet paid ample attention to the role of the state and particularly the FBI in producing such irruptions and iterations of Islamophobia. This chapter explores the reasons for and forms of government surveillance, media manipulation, and finally counter-intelligence behind the making of Islamophobia in the twentieth century. It argues that though Islamophobia may be a social anxiety, its salience in US society is not exclusively the reflection of certain cultural and political interests, including those of *some* evangelical Christians, pro-Israeli activists, academic orientalists, and mass media; Islamophobia is also the product of the state's legal and extra-legal attempts to control, discipline, and punish Muslim American individuals and organizations.

The chapter examines the anatomy of state Islamophobia directed toward African American Muslim groups and other black religious or political activists associated with Muslims or Islamic ideas or symbols. In order to show the dynamic nature of changing state policies toward domestic black Muslim populations, the first section of the chapter, a prologue, charts the federal government's and other interest groups' interactions with enslaved Muslims in the antebellum era. Enslaved US Muslims played key symbolic roles in antebellum debates over slavery and emancipation, market capitalism, and evangelical Christian missions. A few such as Abdul Rahman Ibrahima (ca. 1762–1829) and Lamen Kebe (ca. 1767–?) were genuine American celebrities and the federal government took extraordinary measures to intervene on behalf of individuals whom, despite their long residence on American soil, the government defined as foreigners. These Muslim "foreigners" were the friendly kind—friendly, that is, to the interests of certain antebellum political and religious groups.

When slavery ended in 1865, however, the image of the Muslim as the friendly foreigner disappeared. With the exception of an occasional federal judicial decision regarding the ability of Muslims to integrate into American culture and the banning of polygamists from entering the country in 1891, the federal government seems to have had little to say about its domestic Muslim populations, most of whom were Gilded Age immigrants from the Ottoman Empire. Important legal cases questioning the whiteness and assimilability of Muslim immigrants arose in the period, but there was little guidance from the executive or legislative branches regarding the relatively small numbers of Muslims who lived in the United States.[5]

By the 1920s, this federal silence toward domestic Muslims began to change. The second section of the chapter examines the growth of Islam in various organizational guises during the interwar period, showing how Muslim American groups such as the Moslem Welfare Society of Sunni Muslim missionary Satti Majid, the NOI, and the Moorish Science Temple became targets of the FBI's RACON, a wartime investigation that attempted to collect all-known instances of "Foreign-Inspired Agitation among the American Negroes."[6] Then, the third section analyzes the development of wartime Islamophobia by scrutinizing what I have dubbed the Black Muslim Scare of the 1960s. In the context of the Cold War and the conflict in Vietnam, the NOI, above all other Muslim groups, became the focus of FBI surveillance, disinformation campaigns, and counterintelligence activities. A conclusion examines the reverberation of the Black Muslim Scare in the post-9/11 period.

Prologue: Black Muslims as Friendly Foreigners

Muslims were consequential figures in Anglo-American history from the eighteenth-century onward. Some of them were among the most educated Americans of the era—of any race or class. These elites were literate in Arabic and often fluent in more than one language. They had ties not only to their homelands but also to global Muslim networks of scholarship, trade, diplomacy, and travel. Contrary to the images that most Anglo Americans had of Africa, these Muslims came from cultures that celebrated literacy, scholarship, calligraphy, poetry, and Sufism, the mystical branch of Islam in which Muslims cultivate personal and intimate relationships with God.[7]

Muslims in the 13 colonies and the United States may have numbered in the tens of thousands—though the number of Muslims in other parts of the Americas was surely much higher. Historian Allan Austin has reckoned between 1711 and 1808, about 5–10 percent, perhaps as many as 30,000–40,000 of slaves brought to the 13 colonies and the United States, were Muslims. Austin traces their roots mainly to Senegambia, "the source for the most sought-after slaves, especially by American slavers working fast between the end of the Revolutionary War [in 1783] and January 1, 1808," when the United States officially outlawed the international (but not the domestic) slave trade.[8] Historian Michael Gomez gives similar figures, estimating that 255,000 of the 481,000 first-generation Africans transported to British North America were inhabitants of African locales where Muslims lived or ruled. Gomez has written that thousands or perhaps tens of thousands of African Americans may have been raised as Muslims.[9]

Setting aside the question about population size, the important point is that, whatever their number, educated Muslims had a disproportionate impact on US political discourse in the antebellum period. Since large numbers of Americans, slave or free, were still illiterate in this era, those slaves who could write attracted the attention of planters and other elites, including merchants. Some of these persons became genuine American and even trans-Atlantic celebrities. Long before the United States declared its independence, for example, Job Ben Solomon (c. 1701–c. 1773) became a figure of renown on both sides of the Atlantic. According to his biography, one of the earliest English-language biographies of an African slave, Job was born Ayuba or Hyuba, Boon Salumena Jallo (Job, Son of Solomon, of the Fulbe tribe) around 1701 in Boonda, also known as Bundu, in eastern Senegal.[10] He was the child of an imam, or religious scholar and leader, and thus educated in Qur'anic Arabic and Islamic studies. By the age of 30 years, he had married twice and had four children. Hyuba, like many in Africa, was himself a slave trader. In 1730, on a journey to a port along the Gambia River where he hoped to sell two slaves, Hyuba was abducted and enslaved.

Job was taken to Maryland, where he grew tobacco and herded livestock. He also wrote a letter in Arabic to his father, asking for his help. Through a confusing series of events, James Oglethorpe, a member of the British Parliament and founder of Georgia, discovered this letter and the unusually well-educated man who wrote it. In 1733, Oglethorpe ordered the letter translated into English and was so impressed by Job's story that he purchased Job's bond and had him brought to England, where he introduced him to nobles and members of the Royal Court.

Job was a religious man whose devotions, fasting, temperance, and food preparations—he butchered his own meat in order to make it *halal*, or permissible—were seen as noble by his English hosts. He was an excellent conversation partner who refused to convert to Christianity, despite reading the New Testament in Arabic. Job challenged the doctrine of Trinity, observing that the word "trinity" was not included in the New Testament and expressed his concern that his English brothers and sisters were being led to engage in *shirk*, the association of anything with the one God. Job insisted that God was not three in number but one; even Prophet Jesus, who was born of a virgin and who performed miracles, was not God, he said. If his English sponsors were disappointed by Job's refusal to convert to Christianity, their disappointment was not recorded by Thomas Bluett, Job's biographer. Bluett was happy to note, however, that Job was especially critical of the English Protestants' political and religious rivals, the Roman Catholics, whose African missionaries practiced idolatry, he argued.

Perhaps the lack of disappointment over Job's failure to convert to Christianity was because his sponsors had different plans in mind for Job's future. Around 1734, the Royal African Company transported Job to West Africa, where it was thought that he might be able to advance English commercial interests as an employee of the company. Though this did not occur, Job would live on in Anglophone literature; his biography was one of the earliest published English-language slave narratives.[11]

Job's relationship with his Anglo sponsors was an important precursor to Americans' later patronage of certain Muslim Americans. It helps to identify the differing interests that shaped Anglo and later Anglo-American interactions with the Muslim other in the colonial versus antebellum eras. Job's return to Africa was not made conditional on his promise to convert the "heathen" to Christianity nor was it explained as an expression of antislavery sentiment. Neither Job nor his sponsors seemed to oppose slavery. His return to Africa, like that of later Muslim Americans, was seen instead as having potential economic benefit through the establishment of trade networks. Job's repatriation served the interests of those merchants who wished to develop English-speaking native agents in West Africa, and in so doing, anticipated a larger trend in the antebellum United States.

In a similar fashion, enslaved African American Muslim Abdul Rahman Ibrahima was willing to entertain the idea of working for US business interests once his sponsors sent him and his family back to West Africa. But Ibrahima was willing to go further. He pretended to convert to Christianity and joined his northern abolitionist sponsors in criticizing slavery. His interaction with the state and its competing interests is a tale whose implications are important for understanding antebellum US history and especially the early relationships between the US state and the Muslims under its authority.[12]

This nineteenth-century American celebrity, an ethnic Fulbe, was born the child of a Muslim leader in Futa Jalon, located in the contemporary West African nation of Guinea. Ibrahima studied in both Jenne and Timbuktu, two important centers of Islamic learning. Like many educated people of his era, he could read and write in Arabic. In 1788, during a war to gain new territories for his clan, Ibrahima became a prisoner of war and was enslaved. He was transported to the West Indies and then to New Orleans, Louisiana. He finally settled in Natchez, Mississippi, where he married a Christian woman, Isabella, and had several children.[13]

Though he was apparently known as a "Muslim prince" in his local community, it was not until the 1820s that Ibrahima became a national celebrity. In 1826, he wrote to his father, asking him to pay whatever ransom was required to free him. With the help of local whites, the letter was sent to one of Mississippi's US senators, then to the US consul in Morocco, and finally to Secretary of State Henry Clay. Secretary Clay apparently intervened in the case because he thought that freeing him might help smooth relations with the North African Barbary states with which the United States military had fought two wars—one from 1801 to 1805 and the other from 1815 to 1816. Why did Clay think that the freeing of a Muslim from West Africa might have some effect on North African Muslim leaders? This was no simple error of geography. It was also an expression of Clay's racialist thinking. Like other slave holders, Clay likely thought of Muslim slaves literally as a "breed apart." The elites among them were seen not only as better educated but also as more "civilized" than non-Muslim slaves and thus, it was assumed, these Muslims had to be not only from different religious and ethnic communities but also from different racial stock. Ibrahima could not possibly be of pure "Negro" origins; for Clay and others like him, Ibrahima must have had Arab or Moorish blood in his veins. Some black Americans held to similar views, often analyzing the racial, religious, and ethnic backgrounds of Muslim slaves to account for their "superiority." The New York's *Freedom's Journal*, edited by African American John Russwurm, said in an 1828 article about Ibrahima that "it must be evident to everyone that the Prince is a man superior to the generality of Africans whom we behold in this country."[14]

Secretary of State Clay also supported sending Ibrahima to Africa because of his support for emigrationism, the movement to transport black Americans to Africa. Offering to use federal resources, Clay said that he was willing to provide Abdul Rahman with passage on a ship.[15] Abdul Rahman responded that he would not leave without his wife and children. In 1828, he embarked on a speaking tour through the northern states in which he solicited donations to free his family from slavery and transport them to Africa. The tour attracted a great deal of media attention as northern newspapers embraced this enticing story of an unfortunate prince who has been denied his rightful place in African society. Philanthropist and advocate for the deaf Thomas Gallaudet wrote that "his life appears like a romance, and the incidents would seem incredible if the evidence was not so undeniable."[16] Another source, the *Freedom's Journal*, said that Abdul Rahman was "brought up in luxury and Eastern splendor—but for forty long years [he was] compelled to taste the bitter cup of poverty, and slavery."[17] By referring to the "Eastern splendor" to which Abdul Rahman was supposedly accustomed, the article and others like it played on the stereotype, increasingly important in US literature, popular media, and consumer culture, that the Muslim Orient was a sensual wonderland.

During his tour, Abdul Rahman Ibrahima met some of the nation's most important business, social, and political leaders. Perhaps most notably, Abdul Rahman seems to have been one of the first Muslim or black Americans to have met a US president on a semiofficial visit to the White House. Secretary of Clay arranged for him to meet President John Quincy Adams—a meeting that would become fodder for Andrew Jackson's 1828 campaign against Quincy Adams. The Muslim prince also met Massachusetts Congressman Edward Everett, philanthropists and merchants Charles and Arthur Tappan, and *Star-Spangled Banner* writer Francis Scott Key. Many of these men were supporters of abolitionism, emigrationism, and a burgeoning commercial interest in African goods and markets. Many were also evangelical Christians. Soliciting donations from them all, Abdul Rahman permitted these men to claim him as a supporter of their various causes, including the hope that English-speaking blacks would become agents for white business interests in Liberia.[18]

Political operatives in Mississippi made hay of Abdul Rahman's tour. Supporters of President Quincy Adams's rival, Andrew Jackson, claimed that Adams's meeting with Abdul Rahman was proof that Quincy Adams was "actually exciting the slaves to revolt, by the same species of arguments which produced the massacre of St. Domingo [Haiti]."[19] For planters, slaveowners, and white Southerners more generally, the idea that black slaves in the South would engage in a violent struggle for independence was terrifying, especially since the Haitian revolution had been successful. As the southern states used what by today's standards would be considered fascist or at least dictatorial politics to head off any such revolt, the threat of terrorism—at least in their own minds—seemed to increase. Abdul Rahman had become a symbol of abolitionism, the movement that threatened Southern business interests and the Southern way of life.

But Northerner supporters of Abdul Rahman were not exactly believers in the beloved community, either. They, too, were thoroughly racist in their attitudes toward black people—they just happened to be opposed to slavery because they saw it as a sinful stain on the American soul. Their answer to the problem of freed slaves was to transport them—that is, English-speaking, American-born blacks—to Africa. The freeing of Abdul Rahman and his family did not challenge the views of northern whites; it confirmed the notion that blacks were a foreign element in a white republic. Abdul Rahman Ibrahima was willing to cooperate with such people not because he necessarily shared their political views, but he wanted to raise the funds necessary for his family to emigrate. In this, he was remarkably successful—and given the horrors of slavery, who could blame him for using whatever resources were at his disposal to free him and his family? During his 1828 tour, colonizationists, abolitionists, and others donated approximately US$3,400 toward his cause. In 1829, Abdul Rahman left with his wife, Isabella, from Norfolk, Virginia, and sailed for Liberia, the American colony in West Africa peopled by African American freedmen and women. Some of his children immigrated to Liberia in 1830 while others apparently remained in the United States.[20]

Ibrahima's departure from American soil is an important indication of his friendliness to northern US interests, especially those associated with the administration of President John Quincy Adams. He veiled himself in the social, ethnic, religious, and class differences of a Muslim prince—covering up the fact that he had been in America for approximately three decades. His very marginality within American culture meant that he was a useful vessel for his white allies. Impressing his patrons by writing in Arabic, he could rely on his education to demonstrate the differences between him and most other slaves. Invoking a royal heritage, he set himself apart from other black people. His campaign for liberty was based not on the republican idea that all people deserved to be free, but rather on exceptionalist claims that he was robbed of rightful place in society. His background as a Muslim—who was, still, willing to convert to Christianity—also enabled Abdul Rahman to claim ethnic and racial distance from most other slaves. His extraordinary talents were not seen as indicative of innate black ability; they were seen as expressions of his "Muslim blood." For his white and black American supporters, Islam was not an African religion but an Oriental one, and as such, it embodied a civilization of which black Africans were not capable. Finally, Abdul Rahman Ibrahima lent his imprimatur to the emerging consensus among northern whites that slavery made people bad Christians. According to Cyrus Griffin of the *Natchez Southern Galaxy*, Abdul Rahman argued that the New Testament was "very good law... [but] you no follow it." Slave holders were "greedy after money. You good man, you join the religion? See you want more land, more niggers; you make niggers work hard, make more cotton. Where you find that in your law?"[21] White abolitionists, many of whom were evangelicals, could not have agreed more with such antislavery sentiments.

In sum, this Muslim American was willing to eschew any claims to constitutional rights, to support evangelical Christianity, to buoy white business interests in Africa, to accept white prejudices against blacks, and most importantly, to leave the country. As long as Muslim Americans were willing to behave in this manner, there was no conflict between them and the state. But when Muslim Americans began to agitate for equal rights, to oppose US foreign policy, and to reject racial apartheid, they became downright dangerous.

Interwar Islamic Denominationalism and World War II—Era Repression

Documenting the rise of Islam among black Americans is essential to understand why the FBI became so concerned about Islam in America by the 1930s. It was in the roaring cauldron of 1920s' nativism and white supremacy that African Americans, responding to and working with foreign Muslims from the Caribbean, the Middle

East, South Asia, and Africa, began to join and create a number of different Muslim American organizations. The 1924 National Origins Act, focused on further reducing immigration from non-white lands, was emblematic of the age. This new law expressed concerns among many Anglo-Americans that immigrants from non–Western European countries were bringing both physical and ideological disease to America. Such concerns were amplified in the development of domestic securities agencies such as the nascent FBI, which focused on the spread of "dangerous" groups such as Marcus Garvey's Universal Negro Improvement Association (UNIA) and the Communist Party. As enormous federal, state, and local resources were committed to Jim Crow segregation, a racial apartheid system implemented most strongly in the southern United States but present in the North as well, the fear of America's people of color uniting with colonized people abroad put the growth of Islam among black Americans at the front of the federal government's surveillance and suppression agenda.[22]

To understand the scope of the threat, it is important to remember that in the interwar period, Muslim American history was not as racially divided as it would become in the last three decades of the twentieth century.[23] All Muslim Americans, with the exception of the very few Muslims who were white Americans, were racially oppressed persons in this period. Treated by the executive and judicial branches of the federal government as nonwhites, defined as nonwhite by the National Origins Act, and in at least once instance subject to lynching, Asian Americans, like black Americans, did not succeed in fighting the legal discrimination against them until after 1945.[24] The period between World Wars I and II witnessed instead an alignment of interests among some Muslims Americans who viewed one another as fellow travelers in the fight against white supremacy and colonialism.

This alignment of interests can be seen, for example, in the work of Muhammad Sadiq, the first North American missionary for the Ahmadiyya movement, which formed in the late nineteenth century around the personality and teachings of Ghulam Ahmad. Ahmad was a Muslim reformer believed by his followers to be the long-promised Christian Messiah and the Islamic Mahdi, a figure in Islamic tradition who will bring peace and justice to the world before the Day of Judgment. Many also believed that Ghulam Ahmad was a prophet, a view that conflicted with the Sunni Muslim belief that Muhammad of Arabia is the "seal of the prophets" and the final messenger of God to humanity.[25] These doctrinal disagreements would later restrict the interaction of Ahmadi followers with other Muslim Americans, though in the early 1920s, few communal divisions yet existed among Muslims in America. For example, when Detroit's first purpose-built mosque was opened in the Highland Park area in 1921, Ahmadi missionary Muhammad Sadiq joined Shi'a imam Khalil Bazzy to celebrate the accomplishments of the community and its Sunni imam, Hussien Karoub.[26] Sadiq and Bazzy represented different strands of Islamic religion, but their presence at the opening of a Sunni mosque suggested their willingness to cooperate—as well as to compete—with other Muslim American leaders.

In 1922, Sadiq created a permanent mission along Wabash Avenue on Chicago's South Side in 1922 and founded the *Moslem Sunrise*, a periodical that documents the emergence of the first Muslim American denominational institution that was national in scope.[27] This accomplishment was the result of Sadiq's strategy to target African Americans for conversion. Sadiq brought together the Qur'an and the Sunna, or tradition of the prophet Muhammad, with post–World War I agitation by people of color for freedom from colonialism and Jim Crow segregation. On the one hand, he emphasized the ecumenical appeal of Islam as a religion of social equality; on the other hand, Sadiq argued that Arabic and Islam were part of an explicitly African past that had been taken from blacks when they were enslaved. He endorsed the activities of black nationalist and pan-Africanist Marcus Garvey and sought converts from Garvey's UNIA. In this era of the new nativism, when the Ku Klux Klan rose to political prominence based on a combination of Protestant Christianity, white supremacy, and terrorism, the Ahmadi linking of domestic struggles for racial liberation to what Sadiq and others identified as a rising call for self-determination, the deep spirituality of the Qur'an, and black historical achievements under Islam was a powerful message that convinced over 1,025 mostly African American people to convert to Islam from 1921 to 1925.[28]

Sadiq was only one of several Muslim activists in the 1920s. Dusé Mohamed Ali (1866–1945), the founder of the *African Times and Orient Review*, was another. Ali traveled the United States first as a Shakespearean actor in the nineteenth century and returned from Great Britain to become a foreign affairs columnist for Marcus Garvey's *Negro World* in New York in 1922. Though he worked for the UNIA for only a short while, Ali remained in the United States, establishing entrepreneurial ventures in various American cities. He also helped to create a multiracial and multiethnic group of Muslim worshippers in 1925 Detroit, when, along with Shah Zain ul-Abdein, Joseph Ferris, and S. Z. Abedian, he became involved with the Universal Islamic Society, also known as the Central Islamic Society. In 1926, Ali became secretary of the American Asiatic Association, also called the America–Asia Society, which apparently gained support from the Iranian chargé d'affaires, the mayor of Detroit, and the Egyptian ambassador in Washington. But unlike Sadiq, Ali may have left little evidence of his impact on the development of Islam in the United States when he departed for Nigeria in 1931. Once there, Ali emerged as an elder statesman of the pan-African movement.[29]

Satti Majid (1883–1963), who led groups of Muslim Americans in the 1920s when he advocated on behalf of Yemeni sailors stranded in New York during World War I, had a much greater influence on the development of American Islam. In 1922, he applied to incorporate a benevolent association named the Moslem Welfare Society in Detroit and later established the United Moslem Society in Pittsburgh. His followers in this period included Daoud and Khadija Faisal, who went on to establish the most successful multiracial and multinational Sunni mosque in New York City. In 1927 and 1928, Majid also created the African Moslem Welfare Society in Pittsburgh.[30] After Majid departed the United States on January 31, 1929, for Africa, followers in Pittsburgh sent letters addressed to the "Rev. Magid" and the "Respectable Father Sheich [shaykh, or leader] of Islam in America" there. One of them, composed on February 29, 1932, wanted to know about his goings-on and shared news that Pittsburgh followers remained in contact with Muslims in New York and Cleveland. Helena Kleely, secretary of the Pittsburgh group, was a coauthor of a May 18, 1932, letter, which requested

English translations of the Arabic literature that Majid had forwarded to his followers from abroad. A 1935 letter addressed the Italian occupation of Ethiopia, an event that was closely watched in black America, and speculated that in the future, African Americans would "return back to our homeland Africa," where they would establish a colony. Several followers also lamented the lack of replies to their correspondence.[31]

Missionaries such as Satti Majid were not the only Muslims of African descent to build organizations in the 1920s. American-born converts also established their own groups, some of which seemed to depart from both Ahmadi and Sunni forms of Islam. The most important of these new groups was the Chicago-headquartered Moorish Science Temple of America (MSTA), organized formally in the 1920s by North Carolina-native Timothy Drew. Drew, who took the name Noble Drew Ali (1886–1929), combined his own prophecies with Islamic tropes and symbols, elements of Freemasonry, and themes from American metaphysical movements to establish a new form of Islamic religion. Ali preached that African Americans were Moors, part of a Moroccan nation whose religion was Islam and whose racial heritage was Asian. The MSTA borrowed its Islamic dress, rituals, and other visibly Oriental symbols largely from the Shriners, a Masonic organization. It hoped to establish a community that informed by a strict moral code and the science of "New Thought," a branch of metaphysics that stressed the idea, among other things, that personal health was the product of self-mastery and mental discipline. Human beings, Ali promised, could better their health and their wealth through meditation, prayer, and other spiritual practices. Members of the MSTA understood these teachings to be "Moorish Science," and they thought that such science was both a modern manifestation of ancient wisdom and a new revelation called Islam.[32]

Missionary Satti Majid disagreed. He thought that the group was heretical and wrote to scholars at al-Azhar seminary in Cairo to obtain a fatwa, or learned religious opinion, which condemned the group. In this moment of transnational exchange, Muslim Americans and Muslim visitors looked beyond US borders to appeal to Islamic authority abroad in setting the limits of Islamic authenticity in the United States. Majid wrote that Ali thought himself to be a prophet and composed his own holy scripture, *The Holy Koran of the Moorish Science Temple* (1927), which did not include a single verse from the Qur'an or a single allusion to the Sunna. Al-Azhar responded in November 1931 by releasing an English translation of its fatwa, which declared Ali an "unbeliever or a mentally-deranged person."[33] If the fatwa was ever distributed in the United States—and there is no evidence indicating that it was—it had little impact on the growth of the MSTA, which boasted thousands of members by the 1940s.

The attempt to adjudicate the Islamic authenticity of the MSTA demonstrates the growth and diversity of Muslim Americans and their institutions in the 1920s. Shi'a, Sunni, Ahmadi, and Moorish Muslim institutions had a footprint in the United States by the end of the decade. The beginning of competition among them was an indication that Islam had become a bona fide American religious tradition structured at least in part by larger patterns of denominationalism. Whether born in the United States or just visiting, US Muslims had acknowledged their religious differences, and in taking such notice, they also viewed the Muslim "other" as part of a nascent American religious community. There had been contact, exchange, and conflict in a shared political space.

The rate of such exchanges only accelerated in the 1930s. In 1930, W. D. Fard, a person of color whose background remains contested, founded the NOI, originally called the Allah Temple of Islam, an organization influenced by the Moorish Science Temple. In 1931, Muhammad Ezaldeen (1886–1957), perhaps a former member of the MSTA, went to Cairo, Egypt, and studied Islam under the auspices of the Young Men's Muslim Association. He came back to the United States in 1938 and established the Addeynu Allahe Universal Arabic Association (AAUAA), an African American Sunni Muslim organization that became successful along the East Coast.[34] In 1937, Wali Akram (1904–1994), formerly a leader of the Ahmadiyya movement, created a Sunni mosque in Cleveland.[35] By 1939, Daoud Faisal, Satti Majid's follower, had rented a brownstone for his international, interethnic

Sunni mission on State Street in Brooklyn, New York.[36] Then, in 1943, all of these black-led Sunni organizations convened at the All Moslem and Arab Convention in Philadelphia to form the Uniting Islamic Society of America.[37]

By the end of the 1930s, African Americans had formed the institutions that became the public face, or perhaps more accurately from the point of view of the state security agencies, the potentially dangerous face of American Islam. Based on evidence from membership reports and FBI surveillance, perhaps the MSTA and the Ahmadiyya were the largest religious groups with 10,000 or more members.[38] This estimate does not include the memberships of the AAUAA, the midwestern mosques associated with Wali Akram, the New York-based Islamic Mission of Daoud Ahmed Faisal, and a growing NOI. No matter what the level of membership, this appearance of regional and national Muslim organizations was noted by scholars, the media, the police, and the FBI. In the early 1930s, the Bureau feared that the Moorish Science Temple was a potential threat to the state and initiated covert surveillance on this and other Muslim groups.[39]

But large-scale efforts to track and eventually repress African American Muslim groups did not occur until World War II. The surveillance of black Muslim groups was part of a much larger effort meant to track the potential rise of what FBI director J. Edgar Hoover feared were disloyal African Americans. From June 1942 to August 1943, the FBI conducted a massive investigation, later code-named RACON, that surveyed the full range of African American political dissent. One of Hoover's concerns was that "scheming peddlers of foreign 'isms'" were leading "malcontent" black Americans toward Communism and other putatively anti-American ideologies. The scope of the investigation was broad and the FBI defined disloyalty to United States to include support for the A. Philip Randolph's March on Washington movement and other civil rights activism. As Robert A. Hill, who has compiled and edited the RACON files, notes, "the aim of the investigation was to uncover the source(s) of the rising tide of black resistance to the wave of racial discrimination unleashed by the national defense program."[40] African Americans faced segregation not only in the US armed services, but also among defense contractors.

What alarmed the FBI about African American Muslim groups on the eve of World War II was that many of them, or at least some of their members, saw Japanese people as potential allies. The transnational ties and diasporic consciousness of black Muslim Americans were viewed as increasingly subversive as thousands of African Americans, Muslim or not, put their hopes in the messianic prophecy that the Empire of Japan would liberate them from the cage of American racism through a military invasion. By the 1930s, black Muslims, black Jews, advocates of black emigration to Africa, and black advocates for pan-Asian solidarity declared their public support for a fellow "colored" nation, and a Japanese national, Major Satokata Takahashi, formed a "Development of Our Own" group to galvanize such feelings in Detroit, Chicago, and St. Louis. Several African American leaders appropriated Takahashi's ideas. For example, Mittie Maud Lena Gordon, a former member of Marcus Garvey's Universal Negro Improvement Association, created the Peace Movement of Ethiopia (PME) in 1932. The PME called for the return of black Americans to Africa while also advocating for the war objectives of Japan. The organization's stationery featured an Islamic star and a crescent, and in a June 14, 1942, meeting, Gordon declared that the PME was associated with Islam. Another Chicago-based group created in 1932 that included anticolonial, pro-Japanese leanings was the Pacific Movement of the Eastern World (PMEW), which hoped to ally with the Japanese in order to buoy African American struggles for liberation. Rev. David D. Ervin, a Holiness pastor of the Triumph the Church of the New Age, led the PMEW from 1934 to 1940 and supported the idea that the Japanese should invade the United States to bring about equality. He also sometimes advocated the notion that blacks should immigrate to Japan.[41]

RACON's final report, the *Survey of Racial Conditions in the United States* (1943), reveals the way in which the FBI attempted to discipline religious conduct in the United States. The report creates a profile of pro-Japanese African American organizations that warned of Islam's links to pro-Japanese sentiment. It then attempted to catalog all of the various Muslim groups popular among black Americans as a way of measuring the security risk to the US nation-state. For example, it argued that Satti Majid's

African Moslem Welfare Society of America presented "three of the characteristics common to pro-Japanese negro organizations: the adoption of Mohammedan religion; the identification of Japanese and the negroes as a kindred colored people, and the resettlement of American negroes in negro colonies." The report indicated that while the group's 1927 Pennsylvania incorporation records stated their intent to unite Muslims by eradicating racial differences among them, over a decade later, its members were arguing over whether it should side with Japan in World War II. The FBI characterized this change in the following way: "The society is said to have conducted itself as a religious organization until approximately nine months ago when several persons connected with it exhibited pro-Japanese sympathies."[42] This framing suggests that for the FBI, religion, at least among black people, must be politically quiescent in order to be religion. Once a group began to articulate a position that ran counter to the dominant politics of the Bureau, it stopped being religion proper.[43]

The articulation of pro-Japanese sentiments was evidence of sedition, and as the dream of a Japanese invasion spread among thousands of African Americans in the early 1940s, the government arrested the African American leaders suspected of stoking such feelings. Among the 25 leaders arrested was Elijah Muhammad (1897–1975), leader of the NOI. Muhammad was acquitted of the sedition charge, but was sent away for refusing to register for the military draft.[44] His arrest and prosecution signaled the emergence of a larger pattern for dealing with African American Muslims who criticized the United States. These black Muslims would rarely engage in any genuinely treasonous activity against the United States, but they did capitalize on their imagined ties with foreign states and "foreign" traditions like Islam to resist, at least in rhetorical terms, the policies of the US government toward people of color both at home and abroad. In Elijah Muhammad's sedition case, for example, it was found that Muhammad had called the Japanese "brothers and friends" of black Americans. However, according to all the evidence introduced in the case, there was no record of a Japanese person ever attending the meetings of the NOI nor was there any correspondence indicating "any connection between the leaders of this group of colored people and the Japanese government or any Japanese person."[45]

Given the lack of evidence of any actual treason, one of the few weapons that the Department of Justice possessed to suppress these groups was the Selective Service and Training Act of 1940. In September 1942, 70 members of the NOI were arrested for failure to register for the draft, of which 38 were indicted. Of these, 31 pled guilty, an obviously principled stand against the federal government since it was later determined that seven of these actually did register for the draft.[46] But while members of the NOI were willing to go to jail for their religious beliefs, members of the AAUAA, a black Sunni group, were aware of the trap into which they might fall and they took action to avoid it. All members of the AAUAA registered as conscientious objectors, apparently on the grounds that they could neither consume food that was prepared by the military nor could they be expected to fight their own people, since the Japanese were a fellow "dark race."[47]

Hoover's commitment to curtail not only Communism but all forms of African American protest against racism resulted in a culture of suspicion at the FBI and in the executive branch more generally that sought to monitor and ultimately influence the practice of Islam among African Americans. There is some evidence that agents entertained the possibility that Islamic religion could be practiced in an apolitical way, but at the same time, Islam inevitably came under suspicion because of its association with African American protests against white supremacy. In sweeping Islamic religious practice, of various types, into the machinery of anti-black state suppression, Hoover and the FBI created mechanisms and meanings that framed Islam as a danger to the US nation-state. It did not matter for Hoover's RACON whether black Muslims were explicitly pro-American or not. Islam was a sign for the FBI on the eve of World War II of pro-Japanese sympathy. It was enough to tar Islam as a problematic political symbol that deserved to be disciplined through surveillance, and if possible, prosecution. But the federal government possessed limited tools for the suppression of these movements during World War II. It was only after the war that more aggressive counterintelligence techniques were employed to deal with black Muslims.

The Black Muslim Scare of the 1960s

The government's fear of Islamic political movements after World War II shows the ways in which state power was inscribed and enforced in this period. Islamophobia became a form of government discipline that utilized propaganda, violence, and fear. There was irony in the fact that the government frequently accused Muslims, especially the NOI, of fomenting a race war, when it was the government that actively fashioned Islam as a threat to US domestic peace, international relations, and civil rights. Though government interference in the practice of Islamic religion was limited by US law during World War II, new legal and extralegal techniques were used to discredit the practice of Islam among black Americans after World War II. Restricting the religious freedoms of Muslims, manipulating mainstream media, stoking violent conflict among African American organizations, and even trying to break up marriages, the Department of Justice and the FBI reached into the heart of US society to create hatred of and between Muslim Americans.

Not all of the federal government's techniques for controlling the practice of Islam were successful. One of the government's strategies, for example, was the denial of First Amendment protections to Muslim prisoners. The Justice Department argued that since the NOI was not an authentic religious movement—but rather a "cult" that operated as a political organization—its followers in prison did not have the right to meet or conduct religious services. By redefining Islam as a "cult," the government could avoid the messiness of legal protections for religious expression. But the repression of Islamic practice in both state and federal prisons ended up expanding rather than limiting the rights of prisoners to practice the religion of their choice. The efforts of incarcerated African American Muslims in US courts helped to establish legal precedents and rights for all prisoners. Generally speaking, these cases guaranteed prisoners the right, with conditions, to assemble for religious services, to read religious literature, to wear religious garb, to consume a special diet, and to communicate with religious leaders. For example, the Supreme Court's 1964 decision in *Cooper v. Pate* was one of the first significant prisoners' rights precedents established by the highest court in the land. Thomas Cooper, a member of the NOI sued Illinois prison warden Frank Pate on the grounds that Pate's prejudice against the NOI had resulted in the denial of Cooper's right to the free exercise of his religion. Cooper alleged that Pate denied him the right to read religious literature, communicate with NOI ministers, and to attend religious services. The State of Illinois argued that the NOI was a political rather than a religious organization, a position that the Supreme Court rejected. The court ruled for the first time that prisoners had the right, or the legal standing, to seek relief from religious discrimination and required lower courts to hear the law suits of prisoners that were filed on this basis. The 1964 ruling made clear that prisons must treat prisoners equally, regardless of their particular religious affiliation, unless there was a compelling reason not to do so.[48]

Overall, this and other victories of Muslim prisoners were exceptional checks against the executive branch's ability to repress practices of Islam that it opposed. For the most part, the FBI faced few impediments to suppress the forms of Islam that it found objectionable. Its number one target was the NOI. In 1956, J. Edgar Hoover authorized technical surveillance, including phone taps, of Elijah Muhammad, the leader of the movement. In addition, informants were either recruited from or placed within the NOI.[49] Using the information that it gleaned from its surveillance, the FBI then engaged in a disinformation campaign against the organization. In 1959, the FBI briefed journalists from *Time*, *U.S. News and World Report*, the *Saturday Evening Post*, and other major media outlets about the group, leaking aspects of their surveillance in order to prove its danger to US society. The special agent in charge of the campaign in Chicago wrote that the purpose was to expose the "abhorrent aspects of the organization and its racist, hate type teachings." This was also the year in which Mike Wallace of CBS News produced *The Hate that Hate Produced*, a television program that did as much as any other source to interpret the NOI for millions of Americans. Then, in 1962, the Bureau leaked information about Elijah Muhammad's purchase of automobiles and homes; it forged anonymous letters to the editor accusing the movement of fraud. Finally, the FBI sent anonymous letters to Clara Muhammad, wife of Elijah, exposing the leader's many extramarital affairs.[50]

One of the Bureau's main contentions about the NOI, an argument that echoed the Justice Department's argument about the practice of Islam in US courts, was that the NOI version of Islam was neither real Islam nor legitimate religion. A full-length monograph written within the FBI and circulated to all field offices in the early 1960s concluded that while the NOI purported "adherence to the religious principles of Islam...[and] the spiritual and physical uplift of the Negroes," its "constant emphasis on the vindictive doctrines of the cult results in the propagation of hatred of the white race."[51] The book admitted that while the NOI was not a serious security threat, it should remain an "investigative problem" due to its radical political profile. This remarkable document also included a point-by-point comparison of the "orthodox" teaching of Islam and the "unorthodox" teachings of the NOI.[52] The lack of nuance in this scholarly polemic was helpful in furthering the idea that the NOI lacked Islamic bona fides.

The *real* Muslims of America, according to most in the academy, the media, and the FBI, were the immigrant Muslims. In the 1950s, a large percentage of immigrant Muslims was Syrian-Lebanese, and like their Christian compatriots, they became regarded after World War II as white ethnics. Their immigrant Islam, in contrast with African American Islam, was viewed as a sign by some in the 1950s as a healthy expression of American ethnic identity. As sociologist Will Herberg argued, it was fine for foreign religionists to retain their religious practices as part of their ethnic identity as long as they assimilated to other American values; in fact, it was laudable for them to retain their religious traditions, since this act demonstrated the Cold War claim that America was uniquely free—you could practice whatever religion you liked.[53] But the flip side of that argument was that those indigenous Americans who chose freely to associate with a foreign religion—a religion that was not perceived to be part of their a priori culture—were denying their true ethnic roots as Americans. Mainstream media echoed these claims, framing black Muslims as persons who adopted a false sense of ethnic identity. The black Muslim appropriation of Asia and Allah upset most black and white Americans' racial and religious assumptions. When black Americans depicted themselves as oriental divines, Muslims, Jews, and Hindu spirit mediums, they were seen as having betrayed their real black heritage; they were deluded fakes.[54]

Yet their number continued to grow. Even the FBI admitted internally that drawing additional attention to the NOI may have backfired, making the organization and its leaders Elijah Muhammad and Malcolm X even more popular. There was also a larger context to the movement's growth. The US prosecution of the Cold War, its manipulation of newly independent African and Asian states, the beginning of the Vietnam conflict, and the lack of real progress on social equality at home made the religious and political critique of the NOI convincing to many both inside and outside the movement. On the domestic side, the NOI opposed integration as a solution to racism, perhaps becoming the country's most forceful postwar voice for black political, economic, and cultural self-determination. On the international side, the NOI, in the words of Penny Von Eschen, "permitted a space—for the most part unthinkable in the Cold War era—for an anti-American critique of the Cold War."[55]

But there was no more effective symbol of both domestic and international political resistance to US power than Muhammad Ali, whose principled stand against the Vietnam War resulted in the forfeiture of his world heavyweight boxing crown. Ali, a hero to many people of color and leftists around the world, was seen as a fifth column—the enemy inside the walls—by the US government, which sought to blunt his rising popularity by any means available. In this case, the US Army drafted him. In 1966, at the height of the military conflict in Vietnam, Ali proclaimed that he was willing to give up his boxing crown and go to jail rather than be inducted. He said that he was a conscientious objector whose religion prohibited the killing of innocents. Casting the Vietnam War as a racist and immoral conflict, Ali also stated that the US participation was hypocritical: quipping that "no Vietcong ever called me nigger," Ali pointed out the irony of the United States defending freedom abroad when it still had its own problems with racial equality at home. In 1967, he was convicted of draft evasion and stripped of his boxing title.[56]

That same year, the FBI began a new stage of "operational intensity" in seeking to suppress the NOI. Its tool for doing so was the Counter Intelligence Program, better known as COINTELPRO. Cutting its teeth on the New Left, white hate groups, and the Communist Party in the early 1960s, COINTELPRO expended FBI operations in 1967 to include "Black Nationalist-Hate Groups." It conducted 360 separate operations, becoming the second largest area of all domestic counterintelligence operations. The NOI was perhaps the most popular target of all the black groups.[57] "The purpose of this new counterintelligence endeavor," wrote Hoover on August 25, 1967, "is to expose, disrupt, misdirect, discredit, or otherwise neutralize the activities of black nationalist, hate type organizations and groupings, their leadership, spokesmen, membership and supporters."[58]

In trying to neutralize the NOI, the FBI engaged in activities both disturbing and tragicomic. Agents continued to write anonymous letters about Elijah Muhammad's philandering, but this time they sent them to the leader's daughters as well as to his wife.[59] It persisted in its use of journalists in disinformation campaigns. Agents also sent anonymous letters and used informants to try to pit one black nationalist group against another. In at least six cities, the FBI attempted to cause strife between the Black Panthers and the NOI. Though open conflict arose in Atlanta, tensions between the two groups were generally limited to healthy, spirited debates among African Americans over the best path to black liberation. FBI agents also penned anonymous letters to Elijah Muhammad, accusing his ministers of malfeasance, and planted informants inside mosques to spread rumors about members and leaders at the local level. One of the more amusing instances of this admittedly serious activity was an effort in New York to distribute a "large comic-book type of publication made up to ridicule the leaders" of the mosque.[60] Finally, the FBI's field office may have begun a campaign to install W. D. Mohammed as Elijah Muhammad's successor, writing in one declassified memorandum that Wallace was "the only son of Elijah Muhammad who would have the necessary qualities to guide the NOI in such a manner as would eliminate racist teachings." Whether the FBI's paper support for W. D. Mohammed translated into operational support inside the NOI is not yet known.[61]

The Black Muslim Scare of the 1960s was the pinnacle of pre-9/11 fears about the Muslim threat to the American nation-state. In retrospect, the FBI's efforts seem like an overreaction. Even the FBI admitted in 1960 that Muslims were mounting no serious challenge to the security threat, and still, significant government resources were committed to neutralizing them in the 1960s. In the end, it was not the imminent outbreak of political violence that motivated the state's heavy-handed tactics. It was the symbolic threat, the power of dissent, and the critique of US society and US militarism that led the FBI to wage a counterintelligence war against the NOI. That counter-intelligence campaign constructed an anatomy of Islamophobia in every FBI field office and many local law enforcement agencies. The back-and-forth of memoranda to headquarters in Washington and the Central Research Division's updated "scholarship" on the movement produced habits of fearful surveillance. The FBI spread this Islamophobia to the mainstream media and its consumers through organized and long-running disinformation campaigns. In summary, Islamophobia was not an ignorant reaction of the public to the presence of Muslims in America. It was manufactured.

Variations on the Black Muslim Scare after 9/11

The public face of Muslim America has changed since the 1960s. No longer represented by bow-tied black men hawking copies of *Muhammad Speaks* or the beautiful, semi-naked body of Muhammad Ali, public images of Muslims in America seem instead to rely on old Orientalist tropes like the burka'd woman, the bearded mullah, or the wild-eyed warrior. The Muslim as public enemy is brown rather than black. How that occurred is a long story, one that has to do with the end of the Cold War and the emergence of political resistance in the name of Islam to US empire and US client states among a number of Muslim groups worldwide.[62] Moreover, today's "brown" Muslim, the dissenter, is generally a Sunni rather than a follower of Elijah Muhammad's unique prophecies.

Focusing on doctrinal differences between black and brown, pre- and post-9/11 Muslims, however, covers up a critical link between our current age and that of the Black Muslim Scare. Despite the great differences between the 1960s and the post-9/11 era, there is one critical similarity: Expressions of Islam that make radical critiques of the United States will be suppressed, even if they do not pose a direct security threat to the nation-state. A deep discourse of

Islamophobia within government offices and departments governs the ways in which the state manages Muslim dissent both in the past and in the present.

As in the past, the FBI and the Justice Department—and now the Treasury Department, Homeland Security, and the National Security Administration, among other agencies—seek to reward those versions of Islam that are apolitical and innocuous to US interests while also suppressing even peaceful Islamic resistance to US foreign policy. The USA PATRIOT Act, passed in October 2001, authorized the resurrection of COINTELPRO techniques that had been killed, at least officially, in the post-Watergate era. The federal government reacquired Congressional approval, for example, for aggressive counterintelligence, including so-called sting operations inside religious congregations. The Bush administration detained persons of interest as material witnesses without habeus corpus rights and determined internally that it could wiretap its own citizens without judicial or legislative oversight.[63]

The broad-ranging powers of the government to prevent terrorism have also resulted in the prevention of free speech, assembly, and the free exercise of religion. The federal government and US Army, respectively, falsely accused lawyer Brandon Mayfield and Capt. James Yee of aiding terrorists, and though the names of both men were cleared, the false accusations may have scared some Muslim Americans from publicly voicing their opposition to US foreign policy.[64] Muslim American charities that provided nonmilitary aid to some of the government's declared enemies, groups such as the Palestinian party Hamas were raided and in some cases shut down.[65] In an ultimate insult to the first amendment, the US Supreme Court in 2010 decided in *Holder v. Humanitarian Law Project* that offering training in nonviolent, peaceful protest techniques to groups designated as terrorist organizations by the executive branch could be prosecuted as material aid to terrorists.

As in the 1960s, civil libertarians have challenged the government's increasing power to detain and punish its own citizens without just cause or evidence. Modest victories have been scored in the cases of *Hamdi v. Rumsfeld* (2004), *Hamdan v. Rumsfeld* (2006), and *Boumediene v. Bush* (2008), in which the US Supreme Court acted to check the unlimited power of the executive branch.

But such decisions have done little to retard the increasing powers of the state to persecute political activism in the name of counterterrorism.

President Obama's administration has largely continued the Bush era policies. Guantanamo Bay has remained open; the American mosque has remained a primary target of domestic counterintelligence; and deportation of foreign nationals has actually increased. Obama also personally ordered the assassination of Anwar al-Awlaki and Samir Khan, two US citizens who produced speeches and web materials in support of al-Qaeda. We will never know whether they were guilty of committing terrorist acts because they were killed by drones, an act that many civil libertarians saw as a violation of constitutional guarantees of due process and trial by jury. More recently, the White House gave its support to the National Defense Authorization Act, which allows the executive branch to detain foreigners and perhaps Americans accused of "substantially supporting" terrorism indefinitely without trial. On the domestic side of counterterrorism policy, the Obama administration outlined what it has dubbed the "Strategic Implementation Plan for Empowering Local Partners to Prevent Violent Extremism in United States." One of the primary sites for implementation is the American public school, where teachers and students are supposed to be trained to identity potential terrorists—people who, according to National Security Council official Quintan Wiktorowicz, use the word "infidel," defend Osama bin Laden, and watch extremist videos.[66]

These aggressive approaches to managing Muslim American dissent have been accompanied by simultaneous attempts to "reach out" to Muslims. The administrations of both George W. Bush and Barack Obama have hailed Islam as part of America's religious fabric, using symbolic incorporation to craft Muslim American citizenship as another resource in the prosecution of US interests both at home and abroad. Muslim Americans are among the approximately 15,000 informants employed by the FBI to identify potential terrorist threats in the United States; they often act as an *agent provocateur* attempting to catch fellow Muslims in a sting.[67] In addition, ordinary Muslim Americans are the single greatest source of tips in counterterrorism investigations. They are congratulated for such exemplary work at the same time that the US House of

Representatives Committee on Homeland Security, chaired by Rep. Peter King (R-NY), investigates what he claims is a widespread problem of jihadi extremism in the Muslim American community.

The suppression of politically engaged, critical American Islamic voices is a long tradition. The disciplining of Muslim American politics has been a critical component of US statecraft for decades. In an era in which the government negotiates with, occupies, makes peace, and wages war against more Muslims than ever before, there is little reason to hope that state Islamophobia will end any time soon.

NOTES

1. Robert J. Allison, *The Crescent Obscured: The United States and the Muslim World, 1776–1815* (Chicago, IL: University of Chicago Press, 1995) and Timothy Marr, *The Cultural Roots of American Islamicism* (New York: Cambridge University Press, 2006).
2. Penny M. Von Eschen, *Race against Empire: Black Americans and Anticolonialism, 1937–1957* (Ithaca, NY: Cornell University Press, 1997).
3. Melani McAlister, *Epic Encounters: Culture, Media, and U.S. Interests in the Middle East, 1945–2000* (Berkeley, CA: University of California Press, 2001).
4. Peter Gottschalk and Gabriel Greenberg, *Islamophobia: Making Muslims the Enemy* (Lanham, MD: Rowman and Littlefield, 2008) and Zachary Lockman, *Contending Visions of the Middle East: The History and Politics of Orientalism* (New York: Cambridge University Press, 2004).
5. Kathleen Moore, *Al-Mughtaribun: American Law and the Transformation of Muslim Life in the United States* (Albany, NY: State University of New York, 1995), pp. 19–67.
6. Robert A. Hill, ed., *The FBI's RACON: Racial Conditions in the United States during World War II* (Boston: Northeastern University Press, 1995), p. 4.
7. Edward E. Curtis IV, *Muslims in America: A Short History* (New York: Oxford University Press, 2009), pp. 5–6.
8. Allan D. Austin, *African Muslims in Antebellum America: Transatlantic Stories and Spiritual Struggles* (New York: Routledge, 1997), p. 22.
9. Michael A. Gomez, *Black Crescent: The Experience and Legacy of African Muslims in the Americas* (Cambridge: Cambridge University Press, 2005), p. 166.

10. Thomas Bluett, *Some Memoirs of the Life of Job, the Son of Solomon, the High Priest of Boonda in Africa; Who was a Slave About Two Years in Maryland; and Afterwards Being Brought to England, was Set Free, and Sent to His Native Land in the Year 1734* (London: Printed for R. Ford, 1734), http://docsouth.unc.edu/neh/bluett/menu.html, accessed June 1, 2009.
11. Austin, *African Muslims in Antebellum America*, pp. 50–62.
12. Curtis, *Muslims in America*, pp. 6–10.
13. Terry Alford, *Prince among Slaves* (New York: Oxford University Press, 2007); Allan D. Austin, *African Muslims in Antebellum America: A Sourcebook* (New York: Garland, 1984), pp. 134–240; and Austin, *African Muslims in Antebellum America* (1997), pp. 65–83.
14. "An Afro-American Recalls His Visit to Washington, D.C.," August 29, 1828, as quoted in Austin, *African Muslims in Antebellum America* (1984), pp. 159, 251 n67.
15. Henry Clay to Andrew Marschalk, January 12, 1828, as quoted in ibid., pp. 196–197.
16. "Abduhl Rahahman." *New York Journal of Commerce*, October 16, 1828, as quoted in ibid., pp. 175, 254 n84.
17. "An Afro-American Recalls His Visit to Washington, D.C.," as quoted in ibid., pp. 159, 251n67.
18. *Freedom's Journal*, October 31, 1828, 252, as quoted in ibid., 176–178.
19. Austin, *African Muslims in Antebellum America*, p. 78.
20. Curtis, *Muslims in America*, pp. 9–10.
21. From Cyrus Griffin, "Prince Abduhl Rahahman," *Southern Galaxy* (Natchez, Mississippi), May 29, June 5 and 12, July 5, 1828, as quoted in Austin, *African Muslims in Antebellum America* (1984), p. 142.
22. Edward E. Curtis IV, "United States Foreign Relations," in *Encyclopedia of Muslim-American History* (New York: Facts on File, Inc., 2010), pp. 554–555.
23. Bruce B. Lawrence, *Old Faiths, New Fears: Muslims and Other Asian Immigrants in American Religious Life* (New York: Columbia University Press, 2002), pp. 80–86.
24. Sarah M. A. Gualtieri, *Between Arab and White: Race and Ethnicity in the Early Syrian American Diaspora* (Berkeley, CA: University of California Press, 2009), pp. 113–134.
25. Yohanan Friedmann, *Prophecy Continuous* (Berkeley, CA: University of California Press, 1989).
26. Articles in the *Detroit Free Press*, June 8, 1921, and *Detroit News*, June 9, 1921, as cited by Sally Howell, "Mosques, History," in Jocelyne Cesari, ed., *Encyclopedia of Islam in America*, volume 1 (Westport, CT: Greenwood Press, 2007), p. 432.

27. See Richard Brent Turner, *Islam in the African-American Experience* (2nd edition, Bloomington, IN: Indiana University Press, 2003), pp. 109–146.
28. Ibid., p. 124.
29. Ian Duffield, "Some American Influences on Dusé Mohammed Ali," in *Pan-African Biography*, ed. Robert A. Hill (Los Angeles, CA: Crossroads Press, 1987), pp. 11–56.
30. Patrick D. Bowen, "Satti Majid: A Sudanese Founder of American Islam," *Journal of Africana Religions*, 1:2 (in press).
31. Ahmed I. Abu Shouk, J. O. Hunwick, and R. S. O'Fahey, "A Sudanese Missionary to the United States: Satti Majid, Shaykh al-Islam in North America, and His Encounter with Noble Drew Ali, Prophet of the Moorish Science Temple Movement," *Sudanic Africa* 8 (1997), pp. 137–191.
32. Edward E. Curtis IV, "Debating the Origins of the Moorish Science Temple," in *The New Black Gods: Arthur Huff Fauset and the Study of African Americans Religions*, ed. Edward E. Curtis IV and Danielle BruneSiglers (Bloomington, IN: Indiana University Press, 2009), pp. 70–90.
33. Shouk, Hunwick, and O'Fahey, "Sudanese Missionary," 182.
34. Michael Nash, *Islam among Urban Blacks, Muslims in Newark, NJ: A Social History* (Lanham, MD: University Press of America, 2008).
35. Robert Dannin, *Black Pilgrimage to Islam* (New York: Oxford University Press, 2002), pp. 47–55, 92–96, 108–112, and Mbaye Lo, *Muslims in America: Race, Politics, and Community Building* (Beltsville, MD: Amana Publications, 2004), pp. 55–66.
36. Marc Ferris, "To 'Achieve the Pleasure of Allah': Immigrant Muslims in New York City, 1893–1991," in *Muslim Communities in North America*, ed. Yvonne Yazbeck Haddad and Jane Smith (Albany, NY: State University of New York Press, 1994), p. 212.
37. Dannin, *Black Pilgrimage*, pp. 47–48.
38. Turner, *Islam*, p. 134.
39. "FBI File of the Moorish Science Temple of America," http://vault.fbi.gov/Moorish%20Science%20Temple%20of%20America/Moorish%20Science%20Temple%20of%20America%20Part%201%20of%2031/view (accessed April 26, 2012).
40. Hill, ed., *The FBI's RACON*, p. 4.
41. Ernst Allen, Jr., "When Japan was 'Champion of the Darker Races': Satokata Takahashi and the Flowering of Black Messianic Nationalism," *Black Scholar* 24 (Winter 1994), pp. 23–46.
42. Hill, ed., *FBI's RACON*, pp. 545–546.
43. Sylvester A. Johnson, "Religion Proper and Proper Religion," in *New Black Gods*, ed. Curtis and Sigler, pp. 145–170.

44. Claude Andrew Clegg III, *An Original Man: The Life and Times of Elijah Muhammad* (New York: St. Martin's Press, 1997), pp. 90–93.
45. Hill, ed., *The FBI's RACON*, pp. 544–545.
46. Ibid., pp. 544–545.
47. Ibid., p. 547.
48. Moore, *Al-Mughtaribun*, pp. 69–102.
49. Mattias Gardell, *In the Name of Elijah Muhammad: Minister Louis Farrakhan and the Nation of Islam* (Durham, NC: Duke University Press, 1996), p. 72.
50. Ibid., pp. 73–76.
51. Central Research Section, Federal Bureau of Investigation, "The Nation of Islam: Antiwhite, All-Negro Cult in United States" (October 1960), p. vi.
52. Ibid., pp. 48–67.
53. Will Herberg, *Protestant, Catholic, Jew: An Essay in American Religious Sociology* (Chicago, IL: University of Chicago Press, 1983), pp. 27–28.
54. Edward E. Curtis IV, *Black Muslim Religion in the Nation of Islam, 1960–1975* (Chapel Hill, NC: University of North Carolina Press, 2006), pp. 4–9.
55. Von Eschen, *Race against Empire*, p. 174.
56. William Brown, "Ali, Muhammad." In *Encyclopedia of Muslim-American History*, I, pp. 41–44.
57. Frank T. Donner, *The Age of Surveillance: the Aims and Methods of America's Political Intelligence System* (New York: Knopf, 1980), pp. 178, 212–213.
58. Gardell, *In the Name of Elijah Muhammad*, p. 86.
59. Clegg, *An Original Man*, p. 258.
60. Gardell, *In the Name of Elijah Muhammad*, pp. 87–91.
61. SAC Chicago to FBI Director, 100–35635-B, 4/22/68 quoted in Gardell, *In the Name of Elijah Muhammad*, 101.
62. See further McAlister, *Epic Encounters*, pp. 198–234.
63. See David Cole, *Enemy Aliens: Double Standards and Constitutional Freedoms in the War on Terror*, revised edition (New York: New Press, 2004) and Louise A. Cainkar, *Homeland Insecurity: The Arab American and Muslim American Experience After 9/11* (New York: Russell Sage, 2009).
64. Curtis, ed., *Encyclopedia of Muslim-American History*, pp. 363–364, 597–598.
65. Ibid., pp. 449–452.
66. Dina Temple-Raston, "Officials Detail Plan to Fight Homegrown Terrorism," http://www.npr.org/2011/12/08/143319965/officials-detail-plans-to-fight-terrorism-at-home, accessed December 20, 2011.

67. University of California Graduate School of Journalism, "Journalism School Investigates FBI Use of Informants in Muslim Communities Post 9/11," *Berkeley Research* (August 20, 2011), http://vcresearch. berkeley.edu/news/journalism-school-fellow-investigates-fbi-use-informants-muslim-communities-post-911, accessed September 28, 2011.

Chapter 4

Center Stage
Gendered Islamophobia and Muslim Women
Juliane Hammer

*Why are the images of Muslims as oppressed relegated only to dis-
cussions of the female experience? Why do we assume that images of
Muslims as terrorists reflect general stereotypes of Muslims as a whole,
even though these assumptions are (by and large) being made mainly
about Muslim men? What would it look like for the experiences of
Muslim women (including the stereotypes that we come up against)
to get equal airtime in conversations about "Muslim experiences,"
rather than being limited primarily to the discussions about "Islam and
women"? Or for us to acknowledge the terrorist stereotype as also a
gendered image that mainly encompasses men?*

—*Krista Riley[1]*

The concerns expressed in the quote above are substantial and they
need to be considered for a fuller and more nuanced discussion of
the issue of Islamophobia in America and beyond. Gender as a category of analysis should be but is often not (yet) an integral part of
scholarly inquiry into many topics, among them the study of Islam,
Muslims, and, as in this volume, Islamophobia. It should require no
justification or explanation to state that everything we study and
encounter is in fact gendered: marked by constructed categories of

gender; socially and historically constructed and negotiated gender
roles; and gendered positionality of researchers, journalists, and writers. The aim of this essay is to offer thoughts on the gendered nature
of Islamophobia in several dimensions.

Before proceeding in this direction, I want to offer some clarifica-
tions on how I understand and use the term Islamophobia. Literally
meaning "fear of Islam," Islamophobia is not about innate or natural fear of Islam or Muslims. Rather, it is an ideological construct
produced and reproduced at the nexus of a number of political and
intellectual currents that need to be taken into consideration and
assessed critically in each instance or event of Islamophobic discourse and practice. I see it at the intersection of the following:

- Shifts in domestic politics in which Islam and Muslims become
  tools for renegotiating political allegiances, identities, and power
  structures;
- Imperial wars as extensions of colonial and neocolonial projects;
- Expressions of racism and bigotry in response to shifting demo-
  graphic and political constellations;
- Negotiations of the nature and significance of feminism;
- Political exclusion and discrimination as part of shifting state
  powers and applications of liberal ideology;
- Civilizational discourses on moral and cultural superiority of
  "Western" powers, foremost among them the United States.

It might seem frustrating to fragment the neat and overarching
framework inherent in the ways in which Islamophobia is currently
most often used in academic analysis; and one could argue that such
fragmentation is weakening the political power of the intellectual
critique of Islamophobia. However, it is intellectually more honest
to acknowledge that Islamophobia is not the product of a conspiracy
against Islam and Muslims, originating from one source that can
conveniently be pinpointed and called out. In what follows I attempt
to situate both the victims of Islamophobic discourse and those
producing and disseminating it within the nexus described above.
This requires focusing on specific examples and identifying just
how in each instance, several but not all of these forces are at work.
This kind of nuanced analysis can arguably be more productive in

empowering activist strategies that address the causes and remedies for Islamophobia.

Gendering Islamophobia

How then is Islamophobia gendered? There are several angles to this question that can be explored. Islamophobia is gendered in the way described above, in that gender is inherently part of social construction; thus, there have to be elements of Islamophobia that can be described as gendered. Furthermore, as Krista Riley pointed out above, the genderedness of Islamophobia can productively be explored through a nuanced study of the ways in which Muslims are represented and described as gendered. This genderedness is most obvious in the representation of Muslim men as violent terrorists (both against "us" and Muslim women) and the representation of Muslim women as oppressed and silenced (by Muslim men, Islam, and Muslim culture). Muslim men and women in these representations (or stereotypes) are two sides of the same coin: The violence of oppressive Muslim men is demonstrated in their treatment of their women; and the oppression of Muslim women is perpetrated by violent Muslim men. No other factors or influences can be explored or considered in such a neatly organized scenario.

There is an important connection between gender and sexuality, both in how sexuality is mapped onto Muslim bodies and how Muslim attitudes to sexuality are used to define Muslims as other and as foreign to the United States. Concerns about sexual expression, repression, and control are also part and parcel of debates about Muslim women wearing headscarves or "the veil." The hijab will occasionally appear in my discussion as an outward representation of Muslim women's identity. However, it is a tired trope and one that has been discussed in academic literature in much detail already.[2]

Furthermore, as Jasbir Puar has shown, assumptions about Muslim attitudes to sexuality and gendered bodies have also produced complex and politically productive discourses on homosexuality, homophobia, and American nationalism, or what she terms "homonationalism."[3] In *Terrorist Assemblages*, she discusses in detail the American debate over the Abu Ghraib prisoner abuse scandal. Puar demonstrates that the assumed homophobia of the abused Muslim prisoners is staged against the backdrop of political calculation and in clear contradiction to similarly homophobic debates in the American public sphere. The very discussion of queerness; lesbian, gay, bisexual, transgender, and queer (LGBTQ) rights; and gay marriage becomes flattened into a discourse in which the performance of homonationalism is a sign of American superiority against the homophobia, sexual repression, and general backwardness of Islam and Muslims.

Here I want to explore more specifically how Muslim women are at the center of Islamophobic discourses. This focus on women clearly depends on their relationship with Muslim men; however, masculinity and the threat of dangerous Muslim men is not directly explored as the balance to women in this essay. Much of that work still needs to be done. Thinking about Islamophobia in gendered terms and as a gendered construction is only a first step in this direction.

More specifically, by focusing on women, I advance several interconnected arguments, focusing on Muslim women as objects of Islamophobic discourse; women as producers of Islamophobic discourse; and on some of the complications involved in delineating where Islamophobia begins and ends. I argue that Muslim women occupy "center stage" in Islamophobic discourse in two distinct and contradicting ways: As objects of hate crimes and discrimination, Muslim women have Islamophobia mapped onto them directly and as representations of Muslims in American society; as objects of anti-Islamic discourse Muslim women are represented as victims of their religion, culture, and Muslim men, and thus in need of saving, liberation, and intervention. Women as producers of Islamophobic discourse, both non-Muslim and Muslim, justify the second set of discourses in the service of a range of political goals, and, their own gender matters for the effectiveness and impact of their arguments. Lastly, a thorough analysis of gendered Islamophobia needs to take into consideration the problem of delineating the boundaries of what is identified as Islamophobia as opposed to critical feminist discourse, secular critique, and intra-Muslim reform. In a way then, the last argument also delineates the material discussed in this essay.

Women and Gender in Existing Literature

In surveying available academic literature and other materials about Islamophobia in America and in the global context, it is striking how little has been written directly addressing the role of women and gender in Islamophobic discourse. Many more materials have been made available in recent years, among them studies by Andrew Shryock and Peter Gottschalk (both also in this volume), as well as other book-length treatments of various dimensions of Islamophobia.[4] Several of these works provide some material and thoughts on women. Stephen Sheehi focuses one chapter of his book on the ways in which "Islam's misogyny" is used as a tool in Islamophobic discourse and his book as a whole is focused on the American context. *Thinking through Islamophobia* contains several essays discussing women, veiling, law, and sexuality; however, each of these chapters focuses on European contexts and discourses rather than the United States. The work of Sherene Razack, especially her *Casting Out* (2008)[5] is probably closest to my focus here. However, she develops her arguments primarily based on her work as a lawyer in Canada, and case work in Europe. Important parallels with these contexts should and can be drawn while simultaneously keeping a close eye on the particular circumstances, political dynamics, and Islamophobic constellations in the United States.

Several important investigative reports on the financing and production of Islamophobia have been produced in recent years including "Fear Inc." by the Center for American Progress,[6] "The Right Wing Playbook on Anti-Muslim Extremism" by People for the American Way,[7] as well as "Jihad against Islam" by Robert Steinback from the Southern Poverty Law Center.[8] Each of these follows the financial trail of campaigns, pundits, organizations, and films identified as producing, utilizing, or reproducing Islamophobic discourses identified with neoconservative and right-wing political goals. They focus, however, on the most extreme and obvious forms of Islamophobia and pay less attention to the ways in which politically liberal pundits, journalists, and even scholars can be implicated in the reproduction and spread of Islamophobic discourse. The work of Wendy Brown on toleration and her critique of liberalism as directly implicated in constructing "others" to tolerate and selectively include provides important correctives to the exclusive focus on the most obvious Islamophobes in America.[9]

Rather strikingly, gendered analysis is almost absent from these reports. "Fear Inc." points to equal opportunity Islamophobic networks that include women in their ranks, most notably Pamela Geller, and mentions the oppression of women in connection with that of "gays and religious minorities."[10] The "Right Wing Playbook" mentions the abuse of women, and the dangers for American women in growing Muslim presence in the United States in passing.[11]

In the world of academic journals and articles, gendered Islamophobia has been addressed by a number of scholars, notably though not in the context of the United States.[12] One of the most relevant essays for our consideration here is by Jasmin Zine and discusses experiences of Canadian Muslim Girls with regard to their headscarves. Zine uses the term "gendered Islamophobia" but then somewhat narrowly defines it as "specific forms of ethno-religious and racialized discrimination leveled at Muslim women that proceed from historically contextualized negative stereotypes that inform individual and systematic forms of oppression."[13] Zine points to the impact of Islamophobia "beyond representational politics" as inflicting "epistemic violence," saying that Islamophobia in her view has "material consequences."[14] As I will argue below, the "material consequences" are more than consequences of discourses: They are part and parcel of the broad range of phenomena usually called Islamophobia.

Many of the insights about how Muslim women are objectified and utilized in Islamophobic discourses in other contexts are relevant for a closer analysis of the American contexts and a number of select examples that will provide the necessary context and pretext for deeper analysis. One important connection that has not been explored yet is the connection between media representations of Muslim women and the politics of Islamophobia. The analysis of examples that follows below assumes that there are direct and intentional links between the production and dissemination of media images of oppressed Muslim women, in the United States and elsewhere, the reception of such stereotypes in the public sphere, and the utility of such discourses for domestic and foreign policy making. The media dimensions of Islamophobic discourses and more specifically the representation of Muslim women has been studied extensively, and where appropriate, I draw on available studies and approaches. In my own work, I have argued that there is a particular dynamic at work in the ways in which some American Muslim women have been represented as liberated, outspoken, and "free" in direct opposition to their less "liberated" sisters in the United States as well as abroad. The dynamics at work here will be further explored below.[15]

It is also prudent to acknowledge that casting a wider net will yield significantly different results. This is not only true for expanding our inquiry beyond Islamophobia as a concept and term but also with regard to the intersection of media production, media consumption, and policy making. For example, in this essay, I will describe the use of Islamophobic hate speech against Muslim women and the discrimination and hate crimes produced directly or indirectly by Islamophobic discourse as arguably produced in conjunction with legal, administrative, and domestic policy measures covered under the "War on Terror." Thus, literature on using immigration law for the detention of "suspected terrorists," widespread and legalized surveillance of Muslim communities and individuals, and the reincarnation and expansion of the Patriot Act all can and should be linked in our analysis to the issue of Islamophobia. Of course, this will not solve the chicken and egg conundrum of whether discourses produce media images that produce policies or vice versa, but it will help expand our focus to gain a better understanding of what is an interconnected and complex set of phenomena. An important part of this broader picture is the acknowledgment that Islamophobia today is not isolated from a longer historical trajectory and is certainly not (only) a product of the post-9/11 climate. This is especially true for the consideration of gendered Islamophobia.

Have Muslim women always been at the center of anti-Muslim discourses? This question and its answer are connected to broader debates about the much-discussed clash between "Islam and the West." Bearing in mind that both "Islam" and "the West" are ideological constructs invested with various meanings, boundaries, and definitions by a range of actors in past and present, it is still useful to ponder whether there has "always" been conflict between those constructed entities. Some scholars trace animosity back to the beginnings of Islam and represent the resulting tensions and conflict as a religious battle between Christianity and Islam.[16] Others see a "clash of civilizations" as famously described in the work of Samuel Huntington.[17] Yet others identify more critically the power dimensions of the perceived conflict and situate the representation of Muslims and Islam as other in the context of colonial European ideology.

How long have Muslim women been perceived as oppressed? Leila Ahmed famously described the unholy alliance between Orientalism in the service of (the British) Empire and early British feminism, dating the image of the oppressed Muslim woman in need of liberation at least back to the nineteenth century:

> Broadly speaking, the thesis of the discourse on Islam blending a colonialism committed to male dominance with feminism—the thesis of the new colonial discourse of Islam centered on women— was that Islam was innately and immutably oppressive to women, that the veil and segregation epitomized that oppression, and that these customs were the fundamental reasons for the general and comprehensive backwardness of Islamic societies.[18]

Mohja Kahf has argued in her study of representations of Muslim women in Western literature from the twelfth to the nineteenth century that rather than the image of the Muslim being a feature of all such literature, the particular representation of Muslim women as oppressed is in fact a product of the eighteenth and nineteenth centuries. In previous centuries, other and very different depictions of Muslim women can be found, and the transformation of those images, as Kahf argues, is connected to developments in European societies rather than changing roles of actual Muslim women in their own societies in the same time periods.[19]

Charlotte Weber has offered a detailed analysis of "feminist Orientalism" in the activities of the International Alliance of Women in the first half of the twentieth century and contends that European women in the alliance never regarded their "Middle Eastern sisters" as equal and thus demonstrated the intellectual and political power of Orientalism.[20] These and other scholars have demonstrated that there is indeed a historical legacy of Orientalist depictions of Muslim women focusing on their need for liberation from their cultures and their religion. However, these and other studies also show that the development and application of Orientalist tropes were not the same in all times and places but rather emerged and were produced in specific circumstances and for specific times. Thus, both how particular discourses on Muslim women are produced, by whom, and to what end should not be assumed to be the same. There are patterns of the production and application of knowledge but they are not patterns of sameness. Rather, a repertoire of tropes developed over several centuries in both Europe and North America is at the disposal of those producing contemporary Islamophobic discourses.

Objects of Islamophobic Discourses

Setting the Stage

In a video clip posted on YouTube, the viewer sees small groups of Muslims, men, women, and children, walking in what appears to be early evening toward a building. Police officers stand around the entrance and a man greets the families at the entrance. The camera moves from them to a group off to one side holding American flags and signs in what is clearly a protest of some kind. A man repeatedly shouts through a megaphone: "Muhammad was a pervert, Muhammad was a fraud." Amid screams including "Go home, no shari'a. Do you beat up your wife, too? Are you a molester?" one woman shouts: "Why don't you go beat up your wife like you do every night!" A few seconds later, another one adds: "She probably needs a good beating!"[21]

The video was put together and posted by the regional Southern California office of CAIR (Council on American Islamic Relations), an American Muslim advocacy organization founded in 1994. The event in question was a fund-raising dinner, organized by ICNA Relief, the charity arm of the Islamic Circle of North America, which took place in February 2011 in Yorba Linda, California. The purpose of the dinner was "to raise money for women's shelters, and to help relieve homelessness and hunger in the U.S."[22] The excerpt from the video strikes me as relevant in several ways. One, the insulting statements were yelled exclusively at the Muslim men, despite the fact that women and children were walking alongside them. Thus, Muslim women here were merely objects of a hate discourse that in other incarnations assumes their continued oppression by Islam and violent Muslim men. They are not spoken to, but rather spoken about, a common feature of much of Islamophobic discourse as we have seen it reincarnate in various forms over the last decade. Second, these "statements" demonstrate the centrality of Muslim women as beaten, oppressed, molested, and violated in these discourses. The protesters are familiar with the tropes of such discourse including the accusation that Muhammad married a young girl, that Muslim men routinely abuse their wives, and that the menace of Islam has something to do with "shari'ah." The screamed slogans are at least somewhat ironic when considering the purpose of the event, especially the raising of funds for women's shelters. And the last comment in the paragraph above seems puzzling at least, as it seems to support physical violence against Muslim women, thus implying either their less-than-human status or that physical violence against women in general should be condoned.

The issue of (verbal, physical, systemic) violence inflicted on Muslim women is central in both direct and indirect ways. Verbal violence is directed at Muslims, men directly, and women indirectly, while the shouted statements of the protesters also express "concern" about violence perpetrated by Muslim men against Muslim women. In what follows I distinguish these dimensions as two distinct angles of Islamophobic discourses on Muslim women: the very real experiences of discrimination and hate crimes in relation to hijab and gendered bodies; and discussions of domestic violence, honor killings, and hijab as violence inflicted upon them by Muslim men as represented in Islamophobic discourses.

Inflicting Islamophobia on Muslim Women

When Muslim women are discriminated against in the labor market; when they are treated differently in the public sphere because they are recognizably Muslim; and when they are verbally abused, threatened, and physically assaulted, certain forms of Islamophobic discourses can be discerned as underlying such acts. In discussing select examples of discrimination against Muslim women and hate crimes against them, I want to set the stage for the argument that this type of "Islamophobia" directed against women is part of a larger fear or discomfort with the presence of Muslims in American society; and that it makes sense to see this dimension of the phenomenon in direct relation to racism and fear of nonwhite minorities.

In an essay provocatively titled "Time to Address Violence against Muslim Women," Sahar Aziz argued in late 2011 that it was high time for the American public to take note of the many incidents of physical and verbal harassment leveled against Muslim women in the United States. Aziz lists and links to a series of incidents in which American Muslim women were assaulted, their headscarves pulled of, and insults shouted at them. Aziz argues that "(c)ontrary to popular belief, the biggest threat to Muslin women is no longer limited to domestic violence in the home but rather unprovoked attacks in public places by bigoted strangers. To many, the Muslim woman's headscarf marks her as a terrorist or co-conspirator to terrorism. Meanwhile, her gender marks her as easy prey to cowardly acts by those who seek to violate her body and personal dignity."[23] She continues by calling for "the attention of government officials, women's rights advocates and all Americans concerned with violence against women."[24] Notably, Aziz does not deny that there are other threats to the safety of Muslim women; however, she calls for a reevaluation of such threats as more dangerous to Muslim women than hate crimes. She also points to the ideological use of the trope of the oppressed Muslim woman when the oppression is at the hands of her husband or other Muslim men, which seems to contradict Muslim women's treatment in a discriminatory fashion in the American public sphere. Many of the almost 50 comments to her article in the *Huffington Post* could be cited in analyzing responses to her essay, some supportive of her arguments, many accusing her of ignoring the much larger problem of women's oppression in "Islamic countries." The link between Islamophobic attitudes and discrimination is exemplified in this comment: "Violence cannot be condoned. However, by wearing identity-concealing garments, these women are sending the message that they are victims. They shouldn't be surprised when they are victimized. If they don't take their own rights seriously, then those who are inclined to violence certainly won't."[25]

An episode of the popular ABC show "What would you do?," which aired in early 2008, took up the issue of discrimination against Muslim women through the creation of a situation in which an actress wearing hijab entered a roadside bakery in Waco, Texas, and was refused service by a sales clerk (also an actor) because she was "dressed like that." The reactions of other customers were recorded and some were later approached to discuss and explain their reactions. With the exception of very few responses supportive of the Muslim woman, the overwhelming majority of customers did not react, or supported the verbally offensive clerk. While not a proper measure of public opinion, the episode demonstrates the pervasiveness of negative attitudes to Muslim women in hijab who, in the episode, were invariably coded as foreign, from a different and alien culture, and associated with terrorism by those supporting the discrimination. When the young actress pointed out that she was a native Texan and not foreign at all, she was dismissed and insulted some more. That "What would you do?" is more than a TV show as pointed out in an article about the show on the ABC website:

> The young woman in our experiment was an actor, but many of the hateful words she heard were based on the experiences of Chicago-born Nohayia Javed, who was watching our experiment from the control van. Javed said she has continually suffered verbal abuse and said she has even been physically attacked by fellow Americans—just because she is Muslim.
>
> "They always start off with, 'you're a terrorist, Osama-lover, towel-head, camel jockey' on and on," Javed said. "If I tell them I'm American, they're like, 'No you're not. Just because you were born here doesn't make you American.' And I'm like, 'What makes you American?' "[26]

This discrimination because of wearing hijab is also a legal issue that has been demonstrated by Kathleen Moore in "The Hijab and Religious Liberty: Anti-Discrimination law and Muslim Women in the United States," published in 2000. That her findings from more than a decade ago (and before 9/11) are still relevant is evident in her conclusion where after reviewing a set of cases in which Muslim women sued for religious discrimination, she found that women often fail to win accommodation of their religious and minority needs, especially when employers can reasonably argue that such accommodation would mean a loss of profit on their part.[27]

Discrimination and verbal abuse are also cited as reasons by Muslim women for deciding to remove their hijab. In an NPR feature in 2011 titled "Lifting the Veil: Muslim Women Explain Their Choices," Asma Khalid, the author, profiled 12 Muslim women who had recently decided to remove their head covering. Several of the women cited negative reactions to their hijab by non-Muslims in public as one of the reasons for their decision.[28]

In probably the most stunning example of discriminatory rhetoric, Texas congressman Louie Gohmert took to the floor of the house in June 2010 to argue that Muslims were involved in a plot that would bring women to the United States to give birth to what would later be dubbed "terror babies." He is quoted as saying:

> It appeared they would have young women who became pregnant [and] would get them into the United States to have a baby. They wouldn't even have to pay anything for the baby, ... And then they would return back where they could be raised and coddled as future terrorists. And then one day, 20, 30 years down the road, they can be sent in to help destroy our way of life.[29]

Anderson Cooper debated with Gohmert on his "Keep Them Honest" segment on August 12, 2010. No evidence of Gohmert's claims has ever been presented.[30] However bizarre such claims may seem, and laughable too, they point to a deep-seated distrust and dislike of the presence of Muslims in American society. In addition, Gohmert's remarks link Muslims in the United States and the children born to them to the discussion of "anchor babies" as brought into the conversation by South Carolina Republican Senator Lindsey Graham, also in summer 2010. Graham alleged that illegal immigrants were abusing the 14th Amendment by entering the United States to give birth to US citizens.[31]

In early 2012, Sahar Aziz offered a reassessment of the status of Muslim women (wearing hijab) and argued that they had moved from victims of oppression to potential terrorists through a process that she describes as being stuck in the "crosshairs of intersectionality."[32] Aziz proposes that beyond experiences of discrimination, because of their hijab, and thus their visibility as part of Muslim communities, Muslim women are marked by their headscarves as part of the "suspicious, inherently violent, and forever foreign" terrorist other.[33] Quoting Nadine Strossen, Aziz argues that Muslim women have become "daughters or sisters of terrorists."[34] This permanent suspicion, regardless of actual acts and behaviors, is also marked as racist in Aziz's analysis, an argument that I will explore further below.

In addition to these direct experiences of discrimination, hate speech, and hate crimes, Muslim women have also been affected by legal and political measures that, on the surface, seem to target Muslim men: the Patriot Act, administrative detention measures, and surveillance of "terrorist suspects" among others. Women rarely appear directly affected in this context (which might be a reporting blind spot in some instances); however, it is not difficult to argue that measures targeting Muslim men in American Muslim communities almost always also affect the women of these communities. Women are wives, mothers, sisters, and daughters of the Muslim men taken away and deported for minor immigration infractions, fired for being Muslim, put under surveillance for attending a mosque, forced to endure special registration and random searches at airports, and subject to material support for terrorism trials.[35] Each of these measures targets Muslims for being Muslim and thus affects Muslim women as much as it does Muslim men.

Taken together, these few items of discussion, selected for their merit in demonstrating the breadth of ways in which Muslim women's bodies are at the center of one dimension of Islamophobic discourse, point to the fact that American Muslims indiscriminately and collectively are perceived as foreign, as a fifth column for terrorists, and as threat to the United States. Women's bodies, especially those who visibly identify as Muslim through hijab, bear the brunt of a particular kind of visual profiling that can result in verbal assaults, hate crimes, and exclusion, as well as in increased surveillance of their communities, and insults to their religion.

However, Muslim women also become victims of broader "fears" over shifting race relations, perceptions of racial discrimination, and a very specific fear of nonwhite minorities. Women give birth to the children of these minority communities, and thus their bodies are directly linked to shifting demographic balances as well as the bogus link to terrorism for Muslims specifically.

More specifically, Muslim "cultures" are perceived and represented as foreign, alien, and introducing cultural impurity—thus the need to code Muslim women's bodies as foreign and decidedly not American—which is then directly linked again and again to the threat of terrorism (through Muslim men) and doubts about their loyalty to the United States. These "fears" were reformulated and introduced as legislation in several states through the "creeping shari'ah" campaigns of Islamophobes in 2011.[36]

When William "Jerry" Boykin warned in 2011 that Muslims were such a threat to the United States that he was worried for the "three females" among his six grandchildren because he was "concerned about the day coming when they will be wearing burkas,"[37] he made the link between the presence of Muslim women's bodies (and the garments covering their Muslim bodies) as a threat and the purported oppression of Muslim women by their religion and by Muslim men.

Saving Muslim Women from Islam

This section discusses several examples of Islamophobic discourse in which the oppression of Muslim women by Islam takes center stage. This oppression takes many forms, but it is emphasized, written, and spoken about, and publicized by a range of actors from Newt Gingrich to Pamela Geller and Phyllis Chesler. And it serves a neoconservative and right-wing agenda to mark Islam as a religion not only foreign to the United States but also threatening the very foundations of its society. The assumed gender inequality and oppression of women by Islam is juxtaposed with a quintessentially American gender-egalitarianism and respect for women's rights that can only be described as ironic in the face of recent political developments regarding women's reproductive rights in the months leading up to the 2012 presidential elections.

Nevertheless, pointing out the abysmal situation of Muslim women, their oppression by Islamic Law, their suffering at the hands of Muslim men, and even their own resistance to such oppression, all serve to legitimate Islamophobic rhetoric in both domestic and international affairs. Ironically, the Muslim women that Islamophobes claim to be so concerned about, the women in need of saving, are the same ones rejected as part of the enemy, a fifth column, and the source of Islamic terror from within! The focus of Islamophobic discourses on American Muslim women generates perhaps the greatest irony in how Muslim women are portrayed as in need of liberation from Islam and from Muslim men, while simultaneously alienating and marking as foreign and unwelcome the very women they are trying to liberate. More broadly yet, Islamophobic discourses alienate American Muslims only to then turn around and accuse them of not integrating into American society. Neoconservative pundits and writers have taken up many causes, and have spoken on behalf of Muslim women both in the United States and abroad. In what follows several examples will demonstrate a distinct pattern of focusing on violence against women, "honor killings," and the oppressiveness of "shari'ah" as well as of hijab.

When Aasiya Zubair was murdered by her husband in February 2009, Phyllis Chesler published an article in the *Middle East Quarterly*, refuting the widespread reading of this tragedy as a result of a case of domestic violence.[38] Chesler focuses specifically on cases of murder in Muslim families in North America and describes them as distinct from "normal" domestic violence. She also accuses American Muslim organizations and advocates of trying to shift the blame away from their religion and their communities by insisting that domestic violence is at the core of these killings. Chesler also supported the niqab ban in France, arguing that "apart from being an Islamist act of assertion that involves clear security dangers and creating mental and physical health hazards, the burqa is a flagrant violation of women's most basic human rights."[39]

Chesler is a sophisticated and knowledgeable Islamophobe. In a letter sent to and read at a panel in Toronto titled "Islamism's War against Women" in September 2011, Chesler writes about recent developments after discussing Egyptian scholar and reformer Huda Sha'rawi:

> Huda would weep if she saw how women have been deeply veiled in Egypt and how Islamist forces have taken over—dare I say, colonized?—the Egyptian state. She would be amazed at all the Muslim girls and women living in the west who are veiling too, wearing the suffocating, hot, and heavy totalitarian and fascist flag of Islamism on their heads, faces, and bodies as they walk behind men who are perfectly comfortable in light, modern clothing.
>
> My dear sisters: The hour is late. The body count of female honor killing victims in the west is a mainly Muslim body count. Aqsa Pervez, in Canada, was lured home by her mother and honor murdered by her father for being too Canadian, too western, and for refusing to veil properly enough. Based on my research, the highest torture rate of honor killing victims is not in Pakistan, but in Europe. When Muslim girls and women seek to assimilate, modernize, reject lives of utter subordination, an example must be set so that other Muslim girls and women will not do so.[40]

Pamela Geller, another neoconservative American pundit and feminist, has engaged in countless verbal attacks on Islam and Muslims, often on behalf of oppressed Muslim women. One example is the "Jessica Mokdad Human Rights Conference" convened in Dearborn, Michigan, early May 2012. The conference, organized by the American Freedom Defense Initiative (AFDI) and Stop Islamization of America (SIOA), both of which Geller is involved in, was "dedicated to increasing awareness of honor killings and gendercide under the Shariah."[41] Named after a murder victim Geller and SIOA claim to have been the victim of an honor killing, the conference generated critical responses from Muslim communities and organizations, which were promptly utilized by Geller as fodder for her denunciation campaign against American Muslims. Muslim women appear in her propaganda narrative as abused, beaten, and not infrequently, only become useful to her arguments when they are dead. Geller's arguments are inescapably circular and anyone contradicting her is either a hypocrite or an Islamist. No argument is possible against this representation of Islam, Islamic Law, and

Muslim leaders as misogynist, "standing up for honor killings,"[42] and a threat to Muslim as well as non-Muslim women in the United States and beyond.

The anti-Shari'ah legislation mentioned above has also incorporated the representation of Islam as against equality and women's rights. For example, in the months leading up to the senate vote on a law banning "foreign laws," Kansas lawmakers were inundated with materials that argued that "proclaimed that it was really about protecting 'women's rights.' The bill helps 'women know the rights they have in America,' said state Rep. Peggy Mast (R). 'To me, this is a women's rights issue,' said Sen. Susan Wagle (R)."[43]

By rejecting Islam as foreign to American society and the legal system, by justifying military intervention in Muslim majority countries, and by chastising Muslim communities for insisting on their freedom to practice their religion, this form of Islamophobic discourse inscribes Muslim women's bodies with meaning that they have no control over and uses them as pawns or tools, both in a politics of neoconservative imperialism internationally and a political agenda of scapegoating a conveniently targetable minority population and its religion domestically. Neither allows Muslim women any agency unless they are willing to denounce both their religion and their communities and societies.

Foreign Policy and War

When in March 1999 Mavis Leno, wife of talk show host Jay Leno, took up the plight of Afghan women under the Taliban as a cause on behalf of the Feminist Majority, the oppression of Muslim women in Afghanistan overnight became a cause of concern for celebrities, politicians, and public opinion. Highlighting the horrendous conditions imposed on Afghan women allowed for the construction of a discourse that painted them as helpless victims, and Islamic fundamentalists like the Taliban as brutal oppressors in the name of their religion. The resurrection of this trope conveniently ignored the fact that through the mujahidin, the Taliban had indirectly come into power and military might with the support of the US government which had provided such support to develop a counterweight to the Soviet occupation of Afghanistan.

The awareness created during the "Stop Gender Apartheid in
Afghanistan" campaign in 1999 to 2001 was relatively easily turned
into a tool for justifying the invasion of Afghanistan in the wake of
September 11, 2001. Now it was the First Lady, Laura Bush, who took
to the stage in November 2001 to link the necessity for Operation
Enduring Freedom to the oppression of Afghan women: "Civilized
people throughout the world are speaking out in horror—not only
because our hearts break for the women and children of Afghanistan,
but also because in Afghanistan, we see the world the terrorists would
like to impose on the rest of us."[44] Not unlike the nineteenth-century
British colonial ideology, the misogynist Islam trope here served as a
tool for the justification of and rallying for US wars.[45] In early 2002,
RAWA (Revolutionary Association of the Women of Afghanistan)
criticized the Feminist Majority agenda and rhetoric as counterproductive for the rights and safety of Afghan women and as antifemi-
nist: "Waging war does not lead to the liberation of women anywhere.
Women always disproportionately suffer the effects of war, and to
think that women's rights can be won with bullets and bloodshed
is a position dangerous in its naïveté. The Feminist Majority should
know this instinctively."[46] The contestation of the role of feminism as
both a theoretical and activist approach to Muslim women is demonstrated in this set of events and will be discussed further below.

Much of the discourse on the oppression of Muslim women abroad
is primarily utilized in order to justify war and military intervention.
However, as we have seen above, the oppressive Muslim men and the
oppressed Muslim women (elsewhere) also serve as tools for generating
enough fear of Islam to introduce legal measures against Islamic Law in
US domestic policies. In anti-Muslim discrimination and hate speech,
as well as in "saving Muslim women from Islam and Muslim men"
discourses (Muslim), women are victims, real or imagined. However,
gender considerations are also important in the following discussion of
the role women play as producers of Islamophobic discourses.

Women as Producers of Islamophobic Discourse

Robert Spencer, Daniel Pipes, Newt Ginrich, Steven Emerson, Glenn
Beck, Frank Gaffney—many of the most prominent producers

of Islamophobic discourse are male. Some, like Pamela Geller and
Phyllis Chesler, are women and far from an exception; they constitute part of the organized cadre engaging the creation and dissemination of Islamophobic discourses, sometimes but not always
with a focus on women. The presence and central role of these
women is acknowledged (beyond just gender-inclusive language)
in "Fear Inc.," which on at least two occasions speaks of "men and
women" promoting anti-Muslim sentiments. The report includes
lists of "scholars and activists," "political players," and "validators," and each list contains the names of at least two women.[47]
Beyond displaying famed American gender equality, I want to
argue that the contributions of women to Islamophobic discourse
is rather a characteristic of gendered Islamophobia. The power of
women's empathy for other women and the validation of women's
expression of concern for the rights and welfare of other women,
however unequal, is a potent tool and appeals to both male and
female segments of the public sphere. Perhaps most ironic, women
Islamophobes are otherwise not usually defenders of women's
rights, as reflected in their stances on women's reproductive rights
and, to offer a specific example, the Violence against Women
Act, legislating financial support for domestic violence awareness
and prevention work and law enforcement.[48] Below I discuss several of the women producers of Islamophobic discourse in more
detail.

Pamela Geller

Pamela Geller has already been mentioned above, and probably
gained most fame during the campaign against the Park51 Muslim
community center in Manhattan in 2010. Occasioned by the
upcoming midterm elections, the controversy roused much debate,
generated another wave of Islamophobic discourse, and may have
significantly impacted the elections in October 2010. Muslim
women figure prominently in her arguments, which she most frequently shares in the form of blog entries on her blog "Atlas Shrugs."
A search for Muslim women returns hundreds of entries, many of
them Geller's thoughts, on news items. Three hundred and twenty

blog entries address honor killings. An entry from May 24, 2012, states:

> How many girls are murdered that we don't know about, whose families never reported them missing? I am talking about here in the US, Canada and Europe. Murdered for being too western like Jessica Mokdad in Michigan, Noor Almaleki in Arizona (the first honor killing prosecution in the US), Amina and Sarah Said (their father who shot them execution style is still at large), et al. The only way we can help Islam to reform and renounce the sharia (at least in the West) is to shine a light on these brutal and savage practices. While Muslim groups (i.e. CAIR) in the United States denounce these efforts and aggressively pursue the institution of sharia in America, SIOA and AFDI continue the fight to educate the uninformed American public of this gruesome graveyard of girls. Last month's Jessica Mokdad Human Rights Conference did just that, and was a huge success despite pro-honor killing backlash from CAIR and various Arab groups and media.[49]

Geller has also published a book, *Stop the Islamization of America: A Practical Guide to the Resistance*, and has coauthored at least one other book with Robert Spencer. Geller and Spencer founded a group by the same name—Stop the Islamization of America—in 2009.[50] The group was designated as a hate group by the Anti-Defamation League (ADL) in 2011 and in the Steinback report published by the Southern Poverty Law Center in 2011.[51] Geller has accused Barack Obama and the Obama administration of appointing Muslims into government positions without concern of their ties with Muslim extremists or their ability to undermine the United States, and she has also expressed more than once that Obama seems to have no concern for the rights of Muslim women abroad.[52]

Phyllis Chesler

Phyllis Chesler, also mentioned above, is in some ways a more complex character. A psychologist, former professor at the College of

Staten Island, and well-known feminist thinker, Chesler has made
it her business to warn the American public of the rise in Muslim
honor killings, support the niqab ban in France, and call out feminist academics as secret supporters of Islamist supremacy.[53] Chesler
is significantly more educated, has a much larger array of arguments
at her disposal, and couches her arguments in "facts" and more
sophisticated language. Chesler's 2005 book *The Death of Feminism*
has been described by Robert Spencer:

> Phyllis Chesler here supplies what has been conspicuously lacking
> since 9/11: a comprehensive call to women to defend their equality
> of dignity as human beings against a foe that short-sighted multicul-
> turalists and advocates of political correctness have up to now given
> a pass—despite its obvious threat to them. Chesler here speaks out
> fearlessly, passionately, and profoundly against the dehumanization
> of women that is institutionalized in Islamic Sharia law and mani-
> fested in innumerable ways in Islamic societies—as well as among
> Muslim immigrants to Western countries. This book should not be
> missed by any feminist, but not only feminists: Chesler sounds a call
> that every woman in the Western world, and every man, should heed
> before it's too late.[54]

The book chronicles not only Chesler's move from "left feminism"
to the defense of "right feminism," including support of war and
individualistic rights claims rather than critique of patriarchy and
imperialism, but in it, she also explains some of her hatred for
Muslims and Islam as produced by her 1960s' experience of mar-
rying an Afghan Muslim man and following him to Afghanistan
where she lived for several years.[55] Chesler is also a prime example
of Islamophobic discursive practices that insist on linking Islam and
Muslims to homophobia and hatred of Israel, thus creating an argu-
mentational loop in which someone who rejects Islamophobia is also
homophobic against LGBTQ rights, against the right of Israel to
exist, and a danger to American security and patriotism. In accusing American feminists of "Palestinization" and designating Muslim
organizations as "pro-honor killings," she entangles sets of arguments
that can variably be used for Islamophobic, pro-Israel, prowar, and
many other purposes.[56]

"Native Informants"

In the group that "Fear Inc." has described as validators of Islamophobic discourse, one can find, depending on the definition, a rather long list of names. Men and women who are either laying claim to their Muslim identity and thus speak on behalf and/ or against fellow Muslims, as well as a number of former Muslims who have renounced their affiliation with Islam but claim intimate knowledge of the religion, its practices, and its cultures. Much has been written about the politics of these "critical Muslims" including Irshad Manji, Ayaan Hirsi Ali, Azar Nafisi, Nonie Darwish, and others. Saba Mahmood has argued that the "autobiographical genre attesting to Islam's patriarchal ills... is significant not only for its extensive reliance on the most exhausted and pernicious Orientalist tropes... but also for its unabashed promotion of the right-wing conservative agenda now sweeping Europe and America, particularly in regard to Islam."[57] Mahmood focuses on the writings of Nafisi, Manji, and Hirsi Ali.[58]

Here, too, we find degrees of sophistications and catering to a range of audiences. Manji, Hirsi Ali, and Nafisi have published bestseller books and apply varying degrees of deconstructing critique to their subject Islam, while celebrating Israel, America, and neoconservative ideology and politics including American wars. Phyllis Chesler embraces them thus: "We are in the midst of an Islamic and ex-Muslim feminist uprising. Some names are known to Westerners: Ayaan Hirsi Ali, Nonie Darwish, Irshad Manji, Azar Nafisi, Taslima Nasrin, Asra Q. Nomani, Wafa Sultan—grave, elegant, impish, and fiery spirits who live in exile from their countries, communities, families, or even faith. These heroic feminists have been systematically demonized as 'racists' and 'Islamophobes.' Yes, even those whose skin colors may be brown, black, or olive; some are still religious Muslims but most are secularists, atheists, or apostates."[59] Some, including Taslima Nasrin and Asra Nomani, might be horrified to find themselves in a list with Hirsi Ali and Darwish. Of course, the charge of racism against someone who is not "white" could only be an insult! Women of Muslim background have to varying degrees been coopted into the machinery of Islamophobic discourse and at times it seems hard to know where to draw the lines between those willingly participating in the production of such discourse, for monetary reward and/or to advance their political and intellectual agendas, and scholars, activists, and journalists, "native" or not, who seem to feed into Islamophobic discourse by buying into its premises or by supplying the "machinery" with additional arguments and material.

Complicating the Picture

However, the picture is more complicated, and anti-Muslim neo-conservative rhetoric can be difficult to separate from secular feminist discourse that sometimes but not always aligns itself with neoconservative agendas regarding Islam and Muslim communities. It is at the more complicated intersections, when secular American feminists decide to become spokespersons for Muslim women and against their oppression, that Islamophobic rhetoric and expression becomes somewhat more difficult to debate. Well-intentioned and yet patronizing discourses on "white women saving brown women from brown men" abound and have a distinct history of their own. Such feminist discourses have been described as imperial feminism, as feminist orientalism in relation to Muslim women, and as outright racist. Lila Abu-Lughod in her well-known essay "Do Muslim Women Really Need Saving?" articulated not only a critique of the embedded service to imperial goals provided by some American feminists (related to the invasion of Afghanistan in 2001 and Feminist Majority support for it) but also questioned the theoretical foundation and ethical responsibility of feminist scholars to directly or indirectly participate in US foreign policy.[60]

Furthermore, how can one approach Muslim writers, journalists, and scholars who seem to situate themselves in rather ambivalent positions vis-à-vis the Islamophobic propaganda production? Take the example of a 2012 article by Mona Eltahawy, "Why Do They Hate Us: The Real War on Women is in the Middle East."[61] Eltahawy, who has spoken out in support of the niqab ban in France as well, has been presented as a Muslim feminist reformer, plays the "I am a Muslim woman who lived in Saudi Arabia and wore hijab for ten years" card to claim authenticity, and yet, calling her an Islamophobe does not roll off the tongue. Eltahawy attended and supported the woman-led Friday prayer in New York City in March 2005, which, as I have argued elsewhere, generated an important intra-Muslim debate about gender roles and issues in American Muslim communities and beyond.[62] In the article in question, Eltahawy provides a long list of acts, laws, and behaviors directed against women in various Middle Eastern countries and argues that compared to that list, the debates over women's reproductive rights in the United States (between Democrats and Republicans) are not worth much of the agitation they have produced. She writes, for example:

> Just as regime-appointed clerics lull the poor across the region with promises of justice—and nubile virgins—in the next world rather than a reckoning with the corruption and nepotism of the dictator in this life, so women are silenced by a deadly combination of men who hate them while also claiming to have God firmly on their side. I turn again to Saudi Arabia, and not just because when I encountered the country at age 15 I was traumatized into feminism—there's no other way to describe it—but because the kingdom is unabashed in its worship of a misogynistic God and never suffers any consequences for it, thanks to its double-whammy advantage of having oil and being home to Islam's two holiest places, Mecca and Medina.[63]

The article created a blogosphere backlash and much debate among American Muslims precisely because Eltahawy cannot as easily be resigned to the Islamophobic camp.[64] Is it just profoundly unhelpful in the current climate to argue that Muslim/Arab men hate women and that is why they treat them in this way? Does calling out Salafists and Islamists on their misogogyny and speaking on behalf of Egyptian as well as Muslim women in the "we" form count as reform of Islam from within, or is it rather its deconstruction from within?

Famed philosopher Slavoj Zizek argued in 2012 that Islam needs to repress women because women such as Hagar and Khadija played such important roles as foundational but later repressed figures for Muslim self-understanding. Zizek develops these arguments in comparison to Judaism and Christianity, profoundly influenced by Freud and Jung and thus certainly deconstructing religion more generally as well. "The key element of the genealogy of Islam is this passage *from* the woman as the only one who can verify Truth, *to* the woman who by her nature lacks reason and faith, cheats and lies, provokes men, interposing herself between them and God as a disturbing presence, and who therefore has to be rendered invisible. Woman, in other words, is an ontological scandal, whose public exposure is an affront to God."[65] Sentences such as this leave the reader to ponder whether this is sophisticated resurrection of good old Orientalism discourse and/or an argument supplying fodder for Islamophobic discourse. Furthermore, this is not an academic piece but rather an opinion post of the website of the Australian Broadcasting Corporation's site on "Religions and Ethics." Zizek does not seem like a fan of feminism either, nor religion for that matter; so does he fit into our analysis of gendered Islamophobia? What happens when the charge of Islamophobia (as racism, anti-Muslim hatred, fear of Islam, etc.) becomes a tool for silencing important and necessary debates about women's rights, patriarchy, imperialism, and feminism, among Muslims and in American society at large?

The murder of Shaima Alawadi in March 2012 was one such event in which the fault lines were drawn by a range of actors and pundits, reflecting the complex embeddedness of gendered Islamophobia in broader issues of politics, culture, and religion.

Campaigning for the Victim?

On March 25, 2012, news outlets including CNN reported that a 32-year old Iraqi woman residing in El Cajon, California, had died in the hospital after having been severely beaten with a tire iron. The CNN report quoted CAIR as saying that Alawadi had been taken off life support that day and died. The reports also mentioned that a note telling the family to go home and calling them terrorists had been left at the house.[66] CAIR's involvement at this stage would point to the assumption that the murder had been a hate crime. And while police did not describe the murder as such, the Internet quickly went viral with comparisons of Alawadi's murder and that of Trayvon Martin, the black teenager fatally shot on February 26, 2012, in Florida.

A Facebook page created almost immediately linked the hoodie campaign after the murder of Trayvon Martin (it had been argued that Trayvon Martin's wearing of a hooded sweatshirt had made him look suspicious, feeding into general and racist fear of young black men) to the fact that Shaima Alawadi wore hijab. College students posted group pictures wearing hoods and hijabs in solidarity on their Facebook pages. It certainly seemed like this was yet another example of how hateful, Islamophobic, and xenophobic discourses could turn into criminal acts.

On April 13, 2012, Adele Wilde-Blavatsky, a regular contributor to the *Feminist Wire*, an online discussion site for feminist thinkers and activists, argued that racism should not be conflated with anti-hijab or even anti-Muslim sentiments. In her post, titled "To be Anti-racist is to be Feminist: The Hoodie and the Hijab are Not Equals," accompanied by a picture of a woman wearing niqab and holding a sign saying "The Veil is Women's Liberation" (irony surely?), she argued:

> A "One Million Hoodies" march was organised to demand justice for Martin. As Brendan O'Neill argued, *this use of the hoodie is questionable enough*. The *wearing of "One million hijabs"* to show public solidarity and outrage at the murder of Alwadi? I cannot think of anything more ironic and counter-productive. What I take issue with here is the equating of the hoodie and the hijab as sources of ethnic identity and pride. The hijab, which is discriminatory and rooted in men's desire to control women's appearance and sexuality, is *not* a choice for the majority of women who wear it. The hoodie, on the other hand, is a choice for *everyone* who wears it. The history and origin of these two items of clothing and what they represent could not be more different; like comparing the crippling footbindings of Chinese women with a "Made in China" Nike trainer.[67]

The entry generated hundreds of responses and a debate with Blavatsky on the Facebook page of the *Feminist Wire*. A collective response was authored by a group of women of color including Muslim women denouncing Blavatsky's argument as racist and stuck in second-wave feminism, concerned with saving brown women, stating that her argument "serves to assert white feminist privilege and power by producing a reductive understanding of racial and gendered violence and by denying Muslim women their agency." The group of women argued:

> As feminists deeply committed to challenging racism and Islamophobia and how it differentially impacts black and Muslim (and black Muslim) communities, we wish to open up a dialogue about how to build solidarities across complex histories of subjugation and survival. This space is precisely what is shut down in this article. In writing this letter, we emphasize that our concern is not solely with Adele Wilde-Blavatsky's article but with the broader systemic issues revealed in the publication of a work that prevents us from challenging hierarchies of privilege and building solidarity.[68]

On April 5, 2012, *The New York Times* reported that information had emerged about Elawadi's plans to divorce her husband and that her daughter had felt forced into a marriage to an Iraqi man.[69] Not long after, the Islamophobic blogosphere took up the case, mocking news outlets and writers who had decried the murder as a hate crime.[70] Nina Burleigh tried to balance her previous coverage of the incident by publishing an article on the *Time* website titled, "Shaima Alawadi's Murder: A Hate Crime against Women?," in which she argued that "Domestic violence against women is a plague on all nations and cultures. It is certainly not limited to Islamic-refugee communities. But American authorities need to pay closer attention to the plight of women in these communities."[71]

The Alawadi murder proved an invitation and opportunity, in a macabre kind of way, for those pointing to increasing Islamophobic discourses and acts against Muslim women and to those for whom Alawadi became a poster child of Muslim honor killings and violence against women. The hate crime hypothesis allowed activists and bloggers to link Alawadi's death to racist and anti-immigrant discourses in American society, and even the possibility that Alawadi was murdered by a member of her family, or on their behalf, arguably weakened this discursive possibility. The link to family violence, not proven so far either, gave fodder to the Islamophobic propaganda machine, allowing Phyllis Chesler to name Alawadi as yet another victim of an honor killing, and deflated the hoodies and hijabs activism.

Karen Leslie Hernandez offered a thoughtful and nuanced reflection on this dynamics and concluded:

> As tragic as Alawadi's death is, there's an important conversation happening here. Was this a case of Islamophobia at its worst? Was this a case of a daughter trying to avoid marrying a man she didn't want to marry? Was this a case of a husband who would not let his wife divorce him?

> We cannot forget the most important part of this matter here— Shaima Alawadi is dead.

> Someone killed an innocent woman and they must be held accountable. I can only hope that justice will be brought in her honor and in her memory, and that it happens sooner, rather than later.[72]

Conclusion

The phenomena described as gendered Islamophobia in this essay are examples, most of them no more than a decade old. Is Islamophobia on the rise, and if so, is this a long-term trend, or a passing scapegoating focus on a particular religious minority community in the United States? Are there broader global connections—Islamophobes certainly have them—between developments in the United States, in Europe, and elsewhere, as suggested in much of the literature on Islamophobia? If it is a passing trend, should scholars and activists just wait for the wave to pass and for hatemongers to move on? The answer is clearly no, regardless of how short or long lived the current trends might be. Islamophobia is much more than a discourse, a set of ideas circulated on the Internet and in print. It is an ideological construct that has real impact on real peoples' lives, and thus, cannot and should not be ignored. Focusing on the gendered dimensions of such discourses reveals the complex intersections of feminist, antiracist, and leftist, as well as liberal and neoconservative agendas, and equips those who care with the tools for nuanced responses including analysis of the particular contexts producing and sustaining Islamophobia, and the possibility for informed and effective alliance building. Muslim women have been at the center of this stage for some time and promise to remain a focal point of interest for the foreseeable future. Further study of their role in a variety of Islamophobic discourses should be combined with research on the gendered-ness of representations of Muslim men, Muslim masculinities, and homophobia. Equally important, this essay's findings and conclusions need to be supplemented with a spotlight on Muslim women's agency in responding to Islamophobic discourses and acts. In some places, we have seen such responses, in the form of taking discriminatory employers to court regardless of the outcome; in deciding to take off the hijab; in Muslim women participating in media production, thereby challenging representations of them as oppressed, silent, and without voice.[73]

I want to end with a quote from Saba Mahmood that both raises important questions and offers an answer of sorts:

> Does the confidence of our political vision as feminists ever run up against the responsibility that we incur for the destruction of life forms so that "unenlightedned" women may be taught to live more freely? Do we fully comprehend the forms of life that we want to so passionately to remake so that Muslim women and men may live a more enlightened existence?...Would an intimate knowledge of life worlds that are distinct from, and perhaps even opposed to, our cosmopolitan lifestyles ever lead us to question the certainty with which we prescribe what is good for all humanity? At a time when feminist and democratic politics run the danger of being reduced to a rhetorical display on the placard of Islam's abuses, these questions offer the slim hope that perhaps a dialogue across political and religious differences...can yield a vision of coexistence that does not require making certain life worlds extinct or provisional. It requires us to entertain the possibility...that one does not always know what one opposes and that a political vision at times has to admit its own finitude in order to even comprehend what it has sought to oppose.[74]

NOTES

1. Krista Riley, "Islamophobia—Let's Talk about Gender," *Muslimah Media Watch* (July 14, 2008), www.patheos.com/blogs/mmw/2008/07/islamophobia-lets-talk-about-gender-2/, accessed September 15, 2012.
2. It is so tired a trope that the literature about hijab is beyond reference in a footnote at this point. However, talking about hijab has retained its power to delineate types and shades of right-wing as well as progressive (and secular) feminist discourses and thus should not be underestimated, however, overanalyzed it might be.
3. Jasbir Puar, *Terrorist Assemblages: Homonationalism in Queer Times* (Durham, NC: Duke University Press, 2007).
4. Andrew Shryock, ed., *Islamophobia/Islamophilia: Beyond the Politics of Enemy and Friend* (Bloomington, IN: Indiana University Press, 2010); Peter Gottschalk and Gabriel Greenberg, *Islamophobia: Making Muslims the Enemy* (New York: Rowman & Littlefield, 2007); S. Sayyid and AbdoolKarim Vakil, ed., *Thinking through Islamophobia: Global Perspectives* (New York: Columbia University Press, 2010); John Esposito and Ibrahim Kalin, eds, *Islamophobia: The Challenge of Pluralism in the 21st Century* (New York: Oxford University Press, 2011); Stephen Sheehi, *Islamophobia: The Ideological Campaign against Muslims* (Atlanta, GA: Clarity Press, 2011).
5. Sherene Razack, *Casting Out: The Eviction of Muslims from Western Law and Politics* (Toronto: University of Toronto Press, 2007).
6. Wajahat Ali, Eli Clifton, Matthew Duss, Lee Fang, Scott Keyes, and Faiz Shakir, "Fear Inc.: The Roots of the Islamophobia Network in America" (2011), www.americanprogress.org/issues/2011/08/islamophobia.html, accessed September 15, 2012.
7. "The Right-Wing Playbook on Anti-Muslim Extremism," People for the American Way (2011), www.pfaw.org/rww-in-focus/the-right-wing-playbook-anti-muslim-extremism, accessed September 15, 2012.
8. Robert Steinback, "Jihad against Islam: The Anti-Muslim Inner Circle," Southern Poverty Law Center, Summer 2011, www.splcenter.org/get-informed/intelligence-report/browse-all-issues/2011/summer/jihad-against-islam, accessed September 15, 2012.
9. Wendy Brown, *Regulating Aversion: Tolerance in the Age of Identity and Empire* (Princeton, NJ: Princeton University Press, 2008).
10. "Fear Inc.," 2011.
11. "The Right Wing Playbook," 2011.
12. For other articles and essay on women and Islamophobia in Europe and Australia, see Christina Ho, "Muslim Women's New Defenders:

Women's Rights, Nationalism and Islamophobia in Contemporary Australia." *Women's Studies International Forum* 30:4 (July–August 2007), pp. 290–298; Haleh Afshar, Rob Aitken, and Myfanwy Franks, "Islamophobia and Women of Pakistani Descent in Bradford: The Crisis of Ascribed and Adopted Identities." In *Muslim Diasporas: Gender, Culture, and Identity*, ed. Haideh Moghissi (Abingdon, UK: Routledge, 2006), pp. 167–185; Susan Carland, "Islamophobia, Fear of Loss of Freedom, and the Muslim Woman." *Islam and Muslim-Christian Relations* 22:4 (Fall 2011), pp. 469–473; Aisha Phoenix, "Somali Young Women and Hierarchies of Belonging." *Young* 19:3 (August 2011), pp. 313–331; Tara Povey, "Islamophobia and Arab and Muslim Women's Activism." *Cosmopolitan Civil Societies* 1:2 (2009), pp. 63–76; as well as many others including several essays in *Thinking Through Islamophobia* (see above) by Samia Bano, "Asking the Law Questions: Agency and Muslim Women" (pp. 135–156), Annelies Moors, "Fear of Small Numbers? Debating Face-Veiling in the Netherlands" (pp. 157–164), and Ruvani Ranasinha, "Fundamental Fictions: Gender, Power and Islam in Brasian Diasporic Formations" (pp. 259–264).

13. Jasmin Zine, "Unveiled Sentiments: Gendered Islamophobia and Experiences of Veiling among Muslim Girls in Canadian Islamic School." *Equity and Excellence in Education* 39 (2006), pp. 239–252, 240.

14. Ibid.

15. See Juliane Hammer, "Performing Gender Justice: The 2005 Woman-Led Prayer in New York." *Contemporary Islam*, special issue on Muslims and Media, 4:1 (April 2010), pp. 91–116. For other examples, see Brigitte Nacos and Oscar Torres-Reyna, *Fueling Our Fears: Stereotyping, Media Coverage, and Public Opinion of Muslim Americans* (Lanham, MD: Rowman and Littlefield, 2007); Heather McCafferty, "The Representation of Muslim Women in American Print Media: A Case Study of *The New York Times*," MA thesis, McGill University, August 2005.

16. Norman Daniel is an example for this direction of argument; see Norman Daniel, *Islam and the West: The Making of an Image* (Oxford: Oneworld, 2009).

17. Samuel Huntington, *The Clash of Civilizations and the Remaking of World Order* (New York: Simon and Schuster, 1998).

18. Leila Ahmed, *Women and Gender in Islam* (New Haven, CT: Yale University Press, 1992), especially pp. 150–155.

19. Mohja Kahf, *Western Representations of the Muslim Woman: From Termagant to Odalisque* (Austin, TX: University of Texas Press, 1999).

20. Charlotte Weber, "Unveiling Scheherazade: Feminist Orientalism in the International Alliance of Women, 1911–1950," *Feminist Studies* 27:1 (Spring 2001), pp. 125–157.
21. Video posted by CAIR Southern California, on March 2, 2011, www.youtube.com/watch?v=NutFkykjmbM, accessed September 15, 2012. The video was clearly edited to put together video footage stretching a longer part of the day and contains written quotes from protesters and attendees of the event as published in the local newspaper.
22. Quoted from the video, at 0:05.
23. Sahar Aziz, "Time to Address Violence against Muslim Women," *Huffington Post* (November 2, 2011), www.huffingtonpost.com/sahar-aziz/violence-again-muslim-women_b_1072529.html?view=screen, accessed September 15, 2012.
24. Ibid.
25. Posted by altoplano, at the link above.
26. Ann Sorkowitz and Julie N. Hays, "Witness to Discrimination: What Would You Do?," ABC News (February 26, 2008), http://abcnews.go.com/Primetime/WhatWouldYouDo/story?id=4339476&page=1#. T7_LpPXLkc0, accessed September 15, 2012; one of several copies of the video can be found here: "What would you do? ABC News," www.youtube.com/watch?v=oKKbIsKBs5M, accessed September 15, 2012.
27. Kathleen Moore, "The *Hijab* and Religious Liberty: Anti-Discrimination Law and Muslim Women in the United States." In *Muslims on the Americanization Path?*, ed. Yvonne Yazbeck Haddad and John L. Esposito (New York: Oxford University Press, 2000), pp. 105–127.
28. The title of the feature and the public de-veiling that several women perform on camera seems unfortunate to me in the ways in which both reenforce and reenact the gaze behind the veil and a certain voyeurism on the part of the viewer. While the feature attempts to be "balanced," it succeeds in representing those women who took their headscarves off as more liberated and invested with agency than the many others who do not make that choice. See the full write-up and audio file here: www.npr.org/2011/04/21/135523680/lifting-the-veil-muslim-women-explain-their-choice, accessed September 15, 2012. This link shows pictures of the 12 women, many with before and after photographs: www.npr.org/2011/04/21/135413427/lifting-the-veil, accessed September 15, 2012.
29. Elise Hu, "TX Rep. Louie Gohmert Warns of Terrorist Babies," *Texas Tribune* (June 28, 2010),www.texastribune.org/texas-mexico-border-news/arizona-immigration-law/tx-rep-louie-gohmert-warns-of-terrorist-babies/, accessed September 15, 2012.

30. Daniel Schulman, "Rep. Louie Gohmert's 'Terror Baby' Meltdown," *Mother Jones* (August 13, 2010), www.motherjones.com/mojo/2010/08/rep-louie-gohmerts-terror-baby-meltdown, accessed September 15, 2012.

31. Talk of the Nation (National Public Radio), "The Debate over 'Anchor Babies' and Citizenship," (August 2010), www.npr.org/templates/story/story.php?storyId=129279863, accessed September 15, 2012.

32. Sahar Aziz.

33. Aziz, 2f.

34. Ibid., see Nadine Strossen, "Freedom and Fear Post-9/11: Are We Again Burning Witches and Fearing Women?" *Nova Law Review* 31 (2007), pp. 279–314.

35. Much has been written on particular aspects of the "War on Terror" and the many measures taken. For select examples, see Moustafa Bayoumi, "Racing Religion." *New Centennial Review* 6:2 (Fall 2006), pp. 267–293; Asli Bali, "Scapegoating the Vulnerable: Preventive Detention of Immigrants in America's 'War on Terror.' " *Studies in Law, Politics, and Society* 38 (2006), pp. 25–69.

36. It has been argued that the debate about Shari'a, or Islamic Law, has replaced the earlier hate and fear-mongering about Jihad. Omar Sacirbey argued in March 2012 that many of the legislative and legal initiatives to ban Islamic Law in state courts has died down: Omar Sacirbey, "Anti-Sharia Movement Loses Steam State Legislatures," *Washington Post* (March 22, 2012), www.washingtonpost.com/national/on-faith/anti-shariah-movement-loses-steam-in-state-legislatures/2012/03/22/gIQAphNxTS_story.html, accessed September 15, 2012. For one of many blogs and website warning against "creeping sharia," see http://creepingsharia.wordpress.com/about-2/, accessed September 15, 2012.

37. Quoted in Kyle Mantyla, "Boykin Terrifies Dobson with Dire Warnings of America's Pending Islamification," February 18, 2011, www.rightwingwatch.org/content/boykin-terrifies-dobson-dire-warnings-americas-pending-islamification, accessed September 15, 2012. Boykin also said the following: "You know, it's interesting to me that two of the groups that have not said anything about this—in fact, have kind of been on the other side on this—are the women's groups and the homosexual groups. Both of those groups are discriminated against very heavily, so if there was total sharia law in this country, by sharia law homosexuals would be killed and all the women would be wearing burkas and hijabs and would be subjugated to the authority of men. But these two groups have not come out and said anything."

38. Phyllis Chelser, "Are Honor Killings Simply Domestic Violence?" *Middle East Quarterly* 16:2 (Spring 2009): pp. 61–69, www.meforum.org/2067/are-honor-killings-simply-domestic-violence, accessed September 15, 2012.
39. Phyllis Chesler, "Ban the Burqa? The Argument in Favor." *Middle East Quarterly* 17:4 (Fall 2010), pp. 33–45, www.meforum.org/2777/ban-the-burqa, accessed September 15, 2012.
40. Phyllis Chesler, "No More Harems: The Hidden History of Muslim and Ex-Muslim Feminists" (October 4, 2011), www.phyllis-chesler.com/1040/muslim-feminism, accessed September 15, 2012.
41. Pamela Geller, "Muslim-Americans Stand Up for Honor Killing," *Atlas Shrugs* (May 10, 2012), http://atlasshrugs2000.typepad.com/atlas_shrugs/jessica-mokdad-human-rights-conference/, accessed September 15, 2012.
42. Ibid.
43. Faiz Shakir, "Kansas Legislature Passes Discriminatory Anti-Muslim Bill by Calling it a 'Women's Rights' Issue," *Think Progress* (May 13, 2012), http://thinkprogress.org/justice/2012/05/13/483278/kansas-legislature-passes-discriminatory-anti-muslim-bill-by-calling-it-a-womens-right-issue/, accessed September 15, 2012.
44. Quoted in Saba Mahmood and Charles Hirschkind, "Feminism, the Taliban and Politics of Counter-Insurgency." *Anthropological Quarterly* 75:2 (Spring 2002), pp. 339–354, 341f. Mahmood and Hirschkind's analysis provided both the material and the lines of argument for this section.
45. See Carole Stabile and Deepa Kumar, "Unveiling Imperialism: Media, Gender, and the War on Afghanistan." *Media, Culture & Society* 27:5 (Fall 2005), pp. 765–782.
46. Sonali Kolhatkar and Mariam Rawi, "Why Is a Leading Feminist Organization Lending Its Name to Support Escalation in Afghanistan?," www.rawa.org/rawa/2009/07/08/why-is-a-leading-feminist-organization-lending-its-name-to-support-escalation-in-afghanistano.html, accessed September 15, 2012.
47. Among the scholars and activists: Pamela Geller and Brigitte Gabriel; political players: Republican representatives Sue Myrick and Renee Ellmer (both NC), Michelle Bachmann (MN); and validators: Nonie Darwish, Clare Lopez. See Wajahat Ali et al., "Fear Inc.," 2011.
48. See the 2012 senate and congressional debates about the reauthorization of the Violence Against Women Act of 1994 (VAWA) that resulted in bipartisan bickering and eventually the drafting of an alternative bill HR 4970, which among other modifications restricts support for immigrant victims and women under tribal jurisdiction. See the

National Task Force to End Sexual and Domestic Violence against Women (NTF) statement and critique of HR 4970: http://4vawa.org/pages/fact-sheet-ntf-opposition-to-hr-4970, accessed September 15, 2012.

49. http://atlasshrugs2000.typepad.com/atlas_shrugs/honor_killings_islam_misogyny/, accessed September 15, 2012.

50. Pamela Geller, *Stop the Islamization of America* (n.p.: WND Books, 2011); see also Pamela Geller, Robert Spencer, and John Bolton, *The Post-American Presidency: The Obama Administration's War on America* (New York: Threshold Editions, 2010).

51. "Backgrounder: Stop Islamization of America (SIOA)," Anti-Defamation League (August 26, 2010), www.adl.org/main_extremism/sioa.htm, accessed September 15, 2012.

52. See Geller's interview with FrontPage magazine, another Islamophobic media outlet from February 2011, "Pamela Geller, *Front Page* Magazine Interview: Obama and the Muslim Brotherhood," *Atlas Shrugs,* http://atlasshrugs2000.typepad.com/atlas_shrugs/2011/02/pamela-geller-front-page-magazine-interview-obama-and-the-muslim-brotherhood.html, accessed September 15, 2012.

53. See a discussion of some of her contributions above. In her "The Feminist Politics of Islamic Misogyny," *American Thinker* (November 13, 2010), www.phyllis-chesler.com/900/feminist-politics-islamic-misogyny, accessed September 15, 2012, Chesler specifically attacks Lila Abu-Lughod as a supporter of honor killings, hater of "the West," and connects this support for Islamism to Abu-Lughod's pro-Palestinian politics.

54. Phyllis Chesler, *The Death of Feminism: What's Next in the Struggle for Women's Freedom* (New York: Palgrave, 2005), www.phyllis-chesler.com/books/the-death-of-feminism, accessed September 15, 2012.

55. See also Phyllis Chesler, "A Lesson Learned in Kabul," Human Rights Service, (October 27, 2009), www.phyllis-chesler.com/638/a-lesson-learned-in-kabul, accessed September 15, 2012.

56. Her website has rubrics for her focus areas of writing including Israel, Anti-Semitism, Islamic Apartheid, Jihad/Terrorism, and Feminism, www.phyllis-chesler.com/, accessed September 15, 2012.

57. Saba Mahmood, "Feminism, Democracy, and Empire: Islam and the War on Terror." In *Women's Studies on the Edge,* ed. Joan Scott (Durham, NC: Duke University Press, 2007), pp. 81–114.

58. See also a critique of books by Manji, Chesler, and Oriana Fallaci (a European right-wing Islamophobe) by Sherene Razack in *Casting Out,* pp. 98–106.

59. Chesler, "No More Harems," 2011.

60. Lila Abu-Lughod, "Do Muslim Women Really Need Saving? Anthropological Reflections on Cultural Relativism and Its Others." *American Anthropologist* 103:3 (September 2002), pp. 783–790.
61. Mona Eltahawy, "Why Do They Hate Us?: The Real War on Women is in the Middle East," *Foreign Policy* ("The Sex Issue") (May/June 2012), www.foreignpolicy.com/articles/2012/04/23/why_do_they_hate_us?page=full, accessed September 15, 2012.
62. See Juliane Hammer, *American Muslim Women, Religious Authority, and Activism: More than a Prayer* (Austin, TX: University of Texas Press, 2012).
63. Eltahawy, "Why Do They Hate Us?"
64. See, for example, Mona Kareem, "Why Do They Hate Us? A Blogger's Response," www.al-monitor.com/pulse/originals/2012/al-monitor/in-response-to-mona-eltahawys-ha.html, accessed September 15, 2012; Samia Errazzouki, "Dear Mona Eltahawy, You Do Not Represent 'Us'," www.al-monitor.com/pulse/originals/2012/al-monitor/dear-mona-eltahawy-you-do-not-re.html, accessed September 15, 2012; Dalia Mogahed, "Does Mona Eltahawy's Approach Hurt Women?," *Washington Post* Blog (May 15, 2012), www.washingtonpost.com/blogs/guest-voices/post/does-mona-eltahawys-approach-hurts-women/2012/05/15/gIQAXnqSSU_blog.html, accessed September 15, 2012.
65. Slavoj Zizek, "The Power of the Woman and the Truth of Islam," ABC, Religion and Ethics Blog, posted May 10, 2012, www.abc.net.au/religion/articles/2012/05/10/3500125.htm, accessed September 15, 2012.
66. Maria White, "Iraqi Woman Beaten in Her California Home Dies," CNN (March 25, 2012), http://articles.cnn.com/2012–03–25/justice/justice_california-immigrant-death_1_iraqi-woman-el-cajon-life-support?_s=PM:JUSTICE, accessed September 15, 2012.
67. The article was reposted by Adele Wilde-Blavatsky, "To Be Anti-Racist Is to Be Feminist: The Hoodie and the Hijab Are Not Equals," ZNet (April 19, 2012), www.zcommunications.org/to-be-anti-racist-is-to-be-feminist-the-hoodie-and-the-hijab-are-not-equals-by-adele-wilde-blavatsky, accessed September 15, 2012.
68. Jadaliyya Reports, "A Collective Response to 'To Be Anti-Racist is to Be Feminist: The Hoodie and the Hijab are Not the Same,'" *Jadaliyya* (April 15, 2012), www.jadaliyya.com/pages/index/5064/a-collective-response-to-to-be-anti-racist-is-to-b, accessed September 15, 2012.
69. Will Carless and Ian Lovitt, "Family of Iraqi Woman Killed in California Was in Crisis, Records Show," *The New York Times* (April 5, 2012), www.nytimes.com/2012/04/06/us/shaima-alawadi-court-records-show-family-in-crisis.html, accessed September 15, 2012.

70. See, for example, "Salon Tries to Save Face: Shaima Alawadi Murder Not a Hate Crime, But Hey, There's a Lot of Islamophobia Anyway," Jihad Watch, www.jihadwatch.org/2012/04/salon-tries-to-save-face-shaima-alawadi-murder-not-a-hate-crime-but-hey-theres-a-lot-of-islamophobia.html, accessed September 15, 2012.
71. Nina Burleigh, "Shaima Alawadi's Murder: A Hate Crime against Women?" *Time—Ideas* (April 10, 2012), http://ideas.time.com/2012/04/10/shaima-alawadis-murder-a-hate-crime-against-women/, accessed September 15, 2012.
72. Karen Leslie Hernandez, "Investigating a Muslim's Murder," *OnIslam* (May 16, 2012), www.onislam.net/english/back-to-religion/covering-religion/457118-investigating-a-muslims-murder-.html, accessed September 15, 2012.
73. For a discussion of the dynamics of Muslim women's self-representation, see Hammer, *American Muslim Women,* especially chapters 8 and 9, as well as Hammer, "Performing Gender Justice."
74. Mahmood, "Feminism, Democracy, and Empire," p. 108.

Chapter 5

Attack of the Islamophobes
Religious War (and Peace) in Arab/Muslim Detroit[1]
Andrew J. Shryock

Of Laws and Likenesses

I will begin with a simple claim: current forms of Islamophobia are not based primarily on a fear of Islam or hatred of Muslims. Hostility toward Muslims has a very long history in Western societies, as do admiration for the accomplishments of Islamic civilization and strategic alliances between Muslim and Christian polities.[2] The variants of Islamophobia explored in this volume borrow heavily from this old complex of ideas, but they are more directly related to the ambiguities of nationalism, a modern ideology that blends fellow feeling and cultural difference in complex, often unconvincing ways. National identities are meant to be shared, yet they are always partial. Every member of a nation state has several additional identities that are not fully defined by, or contained within, the national community. A French citizen can be a Muslim or a Jew. US citizens can be black, Latino, or French. Often, the state encourages its citizens to claim additional identities, and its willingness to tolerate and equitably manage social

diversity is generally taken as proof of pluralism and a commitment to civil and human rights.

Contemporary Islamophobes entertain a wild variety of hostile
beliefs about Muslims and Islam, but they tend to agree that Islam,
or some essential version of it, falls outside the acceptable range
of tolerance and equal treatment that comes with membership in
both nation and state. This position assumes that Muslim identity
is so partial that it negates the possibility of true citizenship, a status that is too easy (in theory) and too hard (in practice) to define
with clarity.[3] The laws of citizenship are deceptively formulaic, yet
the logics of national belonging (can we refer to them as "laws"?)
are bewilderingly ad hoc. They send us in search of background
details and behavioral traits. Were you born here? Were your parents? Do you speak the national language without a foreign accent?
Do you dress, eat, walk, play sports, watch movies, and interact,
more or less, like the rest of us? Answering "yes" or "no" to any of
these questions will not definitively settle matters of citizenship and
belonging. Nation states are filled with people who seem local, but
are legally outsiders, and persons who seem foreign, and are treated
as such, but are citizens in good standing. Hence, a mystery lies at
the heart of national identity: It is a compelling reality secured not
by official laws or customary likenesses, but by a constantly renego-
tiated blend of the two.[4]

Islamophobia is symptomatic of our inability—in some cases,
our explicit refusal—to let Muslims take part in the construction
of national identity. By "our inability," I refer to the American case,
but related patterns of exclusion are found across Europe, where
minarets (in Switzerland) and headscarves (in France) are deemed
unacceptable intrusions on public space. Islamophobia is not a sentiment restricted to non-Muslim societies; it is especially acute in
countries like Pakistan, Egypt, and Turkey, where Islamists and
secularists vie for political control. It is also pronounced in countries
with large Muslim minorities, like Nigeria and India.[5] What distin-
guishes Western forms of Islamophobia from anti-Muslim politics
more generally is the tendency to depict Islam as a block to authentic
citizenship. In the United States today, Muslims are typically portrayed as outsiders in contexts of national sharing, even when they
are American-born citizens. Islamophobic discourses are based on

the idea that Islam does not belong in the West and that Muslim immigrants cannot sincerely identify with the nation states in which they live.

A counterpolitics of Muslim inclusion is no less common in American political culture, and it exists in ideological symbiosis with more hostile views. Often, this politics of acceptance is based on a principled commitment to multiculturalism or civil liberties, not on familiarity with Muslims or support for their religious or cultural practices. Islamophobia can also generate Islamophilia, an apologetic and generically affectionate relationship to Islam and Muslims. As I will show, Islamophilia itself can pose serious challenges to the effective incorporation of Muslims in American society. This is so for two reasons. First, advocates and opponents of Muslim inclusion often share underlying assumptions about Islam, citizenship, and national belonging, and a positive or negative spin on those assumptions does little to modify their political effects. Second, popular views of Muslims, and state policies related to Islam, are shaped by historical traumas that have been woven into narratives of national identity. Whether they are interlaced with fear or affection, the narratives of trauma that are commonly applied to Muslims living in the West are peculiar in the extent to which they focus on people and events located outside the time/space of nationhood.

Two Trends, One Process

Any discussion of Islam and national trauma written after 2001 must confront the open wound of the 9/11 attacks. I would insist, however, that zooming in on those events is a grave analytical mistake. Other scars are deeper, and far more important. In Europe, for instance, memory of the vicious religious wars triggered by the Protestant Reformation, and public commemorations of the Holocaust, are used to mobilize both pro- and anti-Muslim politics. In the United States, slavery and the Civil Rights movement, memories of religious persecution abroad, and historical accounts of immigrant struggle play a similar role in bolstering and undermining the incorporation of Muslims. National sins, and our efforts to atone for them, can have ironic and unintended consequences for new immigrant populations. In a fascinating study of memory politics in Germany, the Netherlands, and France, Nancy Foner and Richard Alba show how commemoration of the Holocaust, which is meant to foster tolerance and a protective stance toward the rights of minority populations, has actually shored up prejudice against Muslim immigrants, who are widely portrayed as religiously intolerant, homophobic, sexist, and anti-Semitic.[6] These negative characterizations surface at all points along the political spectrum. In the United States, by contrast, attempts to remedy the effects of centuries of slavery and anti-Black racism have culminated in affirmative action policies and a general ethos of multicultural tolerance from which, Foner and Alba contend, new cohorts of post-1965 immigrants have reaped tremendous benefits, often at the expense of African Americans.

Although Foner and Alba do not make this argument explicitly, I would suggest that US Muslims, and especially Arab Americans (who are routinely assumed to be Muslim), are subject to many of the suspicions reserved for Muslims in post-Holocaust Europe; yet they derive few benefits from the collective remedies that are now an institutionalized aspect of racial politics in the United States. Because they are a religious community and not a racial one, Muslims cannot be counted in the US Census nor do affirmative action policies apply to them. Similarly, because Arabs and most other Middle Eastern immigrant populations are defined as "white" by the US Census, they do not count as a minority population in any official sense. Like Muslims, Arabs cannot benefit from affirmative action programs, and their status as white is fragile; it fades once they are publicly identified as Arab or Muslim, attributions that expose them to unwelcome governmental attention and a wide range of negative stereotypes.[7] American Muslims, like their European counterparts, are associated with premodern sensibilities—with "backward" gender systems and hostility toward freedom of speech and religion—and they are linked to enemies of the United States and its allies. The latter category includes Israel, Zionism, and Jews more generally.

It would seem that Arabs and Muslims in the United States occupy a structural position akin to that of Muslims in Europe. Upon closer inspection, however, the resemblance disappears. In the

United States, Arab and Muslim populations are economically well off compared to the larger society; they are more highly educated; they are politically moderate overall, fiscally liberal, and socially conservative; they express high levels of "pride in being American"; and on measures of confidence in key public institutions, such as the police, the courts, the federal government, and public schools, they actually score higher than the general public.[8] Even more surprising (to some) is the fact that this Americanizing profile is often stronger among new immigrants than it is among Arabs and Muslims who are born or have lived for long periods of time in the United States.[9] On the whole, Arab/Muslim populations in the United States would appear to be mainstreaming rapidly.

In Greater Detroit, home to some of America's largest and oldest Arab and Muslim communities, the aftermath of the 9/11 attacks has done little to alter this trend. If anything, it has reinforced it. No one predicted this outcome in the early days of response to the attacks. Because the principal targets of the War on Terror were commonly understood to be Arab or Muslim—all of the 9/11 hijackers fit this description, as do all of the countries the United States has invaded since 2001—it was inevitable that federal authorities would turn to Detroit in their pursuit of enemies and friends. Within hours of the 9/11 attacks, hundreds of journalists and investigators were on the ground in Detroit, looking for stories, suspects, and informants. The first terror-related arrests were made in Dearborn on September 17, 2001; by early 2002, Dearborn (not New York) was the first American city to have a local office of Homeland Security; by 2003, Federal Bureau of Investigation (FBI) headquarters in Detroit was home to the largest counterterrorism investigation in US history.[10] It seemed that Detroit was being reconfigured as the home front for the War on Terror.

Ten years after the 9/11 attacks, however, the climate has changed in unexpected, sometimes puzzling ways. Detroit's principal Arab American social service organizations and advocacy groups have all grown in budgets and membership. Over 20 new mosques, including the largest in North America, have opened in the city since 2001, bringing the number of local mosques to over 65.[11] There are now 25 judges and elected officials of Arab ancestry in Michigan, and about 36 Arab Americans who have been appointed to public office; the trend is decidedly upward since 2001.[12] New cultural institutions, such as the Arab American National Museum, have opened to great fanfare; arts festivals, concert series, and street fairs are flourishing. The Arab American Chamber of Commerce, whose membership owns most of Detroit's gas stations, grocery, and convenience stores, now brokers international trade deals among the US Department of Commerce, the City of Detroit, and the Arab Gulf states.[13] Finally, greater Detroit's Arab and Middle Eastern (Chaldean, Syriac, and Assyrian) populations have grown steadily over the last decade, rising from 125,000 to over 200,000, even as the city's non-Arab sector, and the state of Michigan as a whole, steadily loses population. Of course, not all of Detroit's Muslims are Arab (about 60 percent are), and most of the city's Arabs (58 percent) are Christians, but these patterns are replicated widely across ethnoracial and religious divides.[14]

During a period of intense Islamophobia, foreign wars against Arab and Muslim countries, and domestic antiterrorism campaigns that target people of Middle Eastern descent, why are Detroit's Arab and Muslim communities doing so well? Why have so many positive things happened in the company, or in the context, of more ominous developments? The answer to this question is that the two trends—the positive and the negative—are part of one process. Over the years, I have given this process several names: mainstreaming, disciplinary inclusion, crisis identity formation. In each case, the central idea is the same. As political constituencies and as sites of local community formation, Detroit's Arab/Muslim populations make substantial gains during times of political crisis in the Middle East, especially when the United States is directly engaged in violent conflict with enemies defined as Arab, Muslim, or both. These gains are possible only to the extent that (and only because) local Arab/Muslim communities are seen as ambiguously American, and ambiguously Other. Attempts to remove this ambiguity in moments of crisis generate mainstreaming effects that are also, of necessity, marginalizing effects. The process is traumatic and empowering; it already has a long history; and the 9/11 attacks were rapidly assimilated to its logic. Before explaining how this process works, I should first provide a glimpse of the distinctive world in which it unfolds.

Breach of the Peace

In April of 2011, Pastor Terry Jones came to Dearborn to protest against "radical Islam and Sharia" and (perhaps) to burn a Qur'an outside the Islamic Center of America, the largest mosque in the United States. A pilgrimage to Dearborn has become a rite of passage for opponents of Islam in America. They descend, like seasonal birds, on the annual Dearborn Arab International Festival, where they wander among tens of thousands of Arab and Muslim revelers, passing out proselytizing leaflets, engaging passersby in religious dispute, and occasionally being arrested for disturbance of the peace. In recent years, the city has provided a fenced off space from which these visitors can shout anti-Muslim slogans through their bullhorns: "Mohammed was a pervert!" "Islam is a false religion!" "Islam is a blood-stained religion!" "Jesus Akbar!" "God has a Son!" They receive return taunts from hundreds of young Lebanese and Yemeni Muslims: "We love Jesus!" "Go home!" "Assholes!" "Muhammad!" "Boo!" Empty water bottles occasionally sail overhead. Police and festival security try to keep things under control, and if the exchanges threaten to become physical, the instigators are arrested or convinced to leave. It is important to remember that all of this is happening at a street fair, where families wait in line for their children to buy cotton candy and take rides on Ferris wheels.[15]

Pastor Jones's visit to "Dearbornistan," as neocon bloggers like to call this Detroit suburb,[16] must have shocked him. The city has 40,000 Arab Muslim residents out of a total population of 100,000, and its municipal government is highly responsive to the needs of this unique constituency. Handling anti-Muslims agitators is a skill savvy local politicians must acquire. By publicly burning the Qur'an, Terry Jones had already caused rioting in Afghanistan that left 12 people dead, and his visit to Dearborn was considered a serious threat to law and order in the city. After legal maneuvering by Dearborn's mayor, Jack O'Reilly, and the Wayne County Prosecutor, Kym Worthy, Pastor Jones was denied permission to hold a rally near the mosque. Invoking antique nineteenth-century ordinances that were resurrected for the occasion, Dearborn District Judge Larry Somers ordered Jones to pay a US$45,000 "peace bond" for the right to hold his protest. When Jones refused to do so, he was found guilty of "breach of the peace," was fined US$1, which he again refused to pay, was jailed, and, to complete the package, he was forbidden to go near the Islamic Center for a period of three years.[17]

None of these legal maneuvers involved even a trace element of shari'ah, but Pastor Jones might easily have concluded that he was being criminalized by a political establishment that was controlled by Arabs, Muslims, and their allies. Many of the security officers Jones encountered in Wayne County, including the Dearborn Chief of Police, Ron Haddad, are of Arab descent. The pastor's most rigorous local defender, Rana Elmir, spokesperson for the Michigan ACLU, is a Lebanese Muslim. "I stand up for his right to express himself because I value my right to express myself," Elmir said. "There's nothing more empowering for me than to defend the right of someone to express themselves when I so passionately disagree with them."[18]

Detroit television news stations subjected Jones to cool questioning, often as he sat uncomfortably next to black-robed imams who were more eloquent, more comfortable with interfaith themes, and on better terms with local reporters.[19] Opponents of Pastor Jones gathered by the hundreds at peaceful ecumenical rallies at which priests, rabbis, Muslim clerics, and a host of elected and appointed officials made joint statements and posed for photographs. The local interfaith establishment spoke with a unified voice: "We, as caring neighbors in southeastern Michigan, stand together in condemning the actions of those who spew hate and fear, and who misuse and desecrate holy books of faith."[20] At a large rally organized by Osama Siblani, publisher of the Dearborn-based *Arab American News*, speakers defended Terry Jones's right to criticize Islam–though none condoned the burning of a Qur'an–and most in attendance believed Jones was simply a misguided, ignorant man.

Across this united front, a companion discourse circulated. Local authorities were eager to prevent Terry Jones from protesting outside the Islamic Center because they believed congregants at the mosque (or militant antiracists[21]) would attack Jones if he burned a Qur'an. When I asked local Arab and Muslim friends if they thought things would turn violent if Jones publicly insulted Islam or the Prophet, all of them said "yes." Local religious leaders urged Muslims not to engage with protestors, to be friendly, to ignore unkind words. Self-policing was intense, as mosque leaders did their best to monitor the behavior of "the *shabab*" (young men). City leaders feared that local Muslims would overreact, that Jones had to be muzzled to protect the community from its own worst impulses, and that if someone killed Jones (this possibility was widely discussed), it would do great harm to the reputation of Dearborn, Detroit, and Muslims in the United States. Among Muslims, feelings were mixed. Many people believed Jones should be at liberty to do and say whatever he wanted, but people understood the desire to defend the Qur'an from injury. As a local school teacher told me, "My son said he would jump in to stop Jones from burning the Qur'an. I could not tell him this was wrong. I was proud of him. I wanted to support the way he felt, but I wanted to defend free speech. It was a strange moment for me." The idea that free speech exists on special terms in Dearborn, or that risking it was imprudent and possibly dangerous, was found among Islamophobes (who like to claim that Dearborn is ruled by Islamic law), among friends of the Arab/Muslim community (some of whom hold their current positions because Arab voters elected them), among members of the local ACLU, who denounced the court's ruling against Jones, and among Muslims who do not think anyone should be allowed to insult the Prophet Muhammad or his teachings.

The choreography of the Jones visit was much more complex than this brief sketch can convey, but it serves well as an example of disciplinary inclusion. The Muslim community was supported during this crisis by institutions of the larger society, and it was carefully controlled in the process. The rejection of Terry Jones represented both a commitment to the Americanness of Dearborn's Muslims, who deserved respect, and an acknowledgment of the (supposed) inability of (some) Muslims to accept certain kinds of free speech. Local Muslims were brought into an ecumenical, public rejection of religious bigotry, all the while being told, directly and indirectly, by Muslims and non-Muslims, that reactions of the Danish cartoon variety—physical attacks, threats, burnings in effigy, angry chants of "death to ____!"—would be counterproductive and would confirm what many Americans believe: that Muslims are irrational and intolerant.

In the end, the Terry Jones affair was considered a public relations triumph for Dearborn and its Muslim citizens. When Jones returned to the city several weeks after his initial arrest, he was heckled by 700 protestors who gathered in front of Dearborn City Hall. As Jones repeatedly recited the Pledge of Allegiance, called for a ban on shari'ah law, and asked the US government to monitor all American mosques, Mayor O'Reilly stood by, urging protestors to remain calm. He personally restrained anyone who tried to break through the barricades that police had erected to separate Jones from the crowd. In an exchange with reporters after the protest, Mayor O'Reilly made these comments:

> We're an easy target because people who hate others, in this case anyone who hates Islam and who hates Muslims, they're going to come here because they figure that this is the place to carry out their hate. It's sad because in this community, we get along. In this community, we're working it out really well, and we're all Americans. But, you know, people from other places who have strange ideas and who have limited information and don't care, they act out, and he's acting out...We had great leadership here, people from our Arab community who communicated and got the situation in hand, along with our police, we got the tempers down, and we got them back where they belonged. This was a very volatile situation. I'm asking everybody to think about things they deeply hold in their heart, things that are so important, vital to their way of life, and having them challenged by an ignorant person. And how do you react? Everybody reacts with passion. Everybody gets upset when someone challenges the most deep held feelings we have, and that's what happened here today, and I think, given the circumstance, people behaved very well.[22]

In November 2011, Wayne County Circuit Court Judge Robert Ziolkowski ruled that Pastor Jones's First Amendment rights had been violated by the Wayne County Prosecutor and the Dearborn District Court, and that he had been denied due process as well.[23] Jones immediately announced his plans for a third visit to Dearborn, an event that triggered new rounds of moral discipline and political support for local Muslims.

Best of Times, Worst of Times

The logic of disciplinary inclusion is pervasive in Detroit's Arab and Muslim communities. The contradictory messages sent to them during the Jones affair were mild by the standards set during the War on Terror. When, after the 9/11 attacks, federal authorities began to freeze the assets of Muslim charities that sent money overseas, area Muslims localized their almsgiving, building new mosques, renovating old ones, and opening Islamic schools in Detroit, thereby enlarging the infrastructure of American Muslim identity. In 2005, Michigan's elected political elite—the governor, state representatives, and local mayors—attended opening-day celebrations for the largest of these construction projects, the Islamic Center of America and the American Moslem Society, which they described in their congratulatory speeches as venerable and very American houses of worship. Congressman John Dingell (D-MI), senior member of the US House of Representatives, congratulated the "hardworking, patriotic, law-abiding citizens" who pooled their resources to build these impressive institutions.[24] Yet in 2003, FBI agents armed with special radiation-detecting equipment were driving by Detroit mosques—to see if dirty bombs were being assembled in them[25]—even as Homeland Security, ICE (Immigration and Customs Enforcement), and FBI officials were reaching out to Arab and Muslim community leaders, whom they interfaced with at regular meetings of ALPACT (Advocates and Leaders for Police and Community Trust) and BRIDGES (Building Respect in Diverse Groups to Enhance Sensitivity). As the friendly acronyms suggest, these organizations were designed to represent community concerns and assist federal agencies in their pursuit of information. They were also used to monitor the Arab and Muslim communities and recruit informants from their ranks.[26]

Since the 9/11 attacks, the FBI has run massive counterterrorism investigations in greater Detroit, sending special agents into mosques and interviewing religious leaders and laypeople. As a result, many immigrant congregations have undergone what can only be described as strategic Americanization campaigns, revamping their boards, replacing older, conservative, Arabic-speaking members with younger, moderate, American-educated professionals, and making a concerted effort to introduce themselves to the larger society through open houses and *da`wa* (missionary and teaching) events. Self-policing is now the norm. Many imams record their Friday sermons, so that they can defend themselves against accusations of anti-Americanism. All the larger mosques have installed state-of-the-art security systems to identify graffiti vandals, window breakers, and, more disturbing by far, the occasional "visitor" who tries to engage worshippers in extremist discourse. In a recent essay that examines these developments in meticulous detail, Sally Howell interviews mosque officials who believe (with good reason) that these "visitors" are FBI provocateurs.[27] Andy Arena, FBI special agent in charge of the Detroit office, has repeatedly told mosque leaders that they have nothing to fear as long as they preach "the true Islam."[28]

To complicate matters further, the US State Department uses Dearborn as a promotional tool in its public diplomacy campaigns abroad, producing high-gloss videos (available on YouTube) that show a robust, influential, unapologetically Arab Muslim city in the heart of the American Midwest.[29] A steady stream of US government officials, military brass, and foreign dignitaries march through the Islamic Center of America, the Arab American National Museum, and the Arab Community Center for Economic and Social Services (ACCESS) during visits to Dearborn. These institutions receive thousands of visitors a year, and each boasts a multimillion dollar annual operating budget. Like most churches and synagogues, the Islamic Center is supported by the offerings of people who pray or send their children to school there. The Arab American National Museum and ACCESS, by contrast, subsist almost entirely on support from major US charitable foundations and funding provided by federal, state, and local governments. In short, it is hard to imagine an American ethnic or religious community that is so enthusiastically embraced by the political and cultural mainstream even as it is relentlessly stigmatized, surveilled, infiltrated, scapegoated, and intimidated by federal law enforcement agencies.

Short Memories, Long Histories

The Americanizing pressures that have settled on Detroit since the 9/11 attacks have been severe, but they are not unprecedented.

In the 1990s, the Arab/Muslim population of Michigan experienced steady increases in political incorporation, even as the United States waged war against Iraq, imposed brutal sanctions on that country, and occasionally lobbed rockets at al-Qaeda targets in Afghanistan and Sudan. Institutions and events now taken as evidence of Arab/Muslim cultural acceptance—for instance, the Arab American National Museum and the Dearborn Arab International Festival—have their origins in the mid-1990s, when Arab American organizations reaped the benefits of increased public- and private-sector funding. The latter came in the wake of the 1993 Oslo Accords, when Israel and the Palestine Liberation Organization (PLO) worked out a tentative peace agreement and Arabs living in the United States were brought into the larger geopolitical control mechanism known as "the peace process." Throughout the 1990s, America's generalized antipathy toward its own Arab/Muslim citizens gave way to Ramadan breakfasts in the White House and brazen attempts by US presidential candidates to woo Michigan's Arab and Muslim votes. George W. Bush, running for president in 1999, told Arab Americans he would end profiling of their community if elected.[30]

Americans have short memories. So do Arab/Muslim Americans. Young scholars and community activists often tell me that Detroit's Arab and Muslim populations were "invisible" before 9/11, or that they avoided political activity. My interlocutors seem unaware that during the first Gulf War (1990–1991), young Arab/Muslim activists and scholars made similar claims about their former invisibility and aversion to politics. Traveling further into the past, we find that Arabs and Muslims also stepped out of obscurity during the Lebanese Civil War (1975–1990), the Iran Hostage crisis (1979–1981), the Israeli invasions of Lebanon (1978, 1982), the Arab Oil Embargo (1973), the Yom Kippur War (1973), the Six Day War (1967), the Suez War (1956), and the first Arab–Israeli War (1948). Only a handful of archival scholars and lay historians know that, going back to the late nineteenth century, both *The Detroit Free Press* and *The Detroit News* have provided continuous coverage of the communities now called Arab and Muslim. Simply put, there has not been a time during the last century when Detroit was unaware of its Middle Eastern communities, and these populations

seem always to be active in public life. Governors attended their
fund-raising banquets in the 1950s; mayors attended their mosque
openings in the 1930s; their political meetings and community protests were dutifully reported by the local press in the 1920s, and the
opening of the Highland Park Mosque in 1921, the handiwork of
Syrian, Turkish, and Balkan Muslims, received several columns—
and a photograph of three turban-wearing, flag-waving imams—in
the big Detroit newspapers.[31]

Why is this history so consistently forgotten, or never learned?
Why are Muslims and non-Muslims both unlikely to know it?
Detroit's Muslim population today is mostly immigrant, and the
majority of the city's African American Muslims are converts (or
they entered the Sunni mainstream in 1975, when Warith Deen
Muhammad reformed the Nation of Islam after the death of his
father, the Honorable Elijah Muhammad).[32] This demographic profile lends credence to the popular assumption that Muslims in the
United States are foreigners, that only African American Muslims
are "indigenous," and that American ways of being Muslim are rare,
new, and involve a necessary movement away from Islam as it is
practiced in the Muslim world (and especially in the Arab world).
This imagery simultaneously marginalizes Islam (it is an alien faith,
not simply a minority faith), and it dehistoricizes Muslims (they are
new, converted, arriving, changing, and foreign). Most Americans
are not predisposed to assume that Muslims were already a highly
mobilized, institution-building population by the 1910s and that,
since at least the 1930s, it has been possible to walk through Muslim
neighborhoods in greater Detroit, find a place to pray, read local
community newspapers in Arabic and English, and talk to Muslims
who have spent most or all of their lives in the city.

Our difficulty in making sense of a historically old and thoroughly American Islam is based, I believe, on a pervasive tendency
to divide Arab/Muslim identity into (1) a quality that exists outside (American) national history and before (Western) modernity
and (2) a quality that, with effort, is Americanizable and can be
recognized, cultivated, and taken into modern, national space. The
first quality is defined by sturdy Orientalist motifs, some dating to
wars between Christendom and the Ottoman Empire, others to the

Crusades, and still others to the clash of Greeks and Persians.[33] The second quality is grounded in redemption and conversion motifs; in its modern, secularized form, it corresponds to the familiar story of assimilation, of "becoming American." The combination of these motifs produces an interpretive framework in which Arabs and Muslims can be recognized as Americans, as a legitimate minority constituency, only insofar as they struggle publicly to transition out of their status as premodern, non-American (or even anti-American) people. As a political project, the creation of Arab and Muslim American identities has been defined by this struggle; it is the result of this struggle; and it continually submerges the trauma of this struggle in new attempts to secure and celebrate Arab/Muslim Americanness during moments of national crisis *for which Arabs and Muslims are thought to be responsible.*

In Detroit, these moments of crisis have increased steadily since the 1965 immigration reforms, which brought new Arab and Muslim immigrants to a country whose support for Israel in the 1967 Arab–Israeli War was enthusiastic, and whose support for dictatorial Middle Eastern oil regimes was firm. As the Civil Rights movement, the ethnic identity revival, and a new willingness to commemorate the Holocaust gained institutional strength in the 1960s and 1970s, the attempts of Arab and Muslim Americans to express their own political identity—to win statehood for Palestinians, to resist American and Israeli interventions in Lebanon, to show their support for the Islamic Revolution in Iran, and to build Muslim reform movements in the United States and abroad—came up against a public culture and a US foreign policy that aligned all of these projects with enemies of America, Jews, Israel, Christianity, women's rights, democracy, and progress itself. Although negative images of the Arab/Muslim Other are many centuries old, the geopolitical interests of the United States as a global superpower, especially its strategies for dominance in the Middle East, have produced an updated Muslim enemy that is now a critical aspect of American national identity.[34] As Pastor Terry Jones and Dearborn Muslims confront each other across the police barricades in Dearborn, this is the shared political reality that motivates them.

The Politics of Inversion: From Phobia to Philia

As stock characters, the Muslim Other and the Islamophobe stand in an ideologically perfect relationship when they see each other, first and last, as "enemies" in exactly the sense described by Carl Schmitt, who argued that politics itself is an activity based on the drawing of fundamental distinctions between enemies and friends.[35] Muslims are enemies (just as Greeks and Persians were, or Communists and Capitalists are) when they are judged to be adversaries who, in Schmitt's words, intend to negate their "opponent's way of life and therefore must be repulsed or fought in order to preserve one's own form of existence."[36] The starkness and analytical utility of this formulation for a discussion of Islamophobia lies in the capacity of "enemy status" to render moral nuance irrelevant, even if the diverse qualities of the enemy can still be discerned. As Schmitt puts it:

> The political enemy need not be morally evil or aesthetically ugly; he need not appear as an economic competitor, and it may even be advantageous to engage with him in business transactions. But he is, nevertheless, the other, the stranger; and it is sufficient for his nature that he is, in a specially intense way, existentially something different and alien, so that in the extreme case conflicts with him are possible.[37]

The decision to cast Muslims in this role is a political act; moreover, it is one that can be contested. Not everyone agrees that Muslims are existentially alien, and Muslims who live as citizens in the United States or France or Canada are not, by strict legal reckoning, Others or strangers, even when their fellow nationals see them as outsiders. This overlap of inside and outside, an artifact of global immigration and modern regimes of citizenship, is what drives Islamophobia and imbues it with missionary zeal. Pastor Jones must remind America that Muslims, even the ones who live here with us, as us, are really Them. Mayor O'Reilly, in response, must remind Pastor Jones that "we're all Americans."

If we grant that Islamophobia poses a real danger not only to Muslims, but also to models of citizenship and human rights that aspire to include Muslims and non-Muslims as equals in the same political community, should we not also be concerned about political distortions that might arise from attempts to offset Islamophobic agendas? This question is difficult to consider, and it is easily misconstrued. To put it differently, the insidious nature of Islamophobia is not located in fear alone, or in hate; nor is it found in the designation of enemies as such. After all, a society or group can define its enemies, or be defined as enemies, for entirely legitimate reasons. One can, for instance, consider al-Qaeda an enemy, fear its policies, and hate the violence it espouses without being an Islamophobe. What is most problematic about Islamophobia is its essentializing and universalizing quality, which casts Islam itself and all Muslims as real or potential enemies.

How can we constructively oppose this essentializing impulse in ways that do not simply reinforce it by cultivating its opposite: namely, the image of the Muslim as "friend," as a figure identified with the Self, characterized as familiar, and with whom legitimate conflict is not possible? This image, too, is impervious to nuance, and it can be coercive when applied to Muslims, who might have differences—with non-Muslims and fellow Muslims alike—they think are worth asserting and maintaining. When "friendship" is subordinated to the demands of sameness, whether conceived in national or human terms, it can be just as coercive, just as prone to misrecognition, as the sentiments of hostility it is meant to correct.

Islamophilia, understood as a generalized affection for Islam and Muslims, comes with its own political costs.[38] If, as some analysts would argue, Islamophobia has little to do with real Islam as practiced by actually existing Muslims, then constructing selectively positive images of Islam in response to Islamophobic propaganda will have less than helpful, and sometimes bizarre, results. One of these, now widely recognized, is the spread of "good Muslim/bad Muslim" binaries, in which the good Muslim (the friend) is the real Muslim, and the bad Muslim (the enemy) is a creature who violates the good Muslim code.[39] The "bad Muslim" can and should be vigorously opposed. Indeed, the most crucial task assigned to the good Muslim by the larger society is to oppose bad Muslims, to reject them, expose them, denounce them, reeducate them, turn them in, and apologize for their misdeeds. Failure to carry out this mission will turn good Muslims into bad ones.

As a stereotype, the "good Muslim" has common features: He tends to be a Sufi (ideally, one who reads Rumi); he is peaceful (and assures us that *jihad* is an inner, spiritual contest, not a struggle to "enjoin the good and forbid the wrong" through force of arms); he treats women as equals, and is committed to choice in matters of hijab wearing (and never advocates the covering of a woman's face); if he is a she, then she is highly educated, works outside the home, is her husband's only wife, chose her husband freely, and wears hijab (if at all) only because she wants to. Good Muslims are also pluralists (they recall fondly the ecumenical virtues of medieval Andalusia and are champions of interfaith activism); they are politically moderate (advocates of democracy, human rights, and religious freedom, opponents of armed conflict against the United States and Israel); finally, good Muslims are likely to be converts, Africans, South Asians, or, more likely still, Indonesians and Malaysians; they are less likely to be Arabs, but, as friends of the "good Muslim" will point out, only a small proportion of Muslims are Arabs anyway.

Islamophilic discourse returns consistently to this array of features, which are found, in varying degrees of completeness, in millions of real Muslims. Of course, these traits are lacking in millions of real Muslims as well, but it is not their empirical presence or absence that matters as much as the moral connotations these traits carry when they are used to define the modern, safe, and acceptable Muslim. The same is true of Islamophobic discourses. There are Muslims who advocate and practice violence, oppress women, hate Jews, would like to see the universal establishment of shari'ah law, and so on. Counting them and calling them out is not as important, or as dangerous, as the categorical stigmatization that occurs when phobic portrayals of Muslims come to dominate a political field, thus setting the terms on which Islam is deemed pre/modern, un/safe, and un/acceptable.

In this light, the resemblance between the good Muslim and the good citizen of the liberal democratic state is all too obvious. The good Muslim is certainly less malign than his evil twin, but the traits that define the good Muslim are just as likely to be based on wishful thinking and a politics of fear. Neither standard is meant to be "fair" or "objective"; instead, each is meant to politicize Muslims, to package them for use in conflict situations. In our rush to identify

Muslim friends who think and act like "us," we risk turning those who think and act differently into enemies. US foreign policy, before and after the War on Terror, has had devastating effects on millions of Muslims around the world, and even "good Muslims" would want to oppose US policy as well as the hate it produces at home and overseas. If we persist in portraying Islamophobia as an irrational force of misperception—the bad citizen's response to the bad Muslim—we will render ourselves oblivious to Islamophobia's ultimate causes, which are not simply ignorance or xenophobia. Pastor Terry Jones is rightly criticized for both, but he has never invaded and occupied an independent (Muslim-majority) nation-state, authorized the torture of (Muslim) alien combatants held in secret prisons, killed hundreds of innocent (Muslim) people in unmanned drone attacks, propped up (Muslim) dictators against the will of their (Muslim) subjects, and given orders to detain, deport, and assassinate (Muslim) terror suspects without trial.

Beyond the Politics of Enemy and Friend

At first glance, Islamophobia would appear to be the product of a rigid, polarized worldview. It demands that Muslims be seen negatively, as threatening figures who want to dominate the West, a geopolitical space in which they do not belong and to which they cannot adapt. Yet appearances are misleading. In practice, Islamophobia owes more to the convergence of cultural and political spaces than to their separation.[40] Polarization is what Islamophobes desire, but cannot quite achieve. Anti-Muslim activists like Terry Jones, Pamela Geller, Robert Spencer, the Bible Believers, and the Westboro Baptist Church are drawn to Dearborn because they see it as an abomination, as a dangerous exception to the American norm. In fact, Dearborn is proof that an alternative American reality, one in which Islam is normal and Muslims enjoy political support, is possible and will become increasingly common in future. The Muslim presence in the West has been growing steadily for over a century, through immigration and conversion. Mosques can be found in every major city of Europe and North America, and the idea that Muslims can only be foreigners is now a position that must be vigorously argued, with obvious ideological bias. At the same time, however, the inclusion of Muslims in Western societies as citizens is a conflicted process, and it too requires immense ideological effort. A generalized affection for Muslims is what Islamophiles desire, but cannot quite achieve, because evidence of Muslim difference persists—in food and dress, in family structures, in gender ideologies, in attitudes toward domestic and foreign policy—and because wars against Muslim-majority states and Islamist militant groups constantly reanimate a time-tested imagery of crusade and jihad.

It is impossible to ignore the enemy–friend binary. Attempts to move beyond it are always self-conscious; they produce a kind of double vision. In the very act of building their own communities and public identities, American Muslims must take into account the prejudices and expectations of an imagined, non-Muslim observer. As a result, new distinctions between Self and Other are constantly woven into Muslim American self-definitions. The irony of disciplinary inclusion is the extent to which it turns phobic and philic sentiments into the very architecture of identity formation. It constructs Muslim enemies even as (or precisely because) it stipulates the qualities of Muslim friends. Disciplinary inclusion encourages the Muslim friend to control and marginalize the Muslim enemy, a contest that unfolds in the Self, the family, the community, the nation-state, and the transregional diaspora. This work is delicate, relentless, and it has given rise to its own class of specialists. Greater Detroit now has a professional class of "go-to" Muslims who can be relied upon to build interfaith alliances, meet with visiting government officials and candidates for public office, lead the mosque tours, talk to reporters and scholars, and, of course, to rebuff Islamophobes. Artfully embracing this role, Imam Hassan Qazwini, spiritual leader of the Islamic Center of America, the largest mosque in the United States, has shown a preternatural skill for this diplomatic role. Although he is more likely to address sitting presidents and members of the elite national media, Imam Qazwini had the following words for Pastor Terry Jones: "Who is he to question our loyalty? Muslims are as American as he is. He has no right to question the loyalty of American Muslims in this country. We are peaceful, patriotic citizens who love this country and care about it as much as any citizen."[41]

Over the last ten years, Muslim Americans have become skilled at sending this message, and even angry street protestors know that the most effective (and confusing) chant to hurl at Islamophobes is, "U-S-A! U-S-A!" Borrowing from the civil rights activism, anti-defamation campaigns, and grassroots constituency politics of other American religious and ethnoracial minorities, Arab and Muslim Americans have turned the trauma of the 9/11 attacks into fuel for their own mobilization as US citizens.[42] The larger society, meanwhile, has become very skilled at raising the bar, at demanding and ignoring yet more evidence that Muslims can be, and long have been, American citizens. I am still frequently asked why American Muslims (or "moderate Muslims") never apologized for the 9/11 attacks, or for the violence of radical Muslims—as if they were somehow collectively responsible—and my standard rejoinder, that Muslim and Arab American organizations have been scrupulous in their denunciation of terrorist attacks, is often met with skepticism. On occasion, my interlocutors insist that these statements are not heartfelt or sincere.

This was the signal sent, bluntly, by the 2011 US congressional hearings on "the radicalization of American Muslims" sponsored by House Representative Peter King (R-NY), who argued that Muslims are not assisting law enforcement officials who are investigating their community; he also claimed that "80% of the mosques in American are controlled by radical imams."[43] The inevitable response to these accusations is to reverse the claims: "Muslims *are* policing themselves. They *are* assisting in efforts to combat terrorism. They *are* loyal, hard-working, patriotic Americans, not radical extremists." According to these counterclaims, Muslim Americans, any Muslims in fact, who embrace radical Islam (what is that?) and terrorism (whose terrorism?) are exceptions to the rule. One could say, and many Muslims do, that the "bad Muslims" are not really Muslims at all. Yet for Peter King, "good Muslims" are of little interest, although they are still suspect. When both bad Muslims and good Muslims are irrelevant and exceptional, something is clearly wrong with the terms of debate. The potential for being ordinary and unmarked disappears, as do the moral gray zones in which most of us are privileged to live, unburdened by the obligation of constantly proving our loyalty and constantly having that loyalty questioned.

As hegemonic as it now seems, the moral peculiarity of these rhetorical positions is revealed immediately, and quite shockingly, if one tries to apply them to Christians or Jews as such. An application of this kind is forbidden in polite, metropolitan society; indeed, the ban defines polite metropolitan society, a space in which a person's enemy or friend status does not follow immediately from his or her status as a Christian or a Jew. The argument that Christianity (or Judaism) is, in key respects, antithetical to democracy, or national identity, or even to modernity, is not often made today, and those who care to pursue the argument in depth will be treated as intolerant cranks, or denounced as anti-Semites.[44] The space given in public discourse—in the United States or elsewhere in the world of Anglophone mass media—to the consideration of Christianity and Judaism as security threats, to the links between these belief systems and terror, and to the difficult task of turning Jews and Christians into viable, constructive members of modern society, is miniscule. Yet talking about Muslims and Islam in this way is normal; indeed, it is hard to imagine a public forum on Islamophobia (or a scholarly forum; or even a theological one) that did not consider security issues—that is, the role of violence in the making of anti-Muslim politics—as necessary to a realistic discussion of how Islamophobia is defined, how it is put to use, and how it can be alleviated.

Increasingly, opponents of anti-Muslim ideologues are realizing that the most effective way to defend Muslims and Islam is to insist that all public debate conform to the same ground rules that apply to discussions of Jews and Christians. In April 2012, a year after the visit of Pastor Terry Jones, Pamela Geller held a highly publicized conference against "Islamic honor killings" in Dearborn. In response, a cross-section of Arab and Muslim leaders, elected officials, and interfaith advocates held a rival symposium called "Rejecting Islamophobia." Despite the occasional invocation of God's name, and a uniformly positive take on Islam, the proceedings were secular in tone and orientation. Over a dozen speakers hammered home the idea that they, the Arab/Muslim community of greater Detroit and its allies, were the true defenders of the US Constitution, the true advocates of freedom, tolerance, and diversity. No attempt was made to defend or even to explain Islamic belief and practice, much less "honor killings." The object of critique was not a specific misrepresentation of Islam, but ignorance, racism, bigotry, and cynical attempts to mobilize the right-wing base of the Republican Party. In a brilliant turning of tables, the speakers at "Rejecting Islamophobia" suggested that the most serious threat to national security and the US Constitution is represented today by Islamophobes, who have rejected the commitment to civil liberties that is central to American political (and religious) life. "We stand for America," said Osama Siblani, publisher of *The Arab American News*, "and they stand against America and the American way of life."[45] The good Muslim, in this perspective, is the good citizen. The object of fear and affection is not Islam, but America itself, an ongoing political experiment that continues to generate racism and intolerance alongside the dream of "liberty and justice for all."

Overlapping Identities, Mutual Respect

As I watched the live stream of the "Rejecting Islamophobia" sympo- sium, I noted the steady references to "racism" and "the legacy of slav- ery." This historical trauma, shared by white and black Americans, was offered as a framework in which to talk about the possibility of Muslim inclusion. The benefits of political participation and coali- tion building, of shared citizenship, were also extolled. The Arab speakers, most of them immigrants or the children of immigrants, stressed their rootedness in Dearborn, the solidity of its Arab/ Muslim institutions, and their contributions to the larger society, themes that offset their image as a new, separatist, and alien popula- tion. Overall, the presentations were more patriotic than religious, and the faith on display was conspicuously ecumenical. Most of the sentiments expressed at the event could have been uttered (or eagerly endorsed) by any civic-minded, liberal, pluralist American, whether Muslim or non-Muslim. Indeed, that seemed to be the point.

I began this essay with the claim that Islamophobia does not spring directly from a fear of Islam, or a hatred of Muslims, but from ambiguities rooted in our dominant models of citizenship and national belonging. The battles being fought in Dearborn by Islamophobes, Arab and Muslim Americans, and their allies and opponents in local government, the media, and the courts are generating new, hotly contested versions of Americanism. All parties to these disputes are learning valuable lessons. The most transformative is that Muslims can be American, already are American, and that the political system—in Dearborn—is a social field over which they can exercise considerable influence. This has nothing to do with shari'ah and everything to do with conventional electoral politics and immigrant incorporation. The second lesson, which has been learned over and over again by the local Arab/Muslim communities, is that inclusion comes at the price of discipline. The presence of a large, well-organized, transnationally connected Arab and Muslim population has drawn unwanted attention to greater Detroit, not only from pilgrims in the cause of Islamophobia, but from suspicious federal authorities, hostile media outlets, and military and business interests intent of recruiting personnel for operations in Iraq, Afghanistan, and other sites in the global War on Terror. After ten years of intense pressure to show loyalty to the state, the result is a public Islam that is on easy terms with American national identity, so much so that it can translate itself into a secular discourse of civil liberties, becoming virtually indistinguishable from the Judeo-Christian ambient in which—in greater Detroit at least—it now thrives.

Is this a success story? Is it yet another traumatic shift in consciousness that Detroit's Arabs and Muslims will forget as normalization is followed by new waves of geopolitical crisis? However one answers these questions, it is clear that the enemy–friend distinction has exposed Arab and Muslim Americans to processes of marginalization and mainstreaming that are abusive and extreme. Because these processes have produced massive governmental agencies that are reshaping the relationship between the United States and other nation-states, and between US citizens and their own state, understanding how these processes work is one of the most important social justice issues of our day. Numerous commentators have argued that, if the twentieth century was defined by problems of race and the color line, the twenty-first century will be defined by Islamophobia and the problem of integrating Muslims into modern, democratic societies, both in the West and in the Muslim world. These grand pronouncements bring with them a multitude of problematic assumptions, and they need to be given the same rigorous intellectual attention that has been devoted to the analysis of racism, class inequality, sexism, and other forms of political oppression. We need to expose the tactical ignorance, malign and benign, which suffuses educated opinion on all things Muslim in America. We also need to create political cultures in which Muslims and non-Muslims can interact on terms of mutual respect. Denouncing the crude bigotry of Islamophobes will not produce a political culture of this kind; neither will polite acceptance of Muslims based on the privatization of their religious and cultural differences. Instead, a politics of mutual respect must be anchored in the realization that Muslims and non-Muslims do not live in separate worlds, in self-constituting and clashing civilizations. Increasingly, we all live in overlapping zones of interaction. This overlap will create new identities—secular, religious, national, regional, and ethnoracial—that are endlessly contested, and are *worth* contesting, because they are shared.

NOTES

1. Parts of this chapter were published previously in Andrew Shryock, "Introduction: Islam as an Object of Fear and Affection." In *Islamophobia/Islamophilia: Beyond the Politics of Enemy and Friend*, ed. Andrew Shryock (Bloomington, IN: Indiana University Press, 2010), pp. 1–27. The material appears with the permission of Indiana University Press, all rights reserved.
2. For an insightful review of the last 1,500 years, see Tomaz Mastnak, "Western Hostility toward Muslims: A History of the Present." In *Islamophobia/Islamophilia: Beyond the Politics of Enemy and Friend*, ed. Andrew Shryock (Bloomington, IN: Indiana University Press, 2010), pp. 29–52.
3. A general treatment of theory and practice is available in Margaret Somers, *Genealogies of Citizenship: Markets, Statelessness, and the Right to Have Rights* (New York: Cambridge University Press, 2008). For a discussion of Arab American citizenship, see Wayne Baker and Andrew Shryock, "Citizenship and Crisis," in Detroit Arab American Study Team, *Citizenship and Crisis: Arab Detroit after 9/11* (New York: Russell Sage Foundation, 2009), pp. 3–32.
4. This blend is often called "cultural citizenship." For formative discussions, see Aihwa Ong, "Cultural Citizenship as Subject Making:

Immigrants Negotiate Racial and Cultural Boundaries in the United States." *Current Anthropology* 37 (1996), pp. 737–762; and Renato Rosaldo, "Cultural Citizenship, Inequality, and Multiculturalism." In *Latino Cultural Citizenship: Claiming Identity, Space, and Rights*, ed. William Flores and Rina Benmayor (Boston, MA: Beacon Press, 1997), pp. 253–261.

5. Several studies of Islamophobia in Muslim societies are offered in *Islamophobia/Islamophilia: Beyond the Politics of Enemy and Friend*, ed. Andrew Shryock (Bloomington, IN: Indiana University Press, 2010).

6. Nancy Foner and Richard Alba, "Immigration and the Legacies of the Past: The Impact of Slavery and the Holocaust on Contemporary Immigrants in the United States and Western Europe." *Comparative Studies in Society and History* 52:4 (2010), pp. 798–819.

7. For analysis of these dynamics, see essays in *Race and Arab Americans before and after 9/11: From Invisible Citizens to Visible Subjects*, ed. Amaney Jamal and Nadine Naber (Syracuse, NY: Syracuse University Press, 2008).

8. These findings have been replicated in numerous surveys and demographic analyses, among them, Ihsan Bagby, *A Portrait of Detroit Mosques: Muslim Views on Policy, Politics and Religion* (Clinton Township, MI: Institute for Social Policy and Understanding, 2004); the Arab American Institute Foundation, *Select Social and Demographic Characteristics for Arab Americans* (Washington, DC: Arab American Institute, 2006); Pew Forum on Religion and Public Life, *Muslim Americans: Middle Class and Mostly Mainstream* (Washington, DC: Pew Research Center, 2007); *Preliminary Findings of the Detroit Arab American Study* (Ann Arbor, MI: Institute for Social Research, 2004).

9. This pattern is closely analyzed in Andrew Shryock and Ann Shih Lin, "The Limits of Citizenship," in Detroit Arab American Study Team, *Citizenship and Crisis*, pp. 265–286.

10. For an early account of post-9/11 developments in Dearborn and greater Detroit, see Andrew Shryock, "New Images of Arab Detroit: Seeing Otherness and Identity through the Lens of September 11." *American Anthropologist* 104 (2002), pp. 917–922. For later accounts, see *Arab Detroit 9/11: Life in the Terror Decade*, ed. Nabeel Abraham, Sally Howell, and Andrew Shryock (Detroit, MI: Wayne State University Press, 2011).

11. Research on Detroit's mosques, past and present, is available on the website *Building Islam in Detroit: Foundations/Forms/Futures*, http://biid.lsa.umich.edu/, accessed September 15, 2012.

12. Abdulkader H. Sinno and Eren Tatari, "Toward Electability: Public Office and the Arab Vote," in *Arab Detroit 9/11: Life in the Terror*

Decade, ed. Nabeel Abraham, Sally Howell, and Andrew Shryock (Detroit, MI: Wayne State University Press, 2011), pp. 315–346.

13. Sally Howell and Andrew Shryock, "Cracking Down on Diaspora: Arab Detroit and America's War on Terror." *Anthropological Quarterly* 76:3 (2003), pp. 443–462.

14. For a detailed and up-to-date demographic analysis, see Kim Schopmeyer, "Arab Detroit after 9/11: A Changing Demographic Portrait." In *Arab Detroit 9/11: Life in the Terror Decade*, ed. Nabeel Abraham, Sally Howell, and Andrew Shryock (Detroit, MI: Wayne State University Press, 2011), pp. 29–63.

15. These encounters must be seen to be believed. For representative YouTube clips, simply search "Dearborn Arab Festival." A good starter is www.youtube.com/watch?v=m_8MO7IIlCw, accessed September 15, 2012, but one must sample several clips to gauge the editorial effect.

16. This label is commonly used on sites run by Pamela Geller (http://atlasshrugs2000.typepad.com/, accessed September 15, 2012) and Debbie Schlussel (www.debbieschlussel.com/, accessed September 15, 2012), which feature a steady stream of anti-Arab and Islamophobic materials.

17. Niraj Warikoo, "Terry Jones Goes Free on $1 Bond after Jailing; Judge Bars Him from Mosque for 3 years," *Detroit Free Press* (April 23, 2011), www.freep.com/article/20110422/NEWS02/110422014/Terry-Jones-goes-free-1-bond-after-jailing-judge-bars-him-from-mosque-3-years, accessed September 15, 2012.

18. Joe Grimm, "Muslim Woman Leads ACLU Fight for Quran-Burning Pastor's Right to Condemn Islam," Freedom Forum Diversity Institute, http://freedomforumdiversity.org/2011/05/02/muslim-woman-leads-aclu-fight-for-quran-burning-pastors-right-to-condemn-islam/, accessed September 15, 2012.

19. Jones appeared twice on "Let It Rip," the appropriately named Fox 2 News interview program. For a sample, go to www.youtube.com/watch?v=QQyBvT66lPM, accessed September 15, 2012.

20. *Dearborn Free Press*, "Interfaith Prayer Vigil Set for April 21st" (April 18, 2011), www.dearbornfreepress.com/2011/04/18/interfaith-prayer-vigil-set-for-april-21st/, accessed September 15, 2012.

21. Members of BAMN (By Any Means Necessary) are likely to engage their opponents physically, pushing them, blocking their movements, and so on.

22. For the full exchange, go to "Dearborn Mayor Blasts Quran-burning Pastor Terry Jones after His Rally Causes Tensions," www.youtube.com/watch?v=Ne046IZ72cU, accessed September 15, 2012.

23. For the view from the Thomas More Law Center, which provided legal counsel for Pastor Jones, see "Victory for Pastor Jones; Court

Rules that Pastor's Constitutional Rights Were Violated by 'Peace Bond' Trial," www.thomasmore.org/press-releases/2011/11/victory-pastor-jones-court-rules-pastor-s-constitutional-rights-were-violated, accessed September 15, 2012.

24. These events are described in Sally Howell and Amaney Jamal, "Belief and Belonging," in Detroit Arab American Study Team, *Citizenship and Crisis*, pp. 103–134.
25. Truth is stranger than fiction. For proof, see Niraj Warikoo, "Nuclear Search Targets Muslims," *Detroit Free Press*, December 24, 2005.
26. A detailed account of these relationships is available in Sally Howell and Amaney Jamal, "Detroit Exceptionalism and the Limits of Political Incorporation." In *Being and Belonging: Muslims in the United States since 9/11*, ed. Katherine Pratt Ewing (New York: Russell Sage Foundation, 2008), pp. 47–79.
27. Sally Howell, "Muslims as Moving Targets: External Scrutiny and Internal Critique in Detroit's Mosques." In *Arab Detroit 9/11: Life in the Terror Decade*, ed. Nabeel Abraham, Sally Howell, and Andrew Shryock (Detroit, MI: Wayne State University Press), pp. 151–185.
28. Ibid., p. 169. With this statement, the head of the FBI becomes the Grand Mufti of Detroit.
29. For a sample, go to "Dearborn, Arab Capital of America," www.youtube.com/watch?v=N5YIRUYPyn8, accessed September 15, 2012.
30. The political efflorescence of Arab/Muslim Detroit in the 1990s is recounted in Sally Howell, "Cultural Interventions: Arab American Aesthetics between the Transnational and the Ethnic." *Diaspora* 9:1 (2000), pp. 59–82; and Ismael Ahmed, "Michigan Arab Americans: A Case Study of Electoral and Non-electoral Empowerment." In *American Arabs and Political Participation*, ed. Phillipa Strum (Washington, DC: Woodrow Wilson International Center for Scholars, 2006), pp. 41–52.
31. The founding of the Highland Park Mosque, and related events in Detroit's Muslim history are chronicled in Sally Howell, "Inventing the American Mosque: Early Muslims and their Institutions in Detroit, 1910–1980," PhD dissertation, Rackham School of Graduate Studies, University of Michigan, 2009.
32. See Ihsan Bagby, *A Portrait of Detroit Mosques* (Clinton Township, MI: Institute for Social Policy and Understanding, 2004); Sally Howell, *Arab Detroit 9/11*; and Andrew Shryock and Ann Chih Lin, "Arab American Identities in Question." In *Citizenship and Crisis: Arab Detroit after 9/11*, ed. Detroit Arab American Study Team (New York: Russell Sage Foundation, 2009), pp. 35–86.
33. The standard and best source on these motifs is still Edward Said's *Orientalism* (New York: Vintage, 1978).

34. How this updated Muslim enemy took shape is explained in Melani McAlister, *Epic Encounters: Culture, Media, and U.S. Interests in the Middle East, 1945–2000* (Berkeley, CA: University of California Press, 2001).
35. Carl Schmitt, *The Concept of the Political* (Chicago, IL: University of Chicago Press, 1996).
36. Ibid., p. 27.
37. Ibid.
38. As a political label, Islamophilia is no more and no less accurate than Islamophobia. Applying it to specific individuals would not clarify matters. Suffice it to say, from the perspective of any so-called Islamophobe, every contributor to this volume would be a so-called Islamophile, although none of us would embrace the label as I describe it here. For a similar discussion of how these labels work as political tags, see my framing essay, "Islam as an Object of Fear and Affection: A Problem for Critical Analysis," in *Islamophobia/Islamophilia: Beyond the Politics of Enemy and Friend*, ed. Andrew Shryock (Bloomington, IN: Indiana University Press, 2009), pp. 1–25.
39. The dichotomy is the focus of Mahmood Mamdani's *Good Muslim, Bad Muslim: America, the Cold War, and the Roots of Terror* (New York: Pantheon Books, 2004).
40. This model of the contemporary world contradicts the imagery developed by Samuel Huntington in *The Clash of Civilization and the Remaking of the World Order* (New York: Simon and Schuster, 1996). One might argue that investment in civilizational models, and the idea of necessary civilizational clashes, is an intellectual attempt to hem in processes of transregional cultural interaction that have become too promiscuous.
41. Niraj Warikoo, "Metro interfaith leaders to unite against Quran-burning pastor," *Detroit Free Press* (April 20, 2011), www.freep.com/article/20110420/NEWS02/104200407/Metro-interfaith-leaders-unite-against-Quran-burning-pastor, accessed September 15, 2012.
42. This argument is made at the national level by Anny Bakalian and Mehdi Borzorgmehr, *Backlash 9/11: Middle Eastern and Muslim Americans Respond* (Berkeley, CA: University of California Press, 2009); by Louise Cainkar in her analysis of events in Chicago, *Homeland Insecurity: The Arab American and Muslim American Experience after 9/11* (New York: Russell Sage Foundation, 2009); and by the Detroit Arab American Study Team in *Citizenship and Crisis: Arab Detroit after 9/11* (New York: Russell Sage Foundation, 2009).
43. Scott Keyes, "Rep. Peter King: '80 Percent of Mosques in This Country Are Controlled by Radical Imams,'" *Think Progress* (January

25, 2011), http://thinkprogress.org/politics/2011/01/25/140549/king-radical-mosques/, accessed September 15, 2012.

44. Despite the market appeal of antireligious manifestoes like Christopher Hitchens's *God is Not Great: How Religion Poisons Everything* (New York: Twelve Books, 2007) or Richard Dawkins's *The God Delusion* (New York: Mariner Books, 2008), such books have almost no policy-making potential, and as intellectual exercises, they are widely portrayed as the products of curmudgeonly minds.

45. The entire event can be watched at www.aaiusa.org/blog/entry/rejecting-islamophobia-a-community-stand-against-hate/, accessed September 15, 2012.

Bibliography

ABC News. "Military Action in Afghanistan." October 8–9, 2001. Retrieved from the iPOLL Databank, the Roper Center for Public Opinion Research, University of Connecticut. Available at http://webapps.ropercenter.uconn.edu/CFIDE/cf/action/ipoll/abstract.cfm?keyword=islam&keywordoptions=1&exclude=&excludeoptions=1&topic=Any&organization=ABC+News&fromdate=1%2F1%2F1935&todate=&sortby=ASC&label=&archno=USABC2001–18499&start=summary&abstract.x=15&abstract.y=11, accessed July 14, 2012.
———. "What Would You Do?" www.youtube.com/watch?v=oKKbIsKBs5M, accessed September 15, 2012.
ABC News/Washington Post. August 30–September 2, 2010. Retrieved from the iPOLL Databank, the Roper Center for Public Opinion Research, University of Connecticut. Available at http://webapps.ropercenter.uconn.edu/CFIDE/cf/action/ipoll/abstract.cfm?keyword=islam&keywordoptions=1&exclude=&excludeoptions=1&topic=Any&organization=ABC+News&fromdate=1%2F1%2F1935&todate=&sortby=ASC&label=&archno=USABCWASH2010–1112&start=summary&abstract.x=14&abstract.y=15, accessed July 14, 2012.
Abraham, Nabeel, Sally Howell, and Andrew Shryock, ed. *Arab Detroit 9/11: Life in the Terror Decade.* Detroit: Wayne State University Press, 2011.
Abu Shouk, Ahmed I., J. O. Hunwick, and R. S. O'Fahey. "A Sudanese Missionary to the United States: Satti Majid, Shaykh al-Islam in North America, and His Encounter with Noble Drew Ali, Prophet of the Moorish Science Temple Movement." *Sudanic Africa* 8 (1997), pp. 137–191.
Abu-Lughod, Lila. "Do Muslim Women Really Need Saving? Anthropological Reflections on Cultural Relativism and Its Others." *American Anthropologist* 103:3 (2002), pp. 783–790.
Ackerman, Spencer. "FBI Teaches Agents: 'Mainstream' Muslims Are 'Violent, Radical,' " *Wired* (September 14, 2011), www.wired.com/dangerroom/2011/09/fbi-muslims-radical/all/, accessed September 15, 2012.

————. "Senior US General Orders Top-to-Bottom Review of Military's Islam Training." *Wired* (April 24, 2012), www.wired.com/dangerroom/2012/04/military-islam-training/, accessed September 15, 2012.

Afshar, Haleh, Rob Aitken, and Myfanwy Franks. "Islamophobia and Women of Pakistani Descent in Bradford: The Crisis of Ascribed and Adopted Identities." In *Muslim Diasporas: Gender, Culture, and Identity*, ed. Haideh Moghissi. New York: Routledge, 2006, pp. 167–185.

Ahmed, Ismael. "Michigan Arab Americans: A Case Study of Electoral and Non-electoral Empowerment." In *American Arabs and Political Participation*, ed. Phillipa Strum. Washington, DC: Woodrow Wilson International Center for Scholars, 2006, pp. 41–52.

Ahmed, Leila. *Women and Gender in Islam*. New Haven, CT: Yale University Press, 1992.

Ahmed, Rafiuddin. *The Bengal Muslims 1871–1906: A Quest for Identity*. New Delhi: Oxford University Press, 1996 (1981).

Alford, Terry. *Prince among Slaves*. 30th anniversary edition. New York: Oxford University Press, 2007.

Ali, Noble Drew. "Moorish Leader's Historical Message to America." *Moorish Literature* (n.p.: 1928), p. 13.

Ali, Wajahat, Eli Clifton, Matthew Duss, Lee Fang, Scott Keyes, and Faiz Shakir. "Fear, Inc.: The Roots of the Islamophobia Network in America" (Center for American Progress, August 26, 2011), www.americanprogress.org/issues/religion/report/2011/08/26/10165/fear-inc/, accessed September 15, 2012.

Allen, Jr., Ernst. "When Japan was 'Champion of the Darker Races': Satokata Takahashi and the Flowering of Black Messianic Nationalism." *Black Scholar* 24 (Winter 1994), pp. 23–46.

Allison, Robert J. *The Crescent Obscured: The United States and the Muslim World, 1776–1815*. New York: Oxford University Press, 1995.

American Civil Liberties Union. "Court Upholds Ruling Blocking Oklahoma Sharia and International Law Ban" (January 10, 2012), www.aclu.org/religion-belief/court-upholds-ruling-blocking-oklahoma-sharia-and-international-law-ban, accessed September 15, 2012.

————. "Map—Nationwide Anti-Mosque Activity," www.aclu.org/maps/map-nationwide-anti-mosque-activity, accessed September 15, 2012.

Anonymous. "Islam and Christian Missions." *The Church Missionary Gleaner* 19 (May 1892), pp. 68–69.

————. "The Hatred of Priests." *Littell's Living Age* 79 (October–December 1863), pp. 164–166.

Anti-Defamation League. "Backgrounder: Stop Islamization of America (SIOA)" (August 26, 2010), www.adl.org/main_Extremism/sioa.htm, accessed September 15, 2012.

Arab American Institute Foundation. *Select Social and Demographic Characteristics for Arab Americans.* Washington, DC: Arab American Institute, 2006.

Arab American Institute. "Watch Live: Rejecting Islamophobia: A Community Stand against Hate," www.aaiusa.org/blog/entry/rejecting-islamophobia-a-community-stand-against-hate/, accessed September 15, 2012.

"Arab International Festival 2012 Dearborn Michigan," www.youtube.com/watch?v=m_8MO7IIlCw, accessed September 15, 2012.

Austin, Allan D. *African Muslims in Antebellum America: A Sourcebook.* New York: Garland, 1984.

Aziz, Sahar. "Time to Address Violence against Muslim Women." *Huffington Post* (November 2, 2011), www.huffingtonpost.com/sahar-aziz/violence-again-muslim-women_b_1072529.html?view=screen, accessed September 15, 2012.

Bagby, Ihsan. *A Portrait of Detroit Mosques: Muslim Views on Policy, Politics and Religion.* Clinton Township, MI: Institute for Social Policy and Understanding, 2004.

Bakalian, Anny and Mehdi Borzorgmehr. *Backlash 9/11: Middle Eastern and Muslim Americans Respond.* Berkeley, CA: University of California Press, 2009.

Baker, Wayne and Andrew Shryock. "Citizenship and Crisis." In Detroit Arab American Study Team, *Citizenship and Crisis: Arab Detroit after 9/11.* New York: Russell Sage Foundation, 2009, pp. 3–32.

Baker, Wayne et al. *Preliminary Findings of the Detroit Arab American Study.* Ann Arbor, MI: Institute for Social Research, 2004.

Bali, Asli. "Scapegoating the Vulnerable: Preventive Detention of Immigrants in America's 'War on Terror.'" *Studies in Law, Politics, and Society* 38 (2006), pp. 25–69.

Bano, Samia. "Asking the Law Questions: Agency and Muslim Women." In *Thinking through Islamophobia: Global Perspectives*, ed. Sayyid, S., and AbdoolKarim Vakil. New York: Columbia University Press, 2010, pp. 135–156.

Barreto, Matt A., Karam Dana, and Kassra Oskooii. "The Park 51 (*sic*) Mosque and Anti-Muslim Attitudes in America." Paper presented at the annual conference of the Midwest Political Science Association, Chicago, IL, September 1–4, 2011.

Barton, James Levi. *Daybreak in Turkey.* Boston: Pilgrim, 1908.

Bartosiewicz, Petra. "To Catch a Terrorist: The FBI Hunts for the Enemy Within." *Harper's Magazine* (August, 2011), http://harpers.org/archive/2011/08/0083545, accessed September 15, 2012.

Bayoumi, Moustafa. "Racing Religion." *New Centennial Review* 6:2 (Fall 2006), pp. 267–293.

Behdad, Ali. *A Forgetful Nation: On Immigration and Cultural Identity in the United States*. Durham, NC: Duke University Press, 2005.

Bellah, Robert. "Civil Religion in America." *Daedalus* 96:1 (Winter 1967), pp. 1–21.

Bluett, Thomas. *Some Memoirs of the Life of Job, the Son of Solomon, the High Priest of Boonda in Africa; Who was a Slave About Two Years in Maryland; and Afterwards Being Brought to England, was Set Free, and Sent to His Native Land in the Year 1734*. London: Printed for R. Ford, 1734, http://docsouth.unc.edu/neh/bluett/menu.html, accessed June 1, 2009.

Bowen, Patrick D. "Satti Majid: A Sudanese Founder of American Islam." *Journal of Africana Religions*, 1/2 (in press).

Boykin, William G. "Sharia Law or Constitution? America Must Choose." *Texas Insider* (February 11, 2011), www.texasinsider.org/?p=42440, accessed September 15, 2012.

Brennan, John. "John Brennan Speaks on National Security at NYU." Conference on "A Dialogue on Our Nation's Security" at New York University on February 13, 2010, www.whitehouse.gov/photos-and-video/video/john-brennan-speaks-national-security-nyu, accessed July 15, 2012.

Brown, Wendy. *Regulating Aversion: Tolerance in the Age of Identity and Empire*. Princeton, NJ: Princeton University Press, 2008.

Buchanan, Claudius. *An Apology for Promoting Christianity in India*. Boston, MA: Nathaniel Willis, 1814.

Building Islam in Detroit: Foundations/Forms/Futures, http://biid.lsa.umich.edu/, accessed September 15, 2012.

Bumiller, Elisabeth. "Watchword of the Day: Beware the Caliphate; White House Letter" in *The International Herald Tribune*, December 12, 2005.

Burleigh, Nina. "Shaima Alawadi's Murder: A Hate Crime against Women?" *Time–Ideas* (April 10, 2012), http://ideas.time.com/2012/04/10/shaima-alawadis-murder-a-hate-crime-against-women/, accessed September 15, 2012.

B[uyers], W[illiam]. *Travels in India: Comprising Sketches of Madras, Calcutta, Benares, and the Principal Places on the Ganges;—Also of the Church of England, Baptist, London Society, and Other Missionary Stations*. London: James Blackwood, 1852. Cainkar, Louise A. *Homeland Insecurity: The Arab American and Muslim American Experience after 9/11*. New York: Russell Sage, 2009.

Carland, Susan. "Islamophobia, Fear of Loss of Freedom, and the Muslim Woman." *Islam and Muslim-Christian Relations* 22:4 (Fall 2011), pp. 469–473.

Carless, Will and Ian Lovitt. "Family of Iraqi Woman Killed in California Was in Crisis, Records Show." *New York Times* (April 5, 2012), www.nytimes.com/2012/04/06/us/shaima-alawadi-court-records-show-family-in-crisis.html, accessed September 15, 2012.

Chelser, Phyllis. "Are Honor Killings Simply Domestic Violence?," *Middle East Quarterly*, 16:2 (spring 2009), pp. 61–69, www.meforum.org/2067/are-honor-killings-simply-domestic-violence, accessed September 15, 2012.

———. "A Lesson Learned in Kabul." *Human Rights Service* (October 27, 2009), www.phyllis-chesler.com/638/a-lesson-learned-in-kabul, accessed September 15, 2012.

———. "Ban the Burqa? The Argument in Favor." *Middle East Quarterly* 17:4 (Fall 2010), pp. 33–45, www.meforum.org/2777/ban-the-burqa, accessed September 15, 2012.

———. "No More Harems: The Hidden History of Muslim and Ex-Muslim Feminists" (October 4, 2011), www.phyllis-chesler.com/1040/muslim-feminism, accessed September 15, 2012.

———. "The Feminist Politics of Islamic Misogyny." *American Thinker* (November 13, 2010), www.phyllis-chesler.com/900/feminist-politics-islamic-misogyny, accessed September 15, 2012.

———. *The Death of Feminism: What's Next in the Struggle for Women's Freedom.* New York: Palgrave, 2005, www.phyllis-chesler.com/books/the-death-of-feminism, accessed September 15, 2012.

———. *The Phyllis Chesler Organization*, www.phyllis-chesler.com/, accessed September 15, 2012.

Cincotta, Thomas. *Manufacturing the Muslim Menace: Private Firms, Public Servants, and the Threat to Rights and Security.* Political Research Associates, 2011, www.publiceye.org/liberty/training/Muslim_Menace_Complete.pdf, accessed September 15, 2012.

Clegg III, Claude Andrew. *An Original Man: The Life and Times of Elijah Muhammad.* New York: St. Martin's Press, 1997.

Cole, David. *Enemy Aliens: Double Standards and Constitutional Freedoms in the War on Terror.* New York: New Press, 2004.

Corrigan, John and Lynn S. Neal, ed. *Religious Intolerance in America: A Documentary History.* Chapel Hill, NC: University of North Carolina Press, 2010.

Council on American-Islamic Relations (CAIR) Southern California. Video posted on March 2, 2011, www.youtube.com/watch?v=NutFkykjmbM, accessed September 15, 2012.

Creeping Sharia blog, http://creepingsharia.wordpress.com/about-2/, accessed September 15, 2012.

Curtis, IV, Edward E., *Black Muslim Religion in the Nation of Islam, 1960–1975*. Chapel Hill, NC: University of North Carolina Press, 2006.

Curtis, IV, Edward E., ed. *Encyclopedia of Muslim-American History*. New York: Facts on File, Inc., 2010.

———, ed. *The Columbia Sourcebook of Muslims in the United States*. New York: Columbia University Press, 2008.

Curtis, IV, Edward E. "Debating the Origins of the Moorish Science Temple." In *The New Black Gods: Arthur Huff Fauset and the Study of African Americans Religions*, ed. Edward E. Curtis IV, and Danielle Brune Sigler. Bloomington, IN: Indiana University Press, 2009, pp. 70–90.

———. *Islam in Black America: Identity, Liberation, and Difference in African-American Islamic Thought*. Albany, NY: State University of New York Press, 2002.

———. *Muslims in America: A Short History*. New York: Oxford University Press, 2009.

Dalton, Edward Tuite. *Descriptive Ethnology of Bengal*. Calcutta: Office of the Superintendent of Government Printing, 1872.

Daniel, Norman. *Islam and the West: The Making of an Image*. Oxford: Oneworld, 2009 (1960).

Dannin, Robert. *Black Pilgrimage to Islam*. New York: Oxford University Press, 2002.

Dawkins, Richard. *The God Delusion*. New York: Mariner Books, 2008.

De Atkine, Norvell B. "Why Arabs Lose Wars." *Middle East Quarterly* (December 1999), www.meforum.org/441/why-arabs-lose-wars, accessed September 15, 2012.

"Dearborn, Arab Capital of America," www.youtube.com/watch?v=N5YIRUYPyn8, accessed September 15, 2012.

"Dearborn Mayor Blasts Quran-burning Pastor Terry Jones after His Rally Causes Tensions," www.youtube.com/watch?v=Ne046IZ72cU, accessed September 15, 2012.

Dearborn Free Press. "Interfaith Prayer Vigil Set for April 21st" (April 18, 2011), www.dearbornfreepress.com/2011/04/18/interfaith-prayer-vigil-set-for-april-21st/, accessed September 15, 2012.

Dickinson, John. *The Political Writings of John Dickinson, Esquire: The Address of Congress to the Inhabitants of Quebec. Dated October 26th, 1774*, Volume 2. Wilmington, DE: Bonsal and Niles, 1801.

Donnelly, Ignatius [Edmund Boisgilbert, M.D.]. *Caesar's Column: A Story of the Twentieth Century*. Chicago, IL: F. J. Shulte & Company, 1890.

Donner, Frank T. *The Age of Surveillance: The Aims and Methods of America's Political Intelligence System*. New York: Knopf, 1980.

Duffield, Ian. "Some American Influences on Dusé Mohammed Ali." In *Pan-African Biography*, ed. Robert A. Hill. Los Angeles, CA: Crossroads Press, 1987, pp. 11–56.

Elkholy, Abdo A. *Arab Moslems in the United States.* New Haven, CT: College & University Press, 1966.

Elliott, Justin. "Whatever Happened to the 'Ground Zero Mosque'?" Salon.com (December 31, 2010), www.salon.com/2010/12/31/park_51_a_look_back/, accessed September 15, 2012.

Eltahawy, Mona. "Why Do They Hate Us?: The Real War on Women is in the Middle East." *Foreign Policy* ("The Sex Issue") (May/June 2012), www.foreignpolicy.com/articles/2012/04/23/why_do_they_hate_us?page=full, accessed September 15, 2012.

Emon, Anver. "Banning Shari'a." *The Immanent Frame: Secularism, Religion, and the Public Sphere,* http://blogs.ssrc.org/tif/2011/09/06/banning-shari'a, accessed July 15, 2012.

Ernst, Carl W. *Following Muhammad: Rethinking Islam in the Contemporary World.* Chapel Hill, NC: University of North Carolina Press, 2004.

Errazzouki, Samia. "Dear Mona Eltahawy, You Do Not Represent 'Us'," www.al-monitor.com/pulse/originals/2012/al-monitor/dear-mona-eltahawy-you-do-not-re.html, accessed September 15, 2012.

Esposito, John L. *The Islamic Threat: Myth or Reality?* New York: Oxford University Press, 1992.

Esposito, John and Ibrahim Kalin, ed. *Islamophobia: The Challenge of Pluralism in the 21st Century.* Oxford University Press, 2011.

Federal Bureau of Investigation, Central Research Section. "The Nation of Islam: Antiwhite, All-Negro Cult in United States" (October 1960).

———. "FBI File of the Moorish Science Temple of America," http://vault.fbi.gov/Moorish%20Science%20Temple%20of%20America/Moorish%20Science%20Temple%20of%20America%20Part%201%20of%2031/view, accessed April 26, 2012.

Ferris, Marc. "To 'Achieve the Pleasure of Allah': Immigrant Muslims in New York City, 1893–1991." In *Muslim Communities in North America*, ed. Yvonne Yazbeck Haddad and Jane Smith. Albany, NY: State University of New York Press, 1994, pp. 209–230.

Foner, Nancy and Richard Alba. "Immigration and the Legacies of the Past: The Impact of Slavery and the Holocaust on Contemporary Immigrants in the United States and Western Europe." *Comparative Studies in Society and History* 52:4 (2010), pp. 798–819.

Fox 2 News. "Full Terry Jones on Let It Rip" (April 21, 2011), www.youtube.com/watch?v=QQyBvT66lPM, accessed September 15, 2012.

Franklin, Benjamin. *Poor Richard's Almanack.* New York: Barnes & Noble Publishing, 2004.

Friedmann, Yohanan. *Prophecy Continuous*. Berkeley, CA: University of California Press, 1989.

Gardell, Mattias. *In the Name of Elijah Muhammad: Minister Louis Farrakhan and the Nation of Islam*. Durham, NC: Duke University Press, 1996.

Geisler, Norman and Abdul Saleeb. *Answering Islam: The Crescent in Light of the Cross*. Grand Rapids, MI: Baker, 2006 (1993).

Geller, Pamela. "Honor Killings: Islam Misogyny." *Atlas Shrugs* (September 6, 2012), http://atlasshrugs2000.typepad.com/atlas_shrugs/honor_killings_islam_misogyny/, accessed September 15, 2012.

———. "Muslim-Americans Stand Up for Honor Killing." *Atlas Shrugs* (May 10, 2012), http://atlasshrugs2000.typepad.com/atlas_shrugs/jessica-mokdad-human-rights-conference/, accessed September 15, 2012.

———. "Pamela Geller, *Front Page* Magazine Interview: Obama and The Muslim Brotherhood." *Atlas Shrugs*, http://atlasshrugs2000.typepad.com/atlas_shrugs/2011/02/pamela-geller-front-page-magazine-interview-obama-and-the-muslim-brotherhood.html, accessed September 15, 2012.

———. *Stop the Islamization of America*. N.p.: WND Books, 2011.

Geller, Pamela, Robert Spencer, and John Bolton. *The Post-American Presidency: The Obama Administration's War on America*. New York: Threshold Editions, 2010.

Ghosh, Bobby. "Islamophobia: Does America Have a Muslim Problem?" *Time Magazine* (August 30, 2010), www.time.com/time/magazine/article/0,9171,2011936,00.html, accessed September 13, 2012.

Goldman, Adam and Matt Apuzzo. "NYPD: Muslim spying led to no leads, terror cases." Associated Press (August 21, 2012), www.ap.org/Content/AP-In-The-News/2012/NYPD-Muslim-spying-led-to-no-leads-terror-cases, accessed September 15, 2012.

Gomez, Michael A. *Black Crescent: The Experience and Legacy of African Muslims in the Americas*. Cambridge: Cambridge University Press, 2005.

Greenwald, Glenn. "Combating Islamophobic Violence," Salon.com (August 9, 2012), www.salon.com/2012/08/09/combating_islamophobic_violence/, accessed September 15, 2012.

Grimm, Joe. "Muslim Woman Leads ACLU Fight for Quran-Burning Pastor's Right to Condemn Islam." Freedom Forum Diversity Institute, http://freedomforumdiversity.org/2011/05/02/muslim-woman-leads-aclu-fight-for-quran-burning-pastors-right-to-condemn-islam/, accessed September 15, 2012.

Gualtieri, Sarah M. A. *Between Arab and White: Race and Ethnicity in the Early Syrian American Diaspora*. Berkeley, CA: University of California Press, 2009.

Haley, Alex. *Roots*. Garden City, NJ: Doubleday, 1976.

Hamilton, Walter. *East-India Gazetteer; Containing Particular Descriptions of the Empires, Kingdoms, Principalities, Provinces, Cities, Towns, Districts, Fortresses, Harbours, Rivers, Lakes, &c of Hindostan, and the Adjacent Countries, India Beyond the Ganges, and the Eastern Archipelago*. Volume I. Delhi: Low Price, 1993 (1828), p. 497.

Hammer, Juliane. *American Muslim Women, Religious Authority, and Activism: More than a Prayer*. Austin, TX: University of Texas Press, 2012.

———. "Performing Gender Justice: The 2005 Woman-Led Prayer in New York," *Contemporary Islam*, special issue on Muslims and Media, 4:1 (April 2010), pp. 91–116.

Hand, R. *Early English Administration of Bihar, 1781–85*. Calcutta: Bengal Secretariat Press, 1894.

Hanson, John Wesley. *The World's Congress of Religions: The Addresses and Papers Delivered Before the Parliament, and an Abstract of the Congresses Held in the Art Institute, Chicago, Aug. 25 to Oct. 15, 1893, Under the Auspices of the World's Columbian Exposition*. Chicago, IL: Monarch Book, 1894.

Hardy, P. *The Muslims of British India*. Cambridge: Cambridge University Press, 1972.

Hayward, John. *The Book of Religions: Comprising the Views, Creeds, Sentiments, or Opinions, of All the Principal Religious Sects in the World, Particularly of All Christian Denominations in Europe and America, to which are Added Church and Missionary Statistics, Together with Biographical Sketches*, 2nd edition, Boston, MA: I. S. Boyd and E. W. Buswell, 1842.

Henshaw, John Prentiss Kewley. *An Inquiry Into the Meaning of the Prophecies Relating to the Second Advent of Our Lord Jesus Christ: In a Course of Lectures, Delivered in St. Peter's Church, Baltimore*. Baltimore, MD: Daniel Brunner, 1842.

Herberg, Will. *Protestant-Catholic-Jew: An Essay in American Religious Sociology*. Chicago, IL: University of Chicago Press, 1955.

Hernandez, Karen Leslie. "Investigating a Muslim's Murder." *OnIslam* (May 16, 2012), www.onislam.net/english/back-to-religion/covering-religion/457118-investigating-a-muslims-murder-.html, accessed September 15, 2012.

Higham, John. "Another Look at Nativism." In *Send These to Me: Jews and Other Immigrants in Urban America*. New York: Atheneum, 1975, pp. 102–115.

Higham, John. *Strangers in the Land: Patterns of American Nativism, 1860–1925*. New Brunswick, NJ: Rutgers University Press, 1988 (1955).

Hill, Robert A., ed. *The FBI's RACON: Racial Conditions in the United States during World War II.* Boston, MA: Northeastern University Press, 1995.

Hitchens, Christopher. *God is Not Great: How Religion Poisons Everything.* New York: Twelve Books, 2007.

Ho, Christina. "Muslim Women's New Defenders: Women's Rights, Nationalism and Islamophobia in Contemporary Australia." *Women's Studies International Forum* 30:4 (July–August 2007), pp. 290–298.

Hodson, T. C. *India. Census Ethnography, 1901–1931.* New Delhi: Government of India Press, 1937.

Howell, Sally. "Cultural Interventions: Arab American Aesthetics between the Transnational and the Ethnic." *Diaspora* 9:1 (2000), pp. 59–82.

———. "Inventing the American Mosque: Early Muslims and their Institutions in Detroit, 1910–1980." PhD dissertation, Rackham School of Graduate Studies, University of Michigan, 2009.

———. "Mosques, History." In *Encyclopedia of Islam in America*, vol. 1, ed. Jocelyne Cesari. Westport, CT: Greenwood Press, 2007, pp. 432–433.

———. "Muslims as Moving Targets: External Scrutiny and Internal Critique in Detroit's Mosques." In *Arab Detroit 9/11: Life in the Terror Decade*, ed. Nabeel Abraham, Sally Howell, and Andrew Shryock. Detroit, MI: Wayne State University Press, 2011, pp. 151–185.

Howell, Sally and Amaney Jamal. "Belief and Belonging." In *Citizenship and Crisis: Arab Detroit after 9/11*, ed. Detroit Arab American Study Team. New York: Russell Sage Foundation, 2009, pp. 103–134.

———. "Detroit Exceptionalism and the Limits of Political Incorporation." In *Being and Belonging: Muslims in the United States since 9/11*, ed. Katherine Pratt Ewing. New York: Russell Sage Foundation, 2008, pp. 47–79.

Howell, Sally and Andrew Shryock. "Cracking Down on Diaspora: Arab Detroit and America's War on Terror." *Anthropological Quarterly* 76:3 (2003), pp. 443–462.

Hu, Elise. "TX Rep. Louie Gohmert Warns of Terrorist Babies," *Texas Tribune* (June 28, 2010), www.texastribune.org/texas-mexico-border-news/arizona-immigration-law/tx-rep-louie-gohmert-warns-of-terrorist-babies/, accessed September 15, 2012.

Hume, Mr. "Letter from Mr. Hume, June 22, 1850" in *The Missionary Herald* 46 (1850), pp. 349–354.

Hunter, W. W. *The Indian Musalmans: Are They Bound in Conscience to Rebel Against the Queen?* 2nd edition, London: Trübner and Company, 1872.

Huntington, Samuel P. *Who Are We? The Challenges to America's National Identity.* New York: Simon & Schuster, 2004.

———. *The Clash of Civilization and the Remaking of the World Order.* New York: Simon and Schuster, 1996.

Hutson, James H. "Founding Fathers and Islam: Library Papers Show Early Tolerance for Muslim Faith." *Library of Congress Information Bulletin* 61:5 (May 2002). www.loc.gov/loc/lcib/0205/tolerance.html, accessed February 14, 2009.

———, ed. *The Founders on Religion: A Book of Quotations.* Princeton, NJ: Princeton University Press, 2007.

India, Government of. Letter, Home Department (Political), to G. Rainy, Chief Secretary, Bihar and Orissa. D.O. No. 1965, Simla, September 17, 1919. Political Department, Special Section. No. 345 of 1919. State Archives of Bihar.

Jadaliyya Reports. "A Collective Response to 'To Be Anti-Racist is to Be Feminist: The Hoodie and the Hijab are Not the Same.' " *Jadaliyya* (April 15, 2012), www.jadaliyya.com/pages/index/5064/a-collective-response-to-to-be-anti-racist-is-to-b, accessed September 15, 2012.

Jamal, Amaney and Nadine Naber, ed. *Race and Arab Americans before and after 9/11: From Invisible Citizens to Visible Subjects.* Syracuse, NY: Syracuse University Press, 2008.

Jefferson, Thomas. *Memoirs, Correspondence, and Private Papers of Thomas Jefferson: Late President of the United States*, volume I, ed. Thomas Jefferson Randolph. London: Henry Colburn and Richard Bentley, 1829.

Jihad Watch. "Salon Tries to Save Face: Shaima Alawadi Murder Not a Hate Crime, But Hey, There's a Lot of Islamophobia Anyway," www.jihad-watch.org/2012/04/salon-tries-to-save-face-shaima-alawadi-murder-not-a-hate-crime-but-hey-theres-a-lot-of-islamophobia.html, accessed September 15, 2012.

Johnson, Sylvester A. "Religion Proper and Proper Religion." In *The New Black Gods: Arthur Huff Fauset and the Study of African Americans Religions*, ed. Edward E. Curtis IV, and Danielle Brune Sigler. Bloomington, IN: Indiana University Press, 2009, pp. 145–170.

Joshi, S. T. *Documents of American Prejudice: An Anthology of Writings on Race from Thomas Jefferson to David Duke.* New York: Basic Books, 1999.

Kahf, Mohja. *Western Representations of the Muslim Woman: From Termagant to Odalisque.* Austin, TX: University of Texas Press, 1999.

Kalkan, Kerem Ozan, Geoffrey C. Layman, and Eric M. Uslander. " 'Bands of Others'? Attitudes toward Muslims in Contemporary American Society." *The Journal of Politics* 71:3 (July 2009), pp. 847–862.

Kareem, Mona. "Why Do They Hate Us? A Blogger's Response," www.al-monitor.com/pulse/originals/2012/al-monitor/in-response-to-mona-eltahawys-ha.html, accessed September 15, 2012.

Keyes, Scott. "Rep. Peter King: '80 Percent Of Mosques In This Country Are Controlled By Radical Imams.'" *Think Progress* (January 25, 2011), http://thinkprogress.org/politics/2011/01/25/140549/king-radical-mosques/, accessed September 15, 2012.

Khalid, Asma. "Lifting the Veil," www.npr.org/2011/04/21/135413427/lifting-the-veil, accessed September 15, 2012.

———. "Lifting The Veil: Muslim Women Explain Their Choice," www.npr.org/2011/04/21/135523680/lifting-the-veil-muslim-women-explain-their-choice, accessed September 15, 2012.

Khan Bahadur, Syed Ahmad. *Review of Dr. Hunter's Indian Musalmans: Are They Bound in Conscience to Rebel Against the Queen?* Benares: Medical Hall Press, 1872.

Kidd, Thomas S. "'Is It Worse to Follow Mahomet than the Devil?' Early American Uses of Islam." *Church History* 72:4 (December 2003), pp. 766–790.

———. *American Christians and Islam: Evangelical Culture and Muslims from the Colonial Period to the Age of Terrorism.* Princeton, NJ: Princeton University Press, 2009.

Kinney, Bruce. *Mormonism: The Islam of America.* Revised edition. New York: Fleming H. Revell, 1912.

Kolhatkar, Sonali and Mariam Rawi. "Why Is a Leading Feminist Organization Lending Its Name to Support Escalation in Afghanistan?" www.rawa.org/rawa/2009/07/08/why-is-a-leading-feminist-organization-lending-its-name-to-support-escalation-in-afghanistano.html, accessed September 15, 2012.

Kurzman, Charles. "Islamic Statements against Terrorism," http://kurzman.unc.edu/islamic-statements-against-terrorism/, accessed September 15, 2012.

———. *The Missing Martyrs: Why There Are So Few Muslim Terrorists.* New York: Oxford University Press, 2011.

Landes, Richard and Steven T. Katz, ed. *The Paranoid Apocalypse: A Hundred-Year Retrospective on the Protocols of the Elders of Zion.* New York: New York University Press, 2012.

Lawrence, Bruce B. *Old Faiths, New Fears: Muslims and Other Asian Immigrants in American Religious Life.* New York: Columbia University Press, 2002.

———. "The Polite Islamophobia of the Intellectual." *Religion Dispatches* (June 1, 2010), www.religiondispatches.org/archive/politics/2635/the_polite_islamophobia_of_the_intellectual_/, accessed September 15, 2012.

Lees, W. Nassau. *Indian Musalmáns: Being Three Letters Reprinted from the "Times" with an Article on the Late Prince Consort, and Four Articles on*

Education, Reprinted from the "Calcutta Englishman." London: Williams and Norgate, 1871.

Leland, Charles Godfrey. *The Egyptian Sketch Book.* New York: Hurd and Houghton, 1874.

LeMesurier, H. Telegram, Government of India, Home Department, Simla, August 21, 1914. Public Special, No. 225 of 1914. State Archives of Bihar.

Lo, Mbaye. *Muslims in America: Race, Politics, and Community Building.* Beltsville, MD: Amana Publications, 2004.

Locke, John. *John Locke: A Letter Concerning Toleration, in Focus*, ed. John P. Horton and Susan Mendus. London: Routledge, 1991.

Lockman, Zachary. *Contending Visions of the Middle East: The History and Politics of Orientalism.* New York: Cambridge University Press, 2004.

Long, J. *How I Taught the Bible to Bengal Peasant-Boys.* London: Gilbert & Rivington, 1875.

Los Angeles Times, February 18–19, 1993. "Los Angeles Times Poll: Clinton's Economic Plan." Retrieved from the iPOLL Databank, the Roper Center for Public Opinion Research, University of Connecticut. Available at http://webapps.ropercenter.uconn.edu/CFIDE/cf/action/catalog/abstract.cfm?label=&keyword=USLAT1993–308&fromDate=&toDate=&organization=Any&type=&keywordOptions=1&start=1&id=&exclude=&excludeOptions=1&topic=Any&sortBy=DESC&archno=USLAT1993–308&abstract=abstract&x=32&y=9, accessed September 14, 2012.

Mahmood, Saba. "Feminism, Democracy, and Empire: Islam and the War on Terror." In *Women's Studies on the Edge*, ed. Joan Scott. Durham, NC: Duke University Press, 2007, pp. 81–114.

Mahmood, Saba and Charles Hirschkind. "Feminism, the Taliban and Politics of Counter-Insurgency." *Anthropological Quarterly* 75:2 (Spring 2002), pp. 339–354.

Mamdani, Mahmood. *Good Muslim, Bad Muslim: America, the Cold War, and the Roots of Terror.* New York: Pantheon Books, 2004.

Mantyla, Kyle. "Boykin Terrifies Dobson with Dire Warnings of America's Pending Islamification," *Right Wing Watch* (February 18, 2011), www.rightwingwatch.org/content/boykin-terrifies-dobson-dire-warnings-americas-pending-islamification, accessed September 15, 2012.

Marr, Timothy. *The Cultural Roots of American Islamicism.* New York: Cambridge University Press, 2006.

Martens, Pam. "The Far Right's Secret Slush Fund to Keep Fear Alive." *Counterpunch* (October 26, 2010), www.counterpunch.com/martens10262010.html, accessed September 15, 2012.

Mastnak, Tomaz. "Western Hostility toward Muslims: A History of the Present." In *Islamophobia/Islamophilia: Beyond the Politics of Enemy and*

Friend, ed. Andrew Shryock. Bloomington, IN: Indiana University Press, 2010, pp. 29–52.

McAlister, Melani. *Epic Encounters: Culture, Media, and U.S. Interests in the Middle East, 1945–2000.* Berkeley, CA: University of California Press, 2001.

McCafferty, Heather. "The Representation of Muslim Women in American Print Media: A Case Study of *The New York Times*." MA thesis, McGill University, August 2005.

Mill, James. *The History of British India*, ed. William Thomas. Chicago, IL: The University of Chicago Press, 1975 (1817).

Mishra, Pankaj. "A Critic at Large: Islamismism—How should Western intellectuals respond to Muslim scholars?," *The New Yorker* (June 7, 2010), www.newyorker.com/arts/critics/atlarge/2010/06/07/100607crat_atlarge_mishra, accessed September 15, 2012.

———. "Does Mona Eltahawy's Approach Hurt Women?" *Washington Post* Blog (May 15, 2012), www.washingtonpost.com/blogs/guest-voices/post/does-mona-eltahawys-approach-hurts-women/2012/05/15/gIQAXnqSSU_blog.html, accessed September 15, 2012.

Moore, Kathleen. "The *Hijab* and Religious Liberty: Anti-Discrimination Law and Muslim Women in the United States." In *Muslims on the Americanization Path?*, ed. Yvonne Yazbeck Haddad and John L. Esposito (New York: Oxford University Press, 2000), pp. 105–127.

———. *Al-Mughtaribun: American Law and the Transformation of Muslim Life in the United States.* Albany, NY: State University of New York, 1995.

Moors, Annelies. "Fear of Small Numbers? Debating Face-Veiling in the Netherlands." In *Thinking through Islamophobia: Global Perspectives*, ed. S. Sayyid, and AbdoolKarim Vakil. New York: Columbia University Press, 2010, pp. 157–164.

Nacos, Brigitte and Oscar Torres-Reyna. *Fueling Our Fears: Stereotyping, Media Coverage, and Public Opinion of Muslim Americans.* Lanham, MD: Rowman and Littlefield, 2007.

Nash, Michael. *Islam among Urban Blacks, Muslims in Newark, NJ: A Social History.* Lanham, MD: University Press of America, 2008.

National Task Force to End Sexual and Domestic Violence against Women. "Fact Sheet: NTF Opposition to HR 4970," http://4vawa.org/pages/fact-sheet-ntf-opposition-to-hr-4970, accessed September 15, 2012.

Nisbet, Erik C., Ronald Ostman, and James Shanahan. "Public Opinion toward Muslim Americans: Civil Liberties and the Role of Religiosity, Ideology, and Media Use." In *Muslims in Western Politics*, ed. Abdulkader H. Sinno. Bloomington, IN: Indiana University Press, 2009, pp. 160–199.

Obama, Barack. "Barack Obama's Speech on Race." *New York Times* (March 18, 2008).

Okin, Susan Moller. "Is Multiculturalism Bad for Women?" In *Is Multiculturalism Bad for Women?*, ed. Joshua Cohen, Matthew Howard, and Martha C. Nussbaum. Princeton, NJ: Princeton University Press, 1999, pp. 7–26.

Ong, Aihwa. "Cultural Citizenship as Subject Making: Immigrants Negotiate Racial and Cultural Boundaries in the United States." *Current Anthropology* 37 (1996), pp. 737–762.

Ose, Erik. "Pro-McCain Group Dumping 28 Million Terror Scare DVDs in Swing States." *Huffington Post* (September 12, 2008), www.huffingtonpost.com/erik-ose/pro-mccain-group-dumping_b_125969.html, accessed September 15, 2012.

Owen, John. "An Address to the Chairman of the East India Company Occasioned by Mr. Twining's Letter to that Gentleman, on the Danger of Interfering in the Religious Opinions of the Natives of India, and on the Views of the British and Foreign Bible Society, as Directed to India." London: Black and Parry, 1807.

Patai, Raphael. *The Arab Mind*, with a new preface by Col. De Atkine ([1973]; reprint edition). New York: Hatherleigh Press, 2007.

Pearson, Harlan O. *Islamic Reform and Revival in Nineteenth-century India: The* Tariqah-i Muhammadiyah. New Delhi: Yoda, 2008.

People for the American Way. "The Right-Wing Playbook on Anti-Muslim Extremism" (2011), www.pfaw.org/rww-in-focus/the-right-wing-playbook-anti-muslim-extremism, accessed September 15, 2012.

Pew Forum on Religion and Public Life. *Muslim Americans: Middle Class and Mostly Mainstream*. Washington, DC: Pew Research Center, 2007.

Pew Research Publications. "Continuing Divide in Views of Islam and Violence" (March 9, 2011), http://pewresearch.org/pubs/1921/poll-islam-violence-more-likely-other-religions-peter-king-congressional-hearings, accessed September 15, 2012.

Phoenix, Aisha. "Somali Young Women and Hierarchies of Belonging," *Young* 19:3 (August 2011), pp. 313–331.

Povey, Tara. "Islamophobia and Arab and Muslim Women's Activism." *Cosmopolitan Civil Societies* 1:2 (2009), pp. 63–76.

"Prejudice." *Oxford English Dictionary* (3rd edition, March 2007), online version June 2012, www.oed.com/view/Entry/150162, accessed September 8, 2012.

Prideaux, Humphrey. *The True Nature of Imposture Fully Display'd in the Life of Mahomet: With a Discourse Annex'd for the Vindication of Christianity from this Charge: Offered to the Consideration of the Deists of the Present Age*, 8th edition. London: E. Curll, 1723.

Puar, Jasbir. *Terrorist Assemblages: Homonationalism in Queer Times.* Durham, NC: Duke University Press, 2007.

Ranasinha, Ruvani. "Fundamental Fictions: Gender, Power and Islam in Brasian Diasporic Formations." In *Thinking through Islamophobia: Global Perspectives,* ed. S. Sayyid and AbdoolKarim Vakil. New York: Columbia University Press, 2010, pp. 259–264.

Razack, Sherene. *Casting Out: The Eviction of Muslims from Western Law and Politics.* Toronto: University of Toronto Press, 2008.

Riley, Krista. "Islamophobia—Let's Talk about Gender," *Muslimah Media Watch,* July 14, 2008, www.patheos.com/blogs/mmw/2008/07/islamophobia-lets-talk-about-gender-2/, accessed September 15, 2012.

Robbins, Tom. "NYPD Cops' Training Included an Anti-Muslim Horror Flick." *The Village Voice* (January 19, 2011), www.villagevoice.com/2011–01–19/columns/nypd-cops-training-included-an-anti-muslim-horror-flick/, accessed September 15, 2012.

Robinson, Francis. *Islam and Muslim History in South Asia.* New Delhi: Oxford University Press, 2000. pp. 192–194.

Roosevelt, Theodore. *Presidential Addresses and State Papers, Volume III: April 7, 1904, to May 9, 1905.* New York: Review of Reviews, 1910.

Rosaldo, Renato. "Cultural Citizenship, Inequality, and Multiculturalism." In *Latino Cultural Citizenship: Claiming Identity, Space, and Rights,* ed. William Flores and Rina Benmayor. Boston: Beacon Press, 1997, pp. 253–261.

Runnymede Trust. *Islamophobia: A Challenge for Us All* (1997), www.runnymedetrust.org/publications/17/32.html, accessed September 15, 2012.

Rushdie, Salman. *The Satanic Verses: A Novel.* New York: Random House, 2008 (1988).

Sacirbey, Omar. "Anti-Sharia Movement Loses Steam State Legislatures," *Washington Post* (March 22, 2012), www.washingtonpost.com/national/on-faith/anti-shariah-movement-loses-steam-in-state-legislatures/2012/03/22/gIQAphNxTS_story.html, accessed September 15, 2012.

Safi, Omid. "Who Put Hate in My Sunday Paper?" (September 29, 2008), http://omidsafi.com/index.php?option=com_content&task=view&id=42&Itemid=9, accessed September 15, 2012.

Said, Edward. *Orientalism.* New York: Vintage, 1978.

Saunders, Doug. *The Myth of the Muslim Tide: Do Immigrants Threaten the West?* New York: Vintage, 2012.

Sayyid, S. and AbdoolKarim Vakil, ed. *Thinking through Islamophobia: Global Perspectives.* New York: Columbia University Press, 2010.

Schachtman, Noah and Spencer Ackerman. "'Institutional Failures' Led Military to Teach War on Islam." *Wired* (June 20, 2012), www.wired.com/dangerroom/2012/06/failure-oversight-war-islam/, accessed September 15, 2012.

————. "US Military Taught Officers: Use 'Hiroshima' Tactics for 'Total War' on Islam." *Wired* (May 10, 2012), www.wired.com/dangerroom/2012/05/total-war-islam/all/, accessed September 15, 2012.

Schanzer, David, Charles Kurzman, and Ebrahim Moosa. *Anti-Terror Lessons of Muslim Americans*. National Institute of Justice Report, 2010, www.sanford.duke.edu/news/Schanzer_Kurzman_Moosa_Anti-Terror_Lessons.pdf, accessed September 15, 2012.

Schmitt, Carl. *The Concept of the Political*. Chicago, IL: University of Chicago Press, 1996.

Schopmeyer, Kim. "Arab Detroit after 9/11: A Changing Demographic Portrait." In *Arab Detroit 9/11: Life in the Terror Decade*, ed. Nabeel Abraham, Sally Howell, and Andrew Shryock. Detroit, MI: Wayne State University Press, 2011, pp. 29–63.

Schulman, Daniel. "Rep. Louie Gohmert's 'Terror Baby' Meltdown." *Mother Jones* (August 13, 2010), www.motherjones.com/mojo/2010/08/rep-louie-gohmerts-terror-baby-meltdown, accessed September 15, 2012.

Shakir, Faiz. "Kansas Legislature Passes Discriminatory Anti-Muslim Bill by Calling it a 'Women's Rights' Issue." *Think Progress* (May 13, 2012), http://thinkprogress.org/justice/2012/05/13/483278/kansas-legislature-passes-discriminatory-anti-muslim-bill-by-calling-it-a-womens-right-issue/, accessed September 15, 2012.

Sheehi, Stephen. *Islamophobia: The Ideological Campaign against Muslims*. Atlanta, GA: Clarity Press, 2011.

Shryock, Andrew, ed. *Islamophobia/Islamophilia: Beyond the Politics of Enemy and Friend*. Bloomington, IN: Indiana University Press, 2010.

————. "Islam as an Object of Fear and Affection: A Problem for Critical Analysis." In *Islamophobia/Islamophilia: Beyond the Politics of Enemy and Friend*, ed. Andrew Shryock. Bloomington, IN: Indiana University Press, 2009, pp. 1–25.

————. "New Images of Arab Detroit: Seeing Otherness and Identity through the Lens of September 11." *American Anthropologist* 104 (2002), pp. 917–922.

Shryock, Andrew and Ann Chih Lin. "The Limits of Citizenship." In Detroit Arab American Study Team, *Citizenship and Crisis: Arab Detroit after 9/11*. New York: Russell Sage Foundation, 2009, pp. 265–286.

Sides, John and Kimberly Gross. "The Origins of Anti-Muslim Stereotyping." Paper presented at the annual conference of the Midwest Political Science Association, Chicago, IL, April 2010.

Sinno, Abdulkader H. and Eren Tatari. "Toward Electability: Public Office and the Arab Vote." In *Arab Detroit 9/11: Life in the Terror Decade*, ed. Nabeel Abraham, Sally Howell, and Andrew Shryock. Detroit, MI: Wayne State University Press, 2011, pp. 315–346.

Skerry, Peter. "The Muslim-American Muddle." *National Affairs*, no. 9 (Fall 2011), www.nationalaffairs.com/publications/detail/the-muslim-american-muddle, accessed September 14, 2012.

Skerry, Peter and Devin Fernandes. "Interpreting the Muslim Vote." *Boston Globe* (November 26, 2004).

Smietana, Bob. "Anti-Muslim Crusaders Make Millions Spreading Fear." *The Tennesseean* (October 24, 2010), www.tennessean.com/article/20101024/NEWS01/10240374/The+price+of+fear, accessed September 15, 2012.

Smith, Eli. "Present Attitude of Mohammedanism, in Reference to the Spread of the Gospel." *The American Quarterly Observer* 1 (July–October 1833), pp. 103–114.

Somers, Margaret. *Genealogies of Citizenship: Markets, Statelessness, and the Right to Have Rights.* New York: Cambridge University Press, 2008.

Sorkowitz, Ann and Julie N. Hays. "Witness to Discrimination: What Would You Do?" ABC News (February 26, 2008), http://abcnews.go.com/Primetime/WhatWouldYouDo/story?id=4339476&page=1#.T7_LpPXLkc0, accessed September 15, 2012.

Spellberg, Denise. "Could a Muslim Be President? An Eighteenth-Century Constitutional Debate." *Eighteenth-Century Studies* 39 (2006), pp. 485–506.

Stabile, Carole and Deepa Kumar. "Unveiling Imperialism: Media, Gender, and the War on Afghanistan." *Media, Culture & Society* 27:5 (Fall 2005), pp. 765–782.

Stalcup, Meg and Joshua Craze. "The Shocking Way US Cops Are Trained to Hate Muslims." *Washington Monthly* (March 10, 2011), www.alternet.org/story/150209/the_shocking_way_us_cops_are_trained_to_hate_muslims?page=entire, accessed September 15, 2012.

Starbuck, Rev. Charles C. "Missions and Civilization. II." *The Andover Review: A Religious and Theological Monthly* 18 (July–December 1892), pp. 69–70.

Steinback, Robert. "Jihad against Islam," Southern Poverty Law Center Intelligence Report (Summer, 2011, Issue Number 142), www.splcenter.org/get-informed/intelligence-report/browse-all-issues/2011/summer/jihad-against-islam, accessed September 15, 2012.

———. "The Anti-Muslim Inner Circle," Southern Poverty Law Center Intelligence Report (Summer, 2011, Issue Number 142), www.splcenter.org/get-informed/intelligence-report/browse-all-issues/2011/summer/the-anti-muslim-inner-circle, accessed September 15, 2012.

Stewart, Robert. *Life and Work in India: An Account of the Conditions, Methods, Difficulties, Results, Future Prospects and Reflex Influence of Missionary Labor in India, Especially in the Punjab Mission of the*

United Presbyterian Church of North America. Philadelphia, PA: Pearl Publishing, 1896.

Strong, Josiah. *Our Country*. Cambridge, MA: Belknap Press of Harvard University Press, 1963 (1891).

Strossen, Nadine. "Freedom and Fear Post-9/11: Are We Again Burning Witches and Fearing Women?" *Nova Law Review* 31 (2007), pp. 279–314.

Takle, John. "Moslem Advance in India." In *Islam and Missions: Being Papers Read at the Second Missionary Conference on Behalf of the Mohammedan World at Lucknow, January 23–28, 1911*, ed. Elwood Morris Wherry, Samuel Marinus Zwemer, and C. G. Mylrea. New York, London: Fleming H. Revell, 1911, pp. 206–219, http://ibri. org/Books/Zwemer/1911-Islam-Missions/htm/doc211.html, accessed September 15, 2012.

Talk of the Nation (National Public Radio). "The Debate over 'Anchor Babies' and Citizenship" (August 2010), www.npr.org/templates/story/ story.php?storyId=129279863, accessed September 15, 2012.

Temple-Raston, Dina. "Officials Detail Plan to Fight Homegrown Terrorism," www.npr.org/2011/12/08/143319965/officials-detail-plans-to-fight-terrorism-at-home, accessed December 20, 2011.

Thomas More Law Center. "Victory for Pastor Jones; Court Rules that Pastor's Constitutional Rights Were Violated by 'Peace Bond' Trial," www.thomasmore.org/press-releases/2011/11/victory-pastor-jones-court-rules-pastor-s-constitutional-rights-were-violated, accessed September 15, 2012.

Thornton, Edward. *A Gazetteer of the Territories under the Government of the East-India Company, and of the Native States on the Continent of India*. Delhi: Low Price Pubications, 1993 (1858).

Tomory, Alexander and K. S. Macdonald. "Bengal." In *Our Church's Work in India*, ed. Alexander Tomory et al. Edinburgh: Oliphant, Anderson & Co., 1910.

Turner, Richard Brent. *Islam in the African-American Experience*, 2nd edition. Bloomington, IN: Indiana University Press, 2003.

Twining, Thomas. *A Letter to the Chairman of the East India Company, on the Danger of Interfering in the Religious Opinions of the Natives of India; and on the Views of the British and Foreign Bible Society as Directed to India*, 2nd edition. London: Hazard and Carthew, 1807.

University of California Graduate School of Journalism. "Journalism School Investigates FBI Use of Informants in Muslim Communities Post 9/11." *Berkeley Research* (August 20, 2011), http://vcresearch.berkeley. edu/news/journalism-school-fellow-investigates-fbi-use-informants-muslim-communities-post-911, accessed September 28, 2011.

Von Eschen, Penny M. *Race against Empire: Black Americans and Anti-colonialism, 1937–1957.* Ithaca, NY: Cornell University Press, 1997.

Walton, Jeremy. "America's Muslim Anxiety: Lessons of *The Third Jihad.*" *The Revealer* (February 2, 2012), http://therevealer.org/archives/10349, accessed September 15, 2012.

Warikoo, Niraj. "Metro interfaith leaders to unite against Quran-burning pastor." *Detroit Free Press* (April 20, 2011), www.freep.com/article/20110420/NEWS02/104200407/Metro-interfaith-leaders-unite-against-Quran-burning-pastor, accessed September 15, 2012.

———. "Nuclear Search Targets Muslims." *Detroit Free Press* (December 24, 2005).

———. "Terry Jones goes free on $1 bond after jailing; judge bars him from mosque for 3 years." *Detroit Free Press* (April 23, 2011), www.freep.com/article/20110422/NEWS02/110422014/Terry-Jones-goes-free-1-bond-after-jailing-judge-bars-him-from-mosque-3-years, accessed September 15, 2012.

Weber, Charlotte. "Unveiling Scheherazade: Feminist Orientalism in the International Alliance of Women, 1911–1950." *Feminist Studies* 27:1 (Spring 2001), pp. 125–157.

Wheeler, D. H. "England and Islam." *The Chautauquan* 5 (October 1884–July 1885), pp. 402–404.

White House, Office of the Press Secretary. "Statement by the President on H.R. 1540," www.whitehouse.gov/the-press-office/2011/12/31/statement-president-hr-1540, accessed on July 15, 2012.

White, Maria. "Iraqi Woman Beaten in Her California Home Dies." CNN (March 25, 2012), http://articles.cnn.com/2012–03–25/justice/justice_california-immigrant-death_1_iraqi-woman-el-cajon-life-support?_s=PM:JUSTICE, accessed September 15, 2012.

Wike, Richard and Brian F. Grim. "Western Views toward Muslims: Evidence from a 2006 Cross-National Survery." *International Journal of Public Opinion Research* 22:1 (2010), pp. 4–25.

Wikipedia. "William G. Boykin," http://en.wikipedia.org/wiki/William_G._Boykin, accessed September 15, 2012.

Wilde-Blavatsky, Adele. "To Be Anti-Racist Is to Be Feminist: The Hoodie and the Hijab Are Not Equals," ZNet (April 19, 2012), www.zcommunications.org/to-be-anti-racist-is-to-be-feminist-the-hoodie-andthe-hijab-are-not-equals-by-adele-wilde-blavatsky, accessed September 15, 2012.

Wilson, W. A. "The Situation in India." In *Islam and Missions: Being Papers Read at the Second Missionary Conference on Behalf of the Mohammedan World at Lucknow, January 23–28, 1911,* ed. Elwood Morris Wherry,

Samuel Marinus Zwemer, and C. G. Mylrea. New York, London: Fleming H. Revell, 1911.

Wiltrout, Kate. "SEAL Training Range Won't Show Woman as Target." *The Virginian-Pilot* (June 30, 2012), http://hamptonroads.com/2012/06/seal-training-range-wont-show-woman-target, accessed September 15, 2012.

X, Malcolm. *The Autobiography of Malcolm X.* New York: Ballantine Books, 1999.

Zine, Jasmin. "Unveiled Sentiments: Gendered Islamophobia and Experiences of Veiling among Muslim Girls in Canadian Islamic School." *Equity and Excellence in Education* 39 (2006), pp. 239–252.

Zizek, Slavoj. "The Power of the Woman and the Truth of Islam." ABC Religion and Ethics Blog (May 10, 2012), www.abc.net.au/religion/articles/2012/05/10/3500125.htm, accessed September 15, 2012.

Zwemer, Samuel M. "The Fulness of Time in the Moslem World." In *Students and the World-wide Expansion of Christianity: Addresses Delivered before the Seventh International Convention of the Student Volunteer Movement for Foreign Missions, Kansas City, Missouri, December 31, 1913 to January 4, 1914*, ed. Fennell Parrish Turner. New York: Student Volunteer Movement for Foreign Missions, 1914.

————. *Islam, a Challenge to Faith: Studies on the Mohammedan Religion and the Needs and Opportunities of the Mohammedan World from the Standpoint of Christian Missions*, 2nd edition. New York: Student Volunteer Movement for Foreign Missions, 1907.

Contributors

Edward E. Curtis IV (Millennium Chair of the Liberal Arts and Professor of Religious Studies at Indiana University/Purdue University Indianapolis) is the author of the *Encyclopedia of Muslim-American History* (Facts on File, 2010).

Carl W. Ernst (William R. Kenan, Jr., Distinguished Professor of Religious Studies, University of North Carolina at Chapel Hill) is the author of *Following Muhammad: Rethinking Islam in the Contemporary World* (UNC Press, 2003).

Kambiz GhaneaBassiri (Associate Professor of Religion and Humanities, Reed College) is the author of *A History of Islam in America: From the New World to the New World Order* (Cambridge University Press, 2010).

Peter Gottschalk (Professor of Religion, Wesleyan University) and **Gabriel Greenberg** (Chaplain, University of California, Berkeley) have jointly authored *Islamophobia: Making Muslims the Enemy* (Rowman & Littlefield, 2007).

Juliane Hammer (Assistant Professor of Religious Studies, University of North Carolina at Chapel Hill) is the author of *American Muslim Women, Religious Authority, and Activism: More than a Prayer* (University of Texas Press, 2012).

Andrew J. Shryock (Professor of Anthropology, University of Michigan) is the editor of *Islamophobia/Islamophilia: Beyond the Politics of Enemy and Friend* (Indiana University Press, 2010).

Index

"Fear Inc." *See* Center for American
    Progress
Federal Bureau of Investigation (FBI),
    5–6, 11, 12, 14, 67, 75, 77, 85;
    COINTELPRO program of, 97–8,
    100; investigations in Detroit, 149,
    155–6; Muslim informants for, 101,
    155; RACON program of, 90–3
Federation of Islamic Associations of
    the United States and Canada, 64
feminism, 128, 132; and colonial
    discourse on Muslim women, 114;
    second wave, 134
Feminist Majority, 124–5, 130
feminists, academic, 128, 130;
    Muslim, 13, 110, 130; white, 134
First Amendment, 4, 7, 11, 60, 63, 66,
    154; protections of, questioned for
    Muslims, 94
Foner, Nancy, 148
Ford, Henry, 62
Fox News TV, 5
Fox, George, 39
Franklin, Benjamin, 42
French revolution, 37

Gaffney, Frank, 4
Gallaudet, Thomas, 82
Gandhi, Mohandas, 34, 35
Garvey, Marcus, 85, 86, 87
Geller, Pamela, 13, 112, 121, 123,
    126–7, 166
gender, 2, 12–13, 107–36
Geneva Conventions, 7
GhaneaBassiri, Kambiz, 2, 7, 9–10
Gingrich, Newt, 121
globalization, 46
Gohmert, Congressman Louie, 119
Gomez, Michael, 78
"good Muslim" stereotype, 15,
    161–3, 165
Gordon, Mittie Maud Lena, 91
Gottschalk, Peter, 2, 8–9

Graham, Sen. Lindsey, 119
Greenberg, Gabriel, 2, 8–9
Ground Zero mosque, 1, 54
Guantanamo Bay, 101
Gulf War, 157

Haley, Alex, 67, 68
Hamilton, Walter, 30
Hammer, Juliane, 2, 7, 12–13
hate crimes, 113, 116, 117, 120
hate speech, against Muslim women,
    113, 118
Haywood, John, 33, 37
Heber, Reginald, 30
Henshaw, John Prentiss Kewley, 41
Herberg Will, 63, 96
Hernandez, Karen Leslie, 135
Higham, John, 59
hijab, 109, 116, 118–19, 120, 130,
    133–4, 137n2
Hill, Robert A., 90
Hindus, 30, 31, 32, 35, 37, 43
Holocaust, 14, 147–8, 159
Homeland Security, 149, 155
homophobia, 109–10, 128, 136
homosexuality, 109–10
"honor killings," 123, 124, 127, 128,
    134, 166
hoodie, 133–4
Hoover, J. Edgar, 90, 93, 95, 97
Hume, Mr., 38, 41
Hunter, W. W., 31, 32, 34–5
Huntington, Samuel, 46, 113, 173n40

Ibrahima, Abdul Rahman, 77, 80–4
immigrants, 59, 61, 63, 68, 77, 85,
    119, 146–7, 160, 1368
Immigration Act of 1924, 60
immigration law, 13
imperialism, 13
"Innocence of Muslims" film trailer, 2
Iqbal, Sir Muhammad, 33, 35
Iranian Revolution, 64, 76